TALLINN MANU
INTERNATIONAL LAW
APPLICABLE TO CYBER
WARFARE

Prepared by the International Group of Experts at the
Invitation of the NATO Cooperative Cyber Defence
Centre of Excellence

General editor
MICHAEL N. SCHMITT

CAMBRIDGE
UNIVERSITY PRESS

CAMBRIDGE UNIVERSITY PRESS
Cambridge, New York, Melbourne, Madrid, Cape Town,
Singapore, São Paulo, Delhi, Mexico City

Cambridge University Press
The Edinburgh Building, Cambridge CB2 8RU, UK

Published in the United States of America by Cambridge University Press, New York

www.cambridge.org
Information on this title: www.cambridge.org/9781107024434

First published 2013
3rd printing 2013

Printed and bound in the United Kingdom by the MPG Books Group

A catalogue record for this publication is available from the British Library

Library of Congress Cataloguing in Publication Data

Tallinn manual on the international law applicable to cyber warfare : prepared by the International
Group of Experts at the invitation of the NATO Cooperative Cyber Defence Centre of Excellence /
general editor Michael N. Schmitt.
pages cm
ISBN 978-1-107-02443-4 (Hardback)
ISBN 978-1-107-61377-5 (Paperback)
1. Information warfare (International law)   2. Cyberterrorism.   I. Schmitt, Michael N.
KZ6718.T35 2013
341.6'3–dc23
2012039599

ISBN 978-1-107-02443-4 Hardback
ISBN 978-1-107-61377-5 Paperback

CONTENTS

          Rule 86 – Humanitarian assistance   236

6 Occupation   239
          Rule 87 – Respect for protected persons in occupied
                    territory   240
          Rule 88 – Public order and safety in occupied
                    territory   242
          Rule 89 – Security of the Occupying Power   244
          Rule 90 – Confiscation and requisition of property   245

7 Neutrality   248
          Rule 91 – Protection of neutral cyber infrastructure   250
          Rule 92 – Cyber operations in neutral territory   251
          Rule 93 – Neutral obligations   252
          Rule 94 – Response by parties to the conflict
                    to violations   254
          Rule 95 – Neutrality and Security Council actions   255

     Glossary   257
     Index   263

THE INTERNATIONAL GROUP OF EXPERTS
AND PARTICIPANTS[1]

International Group of Experts

Director

Professor Michael Schmitt
United States Naval War College

Editorial Committee

Air Commodore (Retired) William H. Boothby
Formerly Deputy Director of Legal Services, Royal Air Force (United Kingdom)

Bruno Demeyere
Catholic University of Leuven

Professor Wolff Heintschel von Heinegg
Europa-Universität Viadrina

Professor James Bret Michael
United States Naval Postgraduate School

Professor Thomas Wingfield
George C. Marshall European Center for Security Studies

Legal Group Facilitators

Professor Eric Talbot Jensen
Brigham Young University Law School

Professor Sean Watts
Creighton University Law School

---

[1] Affiliations during participation in the project.

Legal Experts

Dr Louise Arimatsu
Chatham House

Captain (Navy) Geneviève Bernatchez
Office of the Judge Advocate General, Canadian Forces

Colonel Penny Cumming
Australian Defence Force

Professor Robin Geiß
University of Potsdam

Professor Terry D. Gill
University of Amsterdam, Netherlands Defence Academy, and Utrecht University

Professor Derek Jinks
University of Texas School of Law

Professor Jann Kleffner
Swedish National Defence College

Dr Nils Melzer
Geneva Centre for Security Policy

Brigadier General (Retired, Canadian Forces) Kenneth Watkin
United States Naval War College

Technical Experts

Dr Kenneth Geers
NATO Cooperative Cyber Defence Centre of Excellence

Dr Rain Ottis
NATO Cooperative Cyber Defence Centre of Excellence

Observers

Colonel Gary D. Brown, US Air Force
United States Cyber Command

Dr Cordula Droege
International Committee of the Red Cross

Dr Jean-François Quéguiner
International Committee of the Red Cross

Ulf Häußler
Headquarters, Supreme Allied Commander Transformation, NATO

Peer Reviewers

Professor Geoffrey Corn
South Texas College of Law

Professor Ashley Deeks
University of Virginia

Dr Heather A. Harrison Dinniss
Swedish National Defence College

Commander Clive Dow
Royal Navy (United Kingdom)

Professor Charles Garraway
Human Rights Centre, University of Essex

Group Captain Ian Henderson
Royal Australian Air Force

Dr Gleider Hernandez
Durham University

Professor Chris Jenks
Southern Methodist University School of Law

Dr Noam Lubell
University of Essex

Sasha Radin
University of Melbourne Law School

Commander Paul Walker
United States Navy

Colonel David Wallace, US Army
United States Military Academy

Dr Katharina Ziolkowski
NATO Cooperative Cyber Defence Centre of Excellence

Project Coordinator

Dr Eneken Tikk
NATO Cooperative Cyber Defence Centre of Excellence

Project Manager

Liis Vihul
NATO Cooperative Cyber Defence Centre of Excellence

Rapporteurs

Jean Callaghan
George C. Marshall European Center for Security Studies

Dr James Sweeney
Durham University

Legal Research

Creighton University Law School

Jennifer Arbaugh
Nicole Bohe
Christopher Jackman
Christine Schaad

Emory University Law School

Anand Shah

Chatham House

Hemi Mistry

SHORT FORM CITATIONS

Treaties

Additional Protocol I: Protocol Additional to the Geneva Conventions of 12 August 1949, and Relating to the Protection of Victims of International Armed Conflicts, 8 June 1977, 1125 U.N.T.S. 3.

Additional Protocol II: Protocol Additional to the Geneva Conventions of 12 August 1949, and Relating to the Protection of Victims of Non-International Armed Conflicts, 8 June 1977, 1125 U.N.T.S. 609.

Additional Protocol III: Protocol Additional to the Geneva Conventions of 12 August 1949, and Relating to the Adoption of an Additional Distinctive Emblem, 8 December 2005, 2404 U.N.T.S. 261.

Amended Mines Protocol: Protocol (to the Convention on Prohibitions or Restrictions on the Use of Certain Conventional Weapons Which May Be Deemed to Be Excessively Injurious or to Have Indiscriminate Effects) on Prohibitions or Restrictions on the Use of Mines, Booby-Traps and Other Devices, as amended on 3 May 1996, 2048 U.N.T.S. 133.

Chicago Convention: International Civil Aviation Organization (ICAO), Convention on Civil Aviation, 7 December 1944, 15 U.N.T.S. 295.

Convention on Jurisdictional Immunities: Convention on Jurisdictional Immunities of States and their Property, U.N. Doc. A/59/38 (2 December 2004, not yet in force).

Convention on the Rights of the Child: Convention of the Rights of the Child, 20 November 1989, 1577 U.N.T.S. 3.

Conventional Weapons Convention: Convention on Prohibitions or Restrictions on the Use of Certain Conventional Weapons Which May Be Deemed to Be Excessively Injurious or to Have Indiscriminate Effects, 10 April 1981, 1342 U.N.T.S. 137.

CRC Optional Protocol: Optional Protocol to the Convention on the Rights of the Child on the Involvement of Children in Armed Conflict, 25 May 2000, 2173 U.N.T.S. 222.

Cultural Property Convention: Hague Convention for the Protection of Cultural Property in the Event of Armed Conflict with Regulations for the Execution of the Convention, 14 May 1954, 249 U.N.T.S. 240.

Environmental Modification Convention: Convention on the Prohibition of Military or Any Other Hostile Use of Environmental Modification Techniques ('ENMOD'), 10 December 1976, 1108 U.N.T.S. 151.

Geneva Convention I: Convention (I) for the Amelioration of the Condition of the Wounded and Sick in Armed Forces in the Field, 12 August 1949, 75 U.N.T.S. 31.

Geneva Convention II: Convention (II) for the Amelioration of the Condition of Wounded, Sick and Shipwrecked Members of Armed Forces at Sea, 12 August 1949, 75 U.N.T.S. 85.

Geneva Convention III: Convention (III) Relative to the Treatment of Prisoners of War, 12 August 1949, 75 U.N.T.S. 135.

Geneva Convention IV: Convention (IV) Relative to the Protection of Civilian Persons in Time of War, 12 August 1949, 75 U.N.T.S. 287.

Hague Convention IV: Convention (IV) Respecting the Laws and Customs of War on Land, 18 October 1907, 36 Stat. 2277.

Hague Convention V: Convention (V) Respecting the Rights and Duties of Neutral Powers and Persons in Case of War on Land, 18 October 1907, 36 Stat. 2310.

Hague Convention XIII: Convention (XIII) Concerning the Rights and Duties of Neutral Powers in Naval War, 18 October 1907, 36 Stat. 2415.

Hague Regulations: Convention (IV) Respecting the Laws and Customs of War on Land and its annex: Regulations concerning the Laws and Customs of War on Land, 18 October 1907, 36 Stat. 2277.

ICTR Statute: Statute of the International Criminal Tribunal for Rwanda, S.C. Res. 955 annex, U.N. Doc. S/RES/955 (8 November 1994).

ICTY Statute: Statute of the International Criminal Tribunal for the Former Yugoslavia, S.C. Res. 827 annex, U.N. Doc. S/RES/827 (25 May 1993).

ITU Constitution: Constitution of the International Telecommunications Union, 22 December 1992, 1825 U.N.T.S. 331.

Law of the Sea Convention: United Nations Convention on the Law of the Sea, 10 December 1982, 1833 U.N.T.S. 3.

Mines Protocol: Protocol (to the Convention on Prohibitions or Restrictions on the Use of Certain Conventional Weapons Which May Be Deemed to Be Excessively Injurious or to Have Indiscriminate Effects) on Prohibitions or Restrictions on the Use of Mines, Booby-Traps and Other Devices, 10 October 1980, 1342 U.N.T.S. 168.

Outer Space Treaty: Treaty on Principles Governing the Activities of States in the Exploration and Use of Outer Space, Including the Moon and Other Celestial Bodies, 27 January 1967, 610 U.N.T.S. 205.

Rome Statute: Statute of the International Criminal Court, 17 July 1998, 2187 U.N.T.S. 90.

Second Cultural Property Protocol: Second Protocol to the Hague Convention of 1954 for the Protection of Cultural Property in the Event of Armed Conflict, 26 March 1999, 2253 U.N.T.S. 212.

Sierra Leone Statute: Agreement between the U.N. and the Government of Sierra Leone on the Establishment of a Special Court for Sierra Leone, annex, 16 January 2002, 2178 U.N.T.S. 138.

St Petersburg Declaration: Declaration Renouncing the Use, in Time of War, of Explosive Projectiles Under 400 Grammes Weight, 29 November/11 December 1868, 18 Martens Nouveau Recueil (ser. 1) 474.

United Nations Safety Convention: Convention on the Safety of United Nations and Associated Personnel, 9 December 1994, 2051 U.N.T.S. 363.

Vienna Convention on Diplomatic Relations: Vienna Convention on Diplomatic Relations, 18 April 1961, 500 U.N.T.S. 95.

Case law

Akayesu judgment: *Prosecutor v. Akayesu*, Case No. ICTR-96-4-T, Trial Chamber Judgment (Int'l Crim. Trib. for Rwanda 2 September 1998).

Armed Activities in Congo judgment: *Armed Activities on the Territory of the Congo (Dem. Rep. Congo v. Uganda)*, I.C.J. Reports 2005 (19 December).

Blaškić judgment: *Prosecutor v. Blaškić*, Case No. IT-95-14-A, Appeals Chamber Judgment (Int'l Crim. Trib. for the Former Yugoslavia 29 July 2004).

Corfu Channel case: *Corfu Channel* case (*UK v. Alb.*) 1949 I.C.J. 4 (9 April).

Delalić judgment: *Prosecutor v. Delalić/Mucić*, Case No. IT-96-21-T, Trial Chamber Judgment (Int'l Crim. Trib. for the Former Yugoslavia 16 November 1998).

Galić Trial Chamber judgment: *Prosecutor v. Stanislav Galić*, Case No. IT-98-29-T, Trial Chamber Judgment (Int'l Crim. Trib. for the Former Yugoslavia 5 December 2003).

Galić Appeals Chamber judgment: *Prosecutor v. Galić*, Case No. IT-98-29-A, Appeals Chamber Judgment (Int'l Crim. Trib. for the Former Yugoslavia 30 November 2006).

Genocide case: *Application of the Convention on the Prevention and Punishment of the Crime of Genocide (Bosn. and Herz. v. Serb. and Montenegro)*, 2007 I.C.J. 108 (26 February).

Hadžihasanović judgment: *Prosecutor v. Hadžihasanović*, Case No. IT-01-47-T, Trial Chamber Judgment (Int'l Crim. Trib. for the Former Yugoslavia 15 March 2006).

Haradinaj judgment: *Prosecutor v. Haradinaj*, Case No. IT-04-84-T, Trial Chamber Judgment (Int'l Crim. Trib. for the Former Yugoslavia 3 April 2008).

Kayishema judgment: *Prosecutor v. Kayishema and Ruzindana*, Case No. ICTR 95-1-T, Trial Chamber Judgment (Int'l Crim. Trib. for Rwanda 21 May 1999).

Kosovo Advisory Opinion: *Accordance with International Law of the Unilateral Declaration of Independence in Respect of Kosovo*, Advisory Opinion, 2010 I.C.J. (22 July).

Limaj judgment: *Prosecutor v. Limaj*, Case No. IT-03-66-T, Trial Chamber Judgment (Int'l Crim. Trib. for the Former Yugoslavia 30 November 2005).

Lotus case: *SS 'Lotus'* (*Fr. v. Turk.*), 1927 P.C.I.J. (ser. A) No. 10 (7 September).

Lubanga judgment: *Prosecutor v. Lubanga*, Case No. ICC-01/04-01/06, Trial Chamber Judgment (Int'l Crim. Ct. 14 March 2012).

Martić judgment: *Prosecutor v. Martić*, Case No. IT-95-11-T, Trial Chamber Judgment (Int'l Crim. Trib. for the Former Yugoslavia 12 June 2007).

Milošević decision: *Prosecutor* v. *Milošević*, Case No. IT-02-54-T, Decision on Motion for Judgment of Acquittal (Int'l Crim. Trib. for the Former Yugoslavia 16 June 2004).

Mrkšić judgment: *Prosecutor* v. *Mrkšić*, Case No. IT-95-13/1-T, Trial Chamber Judgment (Int'l Crim. Trib. for the Former Yugoslavia 27 September 2007).

Naulilaa arbitration: *Responsibility of Germany for Damage Caused in the Portuguese Colonies in the South of Africa (Naulilaa Arbitration) (Port.* v. *Ger.),* 2 R.I.A.A. 1011 (1928).

Nicaragua judgment: *Military and Paramilitary Activities in and against Nicaragua (Nicar.* v. *US),* 1986 I.C.J. 14 (27 June).

Nuclear Weapons Advisory Opinion: *Legality of the Threat or Use of Nuclear Weapons,* Advisory Opinion, 1996 I.C.J. 226 (8 July).

Nuremburg Tribunal judgment: *Judgment of the International Military Tribunal Sitting at Nuremberg, Germany (30 September 1946), in* 22 The Trial of German Major War Criminals: Proceedings of the International Military Tribunal Sitting at Nuremberg, Germany (1950).

Oil Platforms judgment: *Oil Platforms (Iran* v. *US),* 2003 I.C.J. 161 (6 November).

Tadić, Decision on the Defence Motion for Interlocutory Appeal: *Prosecutor* v. *Tadić*, Case No. IT-94-1-I, Decision on the Defence Motion for Interlocutory Appeal on Jurisdiction (Int'l Crim. Trib. for the Former Yugoslavia 2 October 1995).

Tadić, Trial Chamber judgment: *Prosecutor* v. *Tadić*, Case No. IT-94-1-T, Trial Chamber Judgment (Int'l Crim. Trib. for the Former Yugoslavia 7 May 1997).

Tadić, Appeals Chamber judgment: *Prosecutor* v. *Tadić*, Case No. IT-94-1-A, Appeals Chamber Judgment (Intl'l Crim. Trib. for the Former Yugoslavia 15 July 1999).

Tehran Hostages case: *United States Diplomatic and Consular Staff in Tehran (US* v. *Iran),* 1980 I.C.J. 3 (24 May).

Wall Advisory Opinion: *Legal Consequences of the Construction of a Wall in the Occupied Palestinian Territory,* Advisory Opinion, 2004 I.C.J. 136 (9 July).

Other sources

AMW Manual: Harvard Program on Humanitarian Policy and Conflict Research, Manual on International Law Applicable to Air and Missile Warfare, with Commentary (2010).

Articles on State Responsibility: International Law Commission, Responsibility of States for Internationally Wrongful Acts, G.A. Res. 56/83 annex, U.N. Doc. A/RES/56/83 (12 December 2001).

Bothe et al.: Michael Bothe et al., New Rules for Victims of Armed Conflicts: Commentary on the Two 1977 Protocols Additional to the Geneva Conventions of 1949 (1982).

Canadian Manual: Canada, Office of the Judge Advocate General, Law of Armed Conflict at the Operational and Tactical Levels, B-GJ-005-104/FP-021 (2001).

Declaration on Friendly Relations: Declaration on Principles of International Law concerning Friendly Relations and Cooperation among States in accordance with the Charter of the United Nations, G.A. Res. 2625 (XXV), U.N. GAOR, 25th Sess., Supp. No. 28, at 121, U.N. Doc. A/8082 (1970).

GERMAN MANUAL: THE FEDERAL MINISTRY OF DEFENCE OF THE FEDERAL REPUBLIC OF GERMANY, HUMANITARIAN LAW IN ARMED CONFLICTS MANUAL (ZDv 15/2) (1992).

Hague Air Warfare Rules: Rules Concerning the Control of Wireless Telegraphy in Time of War and Air Warfare (Drafted by a Commission of Jurists, The Hague, December 1922–February 1923), *reprinted in* DOCUMENTS ON THE LAWS OF WAR 139 (Adam Roberts and Richard Guelff eds., 3rd ed. 2000).

ICRC ADDITIONAL PROTOCOLS COMMENTARY: INTERNATIONAL COMMITTEE OF THE RED CROSS, COMMENTARY ON THE ADDITIONAL PROTOCOLS OF 8 JUNE 1977 TO THE GENEVA CONVENTIONS OF 12 AUGUST 1949 (Yves Sandoz et al. eds., 1987).

ICRC CUSTOMARY IHL STUDY: I INTERNATIONAL COMMITTEE OF THE RED CROSS, CUSTOMARY INTERNATIONAL HUMANITARIAN LAW (Jean-Marie Henckaerts and Louise Doswald-Beck eds., 2005).

ICRC GENEVA CONVENTION I COMMENTARY: COMMENTARY: GENEVA CONVENTION FOR THE AMELIORATION OF THE CONDITION OF THE WOUNDED AND SICK IN ARMED FORCES IN THE FIELD (Jean Pictet ed., 1952).

ICRC GENEVA CONVENTION III COMMENTARY: COMMENTARY: GENEVA CONVENTION RELATIVE TO THE TREATMENT OF PRISONERS OF WAR OF AUGUST 12, 1949 (Jean Pictet ed., 1960).

ICRC GENEVA CONVENTION IV COMMENTARY: COMMENTARY: GENEVA CONVENTION RELATIVE TO THE PROTECTION OF CIVILIAN PERSONS IN TIME OF WAR (Jean Pictet ed., 1958).

ICRC INTERPRETIVE GUIDANCE: INTERNATIONAL COMMITTEE OF THE RED CROSS, INTERPRETIVE GUIDANCE ON THE NOTION OF DIRECT PARTICIPATION IN HOSTILITIES UNDER INTERNATIONAL HUMANITARIAN LAW (Nils Melzer ed., 2009).

NIA GLOSSARY: Committee on National Security Systems (CNSS) Glossary Working Group, National Information Assurance [IA] Glossary, CNSS Instruction No. 4009 (26 April 2010).

NIAC MANUAL: Michael N. Schmitt, Charles H.B. Garraway and Yoram Dinstein, THE MANUAL ON THE LAW OF NON-INTERNATIONAL ARMED CONFLICT WITH COMMENTARY (2006).

Rome Statute Elements of the Crimes: International Criminal Court, Elements of Crimes, U.N. Doc. ICC-ASP/1/3 (9 September 2002).

SAN REMO MANUAL: INTERNATIONAL INSTITUTE OF HUMANITARIAN LAW, SAN REMO MANUAL ON INTERNATIONAL LAW APPLICABLE TO ARMED CONFLICTS AT SEA (Louise Doswald-Beck ed., 1995).

UK ADDITIONAL PROTOCOL RATIFICATION STATEMENT: UK Statement made upon Ratification of Additional Protocols I and II, *reprinted in* DOCUMENTS ON THE LAW OF WAR 510 (Adam Roberts and Richard Guelff eds., 3rd ed. 2000).

UK Manual: UK MINISTRY OF DEFENCE, THE JOINT SERVICE MANUAL OF THE LAW OF ARMED CONFLICT, JSP 383 (2004).

US COMMANDER'S HANDBOOK: US NAVY/US MARINE CORPS/US COAST GUARD, THE COMMANDER'S HANDBOOK ON THE LAW OF NAVAL OPERATIONS, NWP 1-14M/ MCWP 5-12.1/COMDTPUB P5800.7A (2007).

White House Cyber Strategy: The White House, International Strategy for Cyberspace: Prosperity, Security, and Openness in a Networked World (2011).

~

Introduction

In 2009, the NATO Cooperative Cyber Defence Centre of Excellence (NATO CCD COE), an international military organization based in Tallinn, Estonia, and accredited in 2008 by NATO as a 'Centre of Excellence', invited an independent 'International Group of Experts' to produce a manual on the law governing cyber warfare.[1] In doing so, it followed in the footsteps of earlier efforts, such as those resulting in the International Institute of Humanitarian Law's *San Remo Manual on International Law Applicable to Armed Conflicts at Sea*[2] and the Harvard Program on Humanitarian Policy and Conflict Research's *Manual on International Law Applicable to Air and Missile Warfare*.[3] The project brought together distinguished international law practitioners and scholars in an effort to examine how extant legal norms applied to this 'new' form of warfare. Like its predecessors, the *Manual on the International Law Applicable to Cyber Warfare*, or '*Tallinn Manual*', results from an expert-driven process designed to produce a non-binding document applying existing law to cyber warfare.

Cyber operations began to draw the attention of the international legal community in the late 1990s. Most significantly, in 1999 the United States Naval War College convened the first major legal conference on the subject.[4] In the aftermath of the attacks of 11 September 2001, transnational terrorism and the ensuing armed conflicts diverted attention from the topic until the massive cyber operations by 'hacktivists'

---

[1] The NATO CCD COE is neither part of NATO's command or force structure, nor funded by NATO. However, it is part of a wider framework supporting NATO Command Arrangements. Located in Tallinn, its present Sponsoring Nations are Estonia, Germany, Hungary, Italy, Latvia, Lithuania, the Netherlands, Poland, Slovakia, Spain, and the United States.

[2] SAN REMO MANUAL.   [3] AMW MANUAL.

[4] The proceedings were published as COMPUTER NETWORK ATTACK AND INTERNATIONAL LAW, 76 NAVAL WAR COLLEGE INTERNATIONAL LAW STUDIES (Michael N. Schmitt and Brian T. O'Donnell eds., 2002).

against Estonia in 2007 and against Georgia during its war with the Russian Federation in 2008, as well as cyber incidents like the targeting of the Iranian nuclear facilities with the Stuxnet worm in 2010.

These and other events have focused the attention of States on the subject. For instance, in its 2010 *National Security Strategy* the United Kingdom characterized 'cyber attack, including by other States, and by organised crime and terrorists' as one of four 'Tier One' threats to British national security, the others being international terrorism, international military crises between States, and a major accident or natural hazard.[5] The United States' 2010 *National Security Strategy* likewise cited cyber threats as 'one of the most serious national security, public safety, and economic challenges we face as a nation'[6] and in 2011 the US Department of Defense issued its *Strategy for Operating in Cyberspace*, which designates cyberspace as an operational domain.[7] In response to the threat, the United States has now established US Cyber Command to conduct cyber operations.

During the same period, Canada launched *Canada's Cyber Security Strategy*,[8] the United Kingdom issued *The UK Cyber Security Strategy: Protecting and Promoting the UK in a Digitized World*,[9] and Russia published its cyber concept for the armed forces in *Conceptual Views Regarding the Activities of the Armed Forces of the Russian Federation in Information Space*.[10] NATO acknowledged the new threat in its 2010 *Strategic Concept*, wherein it committed itself to 'develop further our ability to prevent, detect, defend against and recover from cyber attacks, including by using the NATO planning process to enhance and coordinate national cyber-defence capabilities, bringing all NATO bodies under centralized cyber protection, and better integrating NATO cyber awareness, warning and response with member nations'.[11]

---

[5] HM Government, *A Strong Britain in an Age of Uncertainty: The National Security Strategy* 11 (2010).

[6] The White House, *National Security Strategy* 27 (2010).

[7] Department of Defense, *Strategy for Operating in Cyberspace* (2011).

[8] Government of Canada, *Canada's Cyber Security Strategy* (October 2010).

[9] HM Government, *The UK Cyber Security Strategy: Protecting and Promoting the UK in a Digitized World* (2011).

[10] Russian Federation, *Conceptual Views Regarding the Activities of the Armed Forces of the Russian Federation in Information Space* (2011).

[11] NATO, *Active Defence, Modern Engagement: Strategic Concept for the Defence and Security of the Members of the North Atlantic Treaty Organization: Active Engagement, Modern Defence* 16–17 (2010).

One of the challenges States face in the cyber environment is that the scope and manner of international law's applicability to cyber operations, whether in offence or defence, has remained unsettled since their advent. After all, at the time the current international legal norms (whether customary or treaty-based) emerged, cyber technology was not on the horizon. Consequently, there is a risk that cyber practice may quickly outdistance agreed understandings as to its governing legal regime.

The threshold questions are whether the existing law applies to cyber issues at all, and, if so, how. Views on the subject range from a full application of the law of armed conflict, along the lines of the International Court of Justice's pronouncement that it applies to 'any use of force, regardless of the weapons employed',[12] to strict application of the Permanent Court of International Justice's pronouncement that acts not forbidden in international law are generally permitted.[13] Of course, the fact that States lack definitive guidance on the subject does not relieve them of their obligation to comply with applicable international law in their cyber operations.[14]

The community of nations is understandably concerned about this normative ambiguity. In 2011, the United States set forth its position on the matter in the *International Strategy for Cyberspace*: 'The development of norms for State conduct in cyberspace does not require a reinvention of customary international law, nor does it render existing international norms obsolete. Long-standing international norms guiding State behavior – in times of peace and conflict – also apply in cyberspace.'[15] Nevertheless, the document acknowledged that the 'unique attributes of networked technology require additional work to clarify how these norms apply and what additional understandings might be necessary to supplement them'.[16]

This project was launched in the hope of bringing some degree of clarity to the complex legal issues surrounding cyber operations, with

---

[12] *Nuclear Weapons* Advisory Opinion, para. 39.

[13] The Permanent Court of International Justice famously asserted that 'The rules of law binding upon States … emanate from their own free will as expressed in conventions or by usages generally accepted as expressing principles of law and established in order to regulate the relations between these co-existing independent communities or with a view to the achievement of common aims.' *Lotus* case at 18.

[14] For the view that the law of armed conflict applies to cyber warfare, see International Committee of the Red Cross, *International Humanitarian Law and Challenges of Contemporary Armed Conflicts*, ICRC Doc. 31IC/11/5.1.2 36–7 (October 2011).

[15] *White House Cyber Strategy* at 9.   [16] *White House Cyber Strategy* at 9.

particular attention paid to those involving the *jus ad bellum* and the *jus in bello*. The result is this '*Tallinn Manual*'.

Scope

The *Tallinn Manual* examines the international law governing 'cyber warfare'.[17] As a general matter, it encompasses both the *jus ad bellum*, the international law governing the resort to force by States as an instrument of their national policy, and the *jus in bello*, the international law regulating the conduct of armed conflict (also labelled the law of war, the law of armed conflict, or international humanitarian law). Related bodies of international law, such as the law of State responsibility and the law of the sea, are dealt with in the context of these topics.

Cyber activities that occur below the level of a 'use of force' (as this term is understood in the *jus ad bellum*), like cyber criminality, have not been addressed in any detail. Nor have any prohibitions on specific cyber actions, except with regard to an 'armed conflict' to which the *jus in bello* applies. For instance, the Manual is without prejudice to other applicable fields of international law, such as international human rights or telecommunications law. The legality of cyber intelligence activities is examined only as they relate to the *jus ad bellum* notions of 'use of force' and 'armed attack', or as relevant in the context of an armed conflict governed by the *jus in bello*. Although individual States and those subject to their jurisdiction must comply with applicable national law, domestic legislation and regulations have likewise not been considered. Finally, the Manual does not delve into the issue of individual criminal liability under either domestic or international law.

In short, this is not a manual on 'cyber security' as that term is understood in common usage. Cyber espionage, theft of intellectual property, and a wide variety of criminal activities in cyberspace pose real and serious threats to all States, as well as to corporations and private individuals. An adequate response to them requires national and international measures. However, the Manual does not address such matters because application of the international law on uses of force and armed conflict plays little or no role in doing so. Such law is no more applicable to these threats in the cyber domain than it is in the physical world.

---

[17] The term 'cyber warfare' is used here in a purely descriptive, non-normative sense.

The *Tallinn Manual*'s emphasis is on cyber-to-cyber operations, *sensu stricto*. Examples include the launch of a cyber operation against a State's critical infrastructure, or a cyber attack targeting enemy command and control systems. The Manual is not intended for use in considering the legal issues surrounding kinetic-to-cyber operations, such as an aerial attack employing bombs against a cyber control centre. It likewise does not address traditional electronic warfare attacks, like jamming. These operations are already well understood under the law of armed conflict.

Finally, the Manual addresses both international and non-international armed conflict. The Commentary indicates when a particular Rule is applicable in both categories of conflict, limited to international armed conflict, or of uncertain application in non-international armed conflict. It should be noted in this regard that the international law applicable to international armed conflict served as the starting point for the legal analysis. An assessment was subsequently made as to whether the particular Rule applies in non-international armed conflict.

The Rules

There are no treaty provisions that directly deal with 'cyber warfare'. Similarly, because State cyber practice and publicly available expressions of *opinio juris* are sparse, it is sometimes difficult to definitively conclude that any cyber-specific customary international law norm exists. This being so, any claim that every assertion in the Manual represents an incontrovertible restatement of international law would be an exaggeration.

This uncertainty does not mean cyber operations exist in a normative void. The International Group of Experts was unanimous in its estimation that both the *jus ad bellum* and *jus in bello* apply to cyber operations. Its task was to determine how such law applied, and to identify any cyber-unique aspects thereof. The Rules set forth in the *Tallinn Manual* accordingly reflect consensus among the Experts as to the applicable *lex lata*, that is, the law currently governing cyber conflict. It does not set forth *lex ferenda*, best practice, or preferred policy.

When treaty law directly on point or sufficient State practice and *opinio juris* from which to discern precise customary international law norms was lacking, the International Group of Experts crafted the Rules broadly. In these cases, the Experts agreed that the relevant principle of law extended into the cyber realm, but were hesitant to draw conclusions as to its exact scope and application in that context. Where different positions as to scope and application existed, they are reflected in the accompanying Commentary.

To the extent the Rules accurately articulate customary international law, they are binding on all States, subject to the possible existence of an exception for persistent objectors. At times, the text of a Rule closely resembles that of an existing treaty norm. For instance, Rule 38 regarding military objectives is nearly identical to the text of Article 52(2) of Additional Protocol I. In such cases, the International Group of Experts concluded that the treaty text represented a reliable and accurate restatement of customary international law. Users of this Manual are cautioned that States may be subject to additional norms set forth in treaties to which they are Party.

The Rules were adopted employing the principle of consensus within the International Group of Experts. All participating experts agreed that, as formulated, the Rules replicate customary international law, unless expressly noted otherwise. It must be acknowledged that at times members of the Group argued for a more restrictive or permissive standard than that eventually agreed upon. The Rule that emerged from these deliberations contains text regarding which it was possible to achieve consensus.

Although the observers (see below) participated in all discussions, the unanimity that was required for adoption of a Rule was limited to the International Group of Experts. Therefore, no conclusions can be drawn as to the position of any entity represented by an Observer with regard to the Rules.

The Commentary

The Commentary accompanying each Rule is intended to identify its legal basis, explain its normative content, address practical implications in the cyber context, and set forth differing positions as to scope or interpretation. Of particular note, the International Group of Experts assiduously sought to capture all reasonable positions for inclusion in the *Tallinn Manual*'s Commentary. As neither treaty application nor State practice is well developed in this field, the Group considered it of the utmost importance to articulate all competing views fully and fairly for consideration by users of the Manual.

Since the Commentary includes a variety of perspectives, users should not conclude that individual members of the International Group of Experts supported any particular position set forth therein. All that should be concluded is that every reasonable position that arose during Group proceedings – as well as those offered by observers, States, and outside experts – is included in the Commentary. For instance, although all members of the International Group of Experts agreed that launching cyber attacks against civilians or civilian objects is unlawful (Rules 32 and 37), views differed as to which operations qualify as 'attacks', as that term is used in the law of armed conflict.

Terminology posed a particular obstacle to the drafting of the *Tallinn Manual*. Many words and phrases have common usage, but also have specific military or legal meanings. For instance, the word 'attack' is commonly used to refer to a cyber operation against a particular object or entity, and in the military sense it usually indicates a military operation targeting a particular person or object. However, attack in the *jus ad bellum* sense, qualified by the word 'armed', refers to a cyber operation that justifies a response in self-defence (Rule 13), whereas the term as used in the *jus in bello* indicates a particular type of military operation that involves the use of violence, whether in offence or defence (Rule 30). Similarly, a 'military objective' in common military usage refers to the goal of a military operation. Yet, as employed in the *jus in bello* the term refers to objects that may be made the lawful object of 'attack', subject to other rules of the law of armed conflict (Rule 38). Users of this Manual are cautioned it employs most terminology in its international law sense, subject to particular meanings set forth in the Glossary.

Significance of sources, citations, and evidence in support of the Rules

Numerous sources were drawn on to develop the Rules and Commentary. Of course, treaty law is cited throughout for the propositions set forth. Customary law posed a greater challenge. In this regard, three sources were of particular importance. The Manual draws heavily on the ICRC Customary IHL Study, as it is a valuable repository of evidence and analysis regarding customary law in both international and non-international armed conflict. The AMW Manual also proved especially valuable because it addresses customary law in both international and non-international law. Finally, the International Group of Experts frequently considered the NIAC Manual when assessing whether a particular Rule applies during non-international armed conflict. With the exception of treaty law, all of the aforementioned sources were persuasive, but not dispositive, evidence of a norm's status as customary international law. Ultimately, the professional knowledge, experience, and expertise of the Experts form the basis for the *Tallinn Manual*'s conclusions as to the customary status of a Rule or its extension into non-international armed conflict.

The International Group of Experts regularly referenced the military manuals of four States – Canada, Germany, the United Kingdom, and the United States. The international legal community generally considers these four manuals to be especially useful during legal research and analysis with respect to conflict issues, although their use should not be interpreted as a comment on the quality of any other such manuals. Moreover, the International Group of Experts included members who participated in the drafting of each of the four manuals. These members were able to provide invaluable insight into the genesis, basis, and meaning of specific provisions. Finally, unlike many other military manuals, these four are all publicly available.

Among the manuals, the US Commander's Handbook served an additional purpose. Unlike Canada, Germany, and the United Kingdom, the United States is not a Party to either of the 1977 Additional Protocols to the 1949 Geneva Conventions, two key sources relied on during the project. The International Group of Experts took the position that the appearance of an Additional Protocol norm in the Handbook was an indication (but not more) of its customary nature. Of course, in doing so they were very sensitive to the fact that the Handbook is a military manual, not a legal treatise, and as such also reflects operational and policy considerations. At the same time, the Experts equally acknowledged that the fact that a State is party to the Additional Protocols does not mean that a provision of its own military manual is reflective only of treaty law.

The International Group of Experts accepted the position held by the International Court of Justice that the 1907 Hague Regulations reflect customary international law[18] and that most of the provisions of the 1949 Geneva Conventions have achieved the same status (a point of lesser significance in light of their universal ratification).[19] These instruments

[18] *Wall* Advisory Opinion, para. 89; *Nuclear Weapons* Advisory Opinion, para. 75. *See also* *Nuremburg* Tribunal judgment at 445.

[19] *Nuclear Weapons* Advisory Opinion, paras. 79, 82. *See also* Report of the Secretary-General Pursuant to Paragraph 2 of Security Council Resolution 808, UN SCOR, para. 35,

were accordingly particularly significant to the Experts in their deliberations regarding the customary status of a Rule.

Lastly, secondary sources, such as law review articles and books, are seldom cited. The International Group of Experts agreed that such citations are generally inappropriate in a manual. They accordingly appear only when particularly relevant on a certain point. Nevertheless, the Experts relied regularly on academic scholarship during their research.

Note that many sources are cited as support for the legal principles set forth in the *Tallinn Manual* (or their interpretation or application). This does not necessarily mean that the International Group of Experts viewed them as legal sources of the Rule or Commentary in question. For instance, the AMW Manual is often cited in order to draw attention to the acceptance of a particular principle in the context of air and missile warfare by the Experts involved in that project. However, the AMW Manual itself does not represent the legal source of any Rules or Commentary contained in the *Tallinn Manual*. Similarly, military manuals are not cited as a source of any particular Rule or Commentary, but rather for the purpose of alerting the reader to a State's acceptance of the general legal principle involved.

The International Group of Experts

Members of the International Group of Experts were carefully selected to include legal practitioners, academics, and technical experts. In particular, the Group's legal practitioners addressed, or had addressed, cyber issues in their professional positions, whereas the academics selected were recognized world-class experts on the *jus ad bellum* and *jus in bello*. This mix is crucial to the credibility of the final product. So too is the inclusion of technical experts who provided input to the discussions and the text to ensure the Manual was practically grounded and addressed key issues raised by actual or possible cyber operations.

Three organizations were invited to provide observers to the process. The observers participated fully in the discussions and drafting of the Manual, but their consent was not necessary to achieve the unanimity required for adoption of a Rule. NATO's Allied Command Transformation provided an observer to provide the perspective of a multinational

---

UN DOC. S/25704 (1993). The Security Council unanimously approved the statute to which the report referred. S.C. Res. 827, UN Doc. S/RES/827 (25 May 1993).

user of the Manual. The US Cyber Command's representative offered the perspective of a relevant operationally mature entity. Finally, the International Committee of the Red Cross was invited to observe and participate in the proceedings in view of the organization's special role *vis-à-vis* the law of armed conflict. Despite the invaluable active participation of the observers in the process, this Manual is not intended to reflect the legal positions or doctrine of any of these three organizations.

Drafting process

In September 2009, a small group met in Tallinn to consider the possible launch of a project to identify the relevant legal norms governing cyber warfare. The group quickly concluded such an effort was worthwhile and, therefore, went on to scope the project and draft a notional table of contents for a manual on the subject.

Based on that work, a larger International Group of Experts was invited to begin the drafting process. Initially, all members of the Group were tasked with researching and preparing proposed Rules on particular topics and an outline of the Commentary that might accompany them. The resulting inputs were combined into a first draft of the Manual.

The text of this draft was then split among three teams of Experts led by Group Facilitators. These teams were charged with refining the first draft. At subsequent meetings of the International Group of Experts, they presented their revised proposed Rules and accompanying Commentary. The meetings were designed to reach consensus on the precise text of the Rules and agreement that the Commentary reflected all reasonable views as to their meaning, scope, and application. At times, the resulting text was sent back into the teams for further consideration. In all, eight plenary meetings of three days each were held in Tallinn between 2010 and 2012.

Upon completion of the plenary sessions, an Editorial Committee drawn from among the International Group of Experts worked on the Manual to ensure the accuracy, thoroughness, and clarity of the Commentary. This team met twelve times in Tallinn or Berlin. The resulting draft was then divided among peer reviewers with deep expertise in the various subjects addressed by the Manual for comment. The Editorial Committee considered these comments and revised the Manual as appropriate. In July 2012, the International Group of Experts convened for a final time in Tallinn to consider the final draft, make any final changes, and approve both the Rules and the Commentary.

Creighton University Law School, Emory University Law School, and Chatham House generously supported the project by funding and supervising advanced law students to perform research and editorial tasks. The London School of Economics' International Humanitarian Law Project and Chatham House's International Security Department both graciously provided facilities for sessions dedicated to final editing of the Manual.

Authority of the Manual

It is essential to understand that the *Tallinn Manual* is not an official document, but is only the product of a group of independent experts acting solely in their personal capacity. The Manual does not represent the views of the NATO CCD COE, its sponsoring nations, or NATO. In particular, it is not meant to reflect NATO doctrine. Nor does it reflect the position of any organization or State represented by observers. Finally, participation in the International Group of Experts by individuals with official positions in their own countries must not be interpreted as indicating that the Manual represents the viewpoints of those countries. Ultimately, the *Tallinn Manual* must be understood as an expression solely of the opinions of the International Group of Experts, all acting in their private capacity.

Professor Michael N. Schmitt
Project Director

PART I

International cyber security law

1.   The term 'international cyber security law' is not a legal term of art. Rather, the object and purpose of its use here is to capture those aspects of public international law that relate to the hostile use of cyberspace, but are not formally an aspect of the *jus in bello*. Hence, the term is only descriptive. In this manual, it primarily refers to the *jus ad bellum*. However, it also incorporates such legal concepts as sovereignty, jurisdiction, and State responsibility insofar as they relate to operation of the *jus ad bellum* and *jus in bello*.

2.   In this regard, the International Group of Experts rejected any assertions that international law is silent on cyberspace in the sense that it is a new domain subject to international legal regulation only on the basis of new treaty law. On the contrary, the Experts unanimously concluded that general principles of international law applied to cyberspace.

1

States and cyberspace

1. The purpose of this chapter is to set forth rules of a general international legal nature detailing the relationship between States, cyber infrastructure, and cyber operations. Section 1 addresses issues relating to State sovereignty, jurisdiction, and control over cyber infrastructure. Section 2 deals with the application of classic public international law rules of State responsibility to cyber operations.

2. Terminology is essential to an accurate understanding of this chapter. 'Cyber infrastructure' refers to the communications, storage, and computing resources upon which information systems operate (Glossary). To the extent States can exercise control over cyber infrastructure, they shoulder certain rights and obligations as a matter of international law. The term 'cyber operations' refers to the employment of cyber capabilities with the primary purpose of achieving objectives in or by the use of cyberspace (Glossary). Under international law, States may be responsible for cyber operations that their organs conduct or that are otherwise attributable to them by virtue of the law of State responsibility. The actions of non-State actors may also sometimes be attributed to States.

3. Except when explicitly noted otherwise, the Rules and Commentary of this chapter apply both in times of peace and in times of armed conflict (whether international or non-international in nature). During an international armed conflict, the law of neutrality also governs the rights and obligations of States with regard to cyber infrastructure and operations (Chapter 7).

SECTION 1: SOVEREIGNTY, JURISDICTION, AND CONTROL

Rule 1 – Sovereignty

A State may exercise control over cyber infrastructure and activities within its sovereign territory.

1.   This Rule emphasizes the fact that although no State may claim sovereignty over cyberspace *per se*, States may exercise sovereign prerogatives over any cyber infrastructure located on their territory, as well as activities associated with that cyber infrastructure.

2.   The accepted definition of 'sovereignty' was set forth in the *Island of Palmas* Arbitral Award of 1928. It provides that 'Sovereignty in the relations between States signifies independence. Independence in regard to a portion of the globe is the right to exercise therein, to the exclusion of any other State, the functions of a State.'[1]

3.   It is the sovereignty that a State enjoys over territory that gives it the right to control cyber infrastructure and cyber activities within its territory. Accordingly, cyber infrastructure situated in the land territory, internal waters, territorial sea (including its bed and subsoil), archipelagic waters, or national airspace is subject to the sovereignty of the territorial State.[2]

4.   Sovereignty implies that a State may control access to its territory and generally enjoys, within the limits set by treaty and customary international law, the exclusive right to exercise jurisdiction and authority on its territory. Exceptions include the use of force pursuant to the right of self-defence (Rule 13) and in accordance with actions authorized or mandated by the United Nations Security Council (Rule 18).

5.   A State's sovereignty over cyber infrastructure within its territory has two consequences. First, that cyber infrastructure is subject to legal and regulatory control by the State.[3] Second, the State's territorial sovereignty protects such cyber infrastructure. It does not matter whether it belongs to the government or to private entities or individuals, nor do the purposes it serves matter.

6.   A cyber operation by a State directed against cyber infrastructure located in another State may violate the latter's sovereignty. It certainly does so if it causes damage. The International Group of Experts could achieve no consensus as to whether the placement of malware that causes no physical damage (as with malware used to monitor activities) constitutes a violation of sovereignty.

---

[1] *Island of Palmas (Neth. v. US)* 2 R.I.A.A. 829, 838 (Perm. Ct. Arb. 1928).

[2] On sovereignty over waters and airspace above waters, see Law of the Sea Convention, Art. 2; on sovereignty over airspace, see Chicago Convention, Arts. 1–3. With regard to cyber infrastructure in outer space, see Rules 3 and 4 and accompanying Commentary.

[3] In the 1949 *Corfu Channel* case, Judge Alejandro Alvarez appended a separate opinion in which he stated: 'By sovereignty, we understand the whole body of rights and attributes which a State possesses in its territory, to the exclusion of all other States, and also in its relations with other States. Sovereignty confers rights upon States and imposes obligations upon them.' *Corfu Channel* case at 43 (individual opinion of Judge Alvarez).

7. If such cyber operations are intended to coerce the government (and are not otherwise permitted under international law), the operation may constitute a prohibited 'intervention'[4] or a prohibited 'use of force' (Rules 10 to 12). A cyber operation that qualifies as an 'armed attack' triggers the right of individual or collective self-defence (Rule 13). Actions not constituting an armed attack but that are nevertheless in violation of international law may entitle the target State to resort to countermeasures (Rule 9). Security Council-mandated or authorized actions under Chapter VII of the United Nations Charter (Rule 18), including those involving cyber operations, do not constitute a violation of the target State's sovereignty.

8. A State may consent to cyber operations conducted from its territory or to remote cyber operations involving cyber infrastructure that is located on its territory. Consider a case in which non-State actors are engaged in unlawful cyber activities on State A's territory. State A does not have the technical ability to put an end to those activities and therefore requests the assistance of State B. State B's ensuing cyber operations on State A's territory would not be a violation of the latter's sovereignty. Consent may also be set forth in a standing treaty. For example, a basing agreement may authorize a sending State's military forces to conduct cyber operations from or within the receiving State's territory.

9. Customary or treaty law may restrict the exercise of sovereign rights by the territorial State. For example, international law imposes restrictions on interference with the activities of diplomatic premises and personnel. Similarly, a State's sovereignty in the territorial sea, archipelagic waters or straits used for international navigation is limited under customary international law by the rights of innocent passage, archipelagic sea lanes passage, and transit passage, respectively.[5]

10. In the cyber context, the principle of sovereignty allows a State to, inter alia, restrict or protect (in part or in whole) access to the Internet, without prejudice to applicable international law, such as human rights or international telecommunications law.[6] The fact that cyber infrastructure located in a given State's territory is linked to the global telecommunications network cannot be interpreted as a waiver of its sovereign rights over that infrastructure.

11. A coastal State's sovereignty over the seabed lying beneath its territorial sea allows that State full control over the placement of any submarine cables thereon. This is a critical right in light of the fact that

---

[4] UN Charter, Art. 2(1).   [5] Law of the Sea Convention, Arts. 17–19, 37–8, 52, 53.
[6] *E.g.*, the ITU Constitution.

submarine cables currently carry the bulk of international Internet communications. As to submarine cables beyond the territorial sea, Article 79(2) of the Convention on the Law of the Sea limits the extent to which a coastal State may interfere with submarine cables on its continental shelf.[7]

12.   Although States may not exercise sovereignty over cyberspace *per se*, States may exercise their jurisdiction *vis-à-vis* cyber crimes and other cyber activities pursuant to the bases of jurisdiction recognized in international law (Rule 2).[8]

13.   With regard to cyber infrastructure aboard sovereign immune platforms, see Rule 4.

14.   Traditionally, the notion of the violation of sovereignty was limited to actions undertaken by, or attributable to, States. However, there is an embryonic view proffered by some scholars that cyber operations conducted by non-State actors may also violate a State's sovereignty (in particular the aspect of territorial integrity).

Rule 2 – Jurisdiction

Without prejudice to applicable international obligations, a State may exercise its jurisdiction:

(a) over persons engaged in cyber activities on its territory;
(b) over cyber infrastructure located on its territory; and
(c) extraterritorially, in accordance with international law.

1.   The term 'jurisdiction' encompasses the authority to prescribe, enforce, and adjudicate. It extends to all matters, including those that are civil, criminal, or administrative in nature. The various general bases of jurisdiction are discussed below.

2.   The principal basis for a State to exercise its jurisdiction is physical or legal presence of a person (*in personam*) or object (*in rem*) on its territory. For instance, pursuant to its *in personam* jurisdiction a State may adopt laws and regulations governing the cyber activities of individuals on its territory. It may also regulate the activities of privately owned entities registered (or otherwise based as a matter of law) in its jurisdiction but physically operating abroad, such as Internet service providers ('ISPs'). *In rem* jurisdiction would allow it to adopt laws governing the operation of cyber infrastructure on its territory.

---

[7] Law of the Sea Convention, Art. 79(2).
[8] *See, e.g.*, Council of Europe, Convention on Cybercrime, 23 November 2001, Eur. T.S. No. 185.

3. It may be difficult to determine jurisdiction within cyberspace because cloud or grid distributed systems can span national borders, as can the replication and dynamic relocation of data and processing. This makes it challenging at any particular time to determine where all of a user's data and processing reside since such data can be located in multiple jurisdictions simultaneously. These technical challenges do not deprive a State of its legal right to exercise jurisdiction over persons and cyber infrastructure located on its territory.

4. With regard to jurisdiction based upon territoriality, it must be noted that although individuals using information and communications technology have a specific physical location, the location of mobile devices can change during a computing session. For instance, a person with a mobile computing device (e.g., a tablet or smartphone) can initiate several database queries or updates for processing by a cloud-based service. As those queries and updates take place, the user may move to another location. Any State from which the individual has operated enjoys jurisdiction because the individual, and the devices involved, were located on its territory when so used.

5. Even with technology such as mobile cloud computing, the devices from which the human user is initiating requests can be geo-located; software services and applications may track the geo-coordinates of the computing devices (e.g., Wi-Fi connection location or the device's global positioning system (GPS) location). It must be cautioned that it is possible under certain circumstances for someone who does not wish to be tracked to spoof the geo-coordinates advertised by his or her computing device. It is also possible that user-location will not be made available by the infrastructure or service provider, or by the application or device itself. Actual physical presence is required, and sufficient, for jurisdiction based on territoriality; spoofed presence does not suffice.

6. Territorial jurisdiction has given rise to two derivative forms of jurisdiction.[9] Subjective territorial jurisdiction involves the application

---

[9] The European Court of Justice Attorney General has explained the doctrine as follows: 'Territoriality ... has given rise to two distinct principles of jurisdiction: (i) *subjective* territoriality, which permits a State to deal with acts which originated within its territory, even though they were completed abroad, (ii) *objective* territoriality, which, conversely, permits a State to deal with acts which originated abroad but which were completed, at least in part, within its own territory ... [from the principle of objective territoriality] is derived the effects doctrine, which, in order to deal with the effects in question, confers jurisdiction upon a State even if the conduct which produced them did not take place within its territory.' Opinion of Mr Advocate General Darmon, Joined Cases 89, 104, 114,

of the law of the State exercising jurisdiction to an incident that is initiated within its territory but completed elsewhere. It applies even if the offending cyber activities have no effect within the State exercising such jurisdiction. Objective territorial jurisdiction, by contrast, grants jurisdiction over individuals to the State where the particular incident has effects even though the act was initiated outside its territory.[10]

7.   Objective territorial jurisdiction is of particular relevance to cyber operations. For example, in 2007, Estonia was targeted in cyber operations initiated at least partially from abroad. As to those acts which violated Estonian law, Estonia would at a minimum have been entitled to invoke jurisdiction over individuals, wherever located, who conducted the operations. In particular, its jurisdiction would have been justified because the operations had substantial effects on Estonian territory, such as interference with the banking system and governmental functions. Similarly, civilians involved in cyber operations against Georgia during that State's international armed conflict with the Russian Federation in 2008 would have been subject to Georgian jurisdiction on the basis of significant interference with websites and disruption of cyber communications in violation of Georgian law.[11]

8.   Other recognized bases for extraterritorial jurisdiction, albeit with certain restrictions, include: (i) nationality of the perpetrator (active personality); (ii) nationality of the victim (passive personality); (iii) national security threat to the State (protective principle); and (iv) violation of a universal norm of international law, such as a war crime (universal jurisdiction). For example, any significant cyber interference with a State's military defensive systems (e.g., air defence and early warning radars) constitutes a threat to national security and accordingly is encompassed by the protective principle.

9.   In light of the variety of jurisdictional bases in international law, two or more States often enjoy jurisdiction over the same person or object in respect of the same event. Consider the case of a terrorist group that launches a cyber operation from the territory of State A designed to cause physical damage to State B's electricity generation plants. The terrorists

---

116, 117 and 125–9, *Ahlström Osakeyhtiö and Others* v. *Comm'n [In re Wood Pulp Cartel]*, paras. 20–1, 1994 E.C.R I-100.

[10] While the effects doctrine has reached a general level of acceptance, its exercise in a number of situations has led to controversy. AMERICAN LAW INSTITUTE, THIRD RESTATEMENT OF FOREIGN RELATIONS LAW § 402(1)(c) (1987).

[11] Civilians are not entitled to combatant immunity under the law of armed conflict and therefore are fully susceptible to the traditional bases of jurisdiction dealt with here.

employ a cyber weapon against the plant's control systems, triggering an explosion that injures workers. Members of the cell are from various States. State A may claim jurisdiction on the basis that the operation occurred there. State B enjoys jurisdiction based on passive personality and objective territorial jurisdiction. Other States have jurisdiction on the grounds of an attacker's nationality.

10.   The phrase 'without prejudice to applicable international obligations' is included to recognize that, in certain circumstances, international law may effectively limit the exercise of jurisdiction over certain persons or objects on a State's territory. Examples include immunity (e.g., combatant and diplomatic immunity) and the grant of primary jurisdiction to one of two States enjoying concurrent jurisdiction over a person or particular offence (e.g., through the application of a Status of Forces Agreement).

Rule 3 – Jurisdiction of flag States and States of registration

Cyber infrastructure located on aircraft, ships, or other platforms in international airspace, on the high seas, or in outer space is subject to the jurisdiction of the flag State or State of registration.

1.   The term 'international airspace' relates to the airspace above the high seas.[12] For the purposes of this Manual, the term 'high seas' denotes all sea areas beyond the outer limit of the territorial sea of coastal States and includes the exclusive economic zone,[13] while 'outer space' refers to the area above an altitude of approximately 100 km.[14]

2.   On the high seas, in international airspace, or in outer space, cyber infrastructure will regularly be located on board such platforms as vessels, offshore installations, aircraft, and satellites. For instance, modern commercial large-tonnage ships are heavily dependent on shipboard cyber infrastructure to control propulsion, navigation, and other on-board systems and rely on land-based cyber systems for a variety of purposes, such as remote maintenance (i.e., monitoring, diagnostics, and repair), weather reports, and navigation. An example of ship-to-ship and ship-to-shore reliance on cyber infrastructure is the use of the Automatic

---

[12] Law of the Sea Convention, Art. 2; US COMMANDER'S HANDBOOK, para. 1.9.

[13] Law of the Sea Convention, Art. 86; US COMMANDER'S HANDBOOK, para. 1.3.5. Although the Law of the Sea Convention provides that the high seas begin at the outer limit of the exclusive economic zone, as used in this Manual, the term includes the exclusive economic zone (in light of its general international character with respect to sovereignty).

[14] *See* US COMMANDER'S HANDBOOK, para. 1.10; UK MANUAL, para. 12.13; AMW MANUAL, commentary accompanying Rule 1(a).

Identification System, whereby ships broadcast their location and receive position updates from other ships.

3.   Jurisdiction (Rule 2) over the platforms on which cyber infrastructure is located is based upon the flag State principle in the case of ships[15] and on the State of registration for aircraft and space objects.[16] With regard to offshore installations, jurisdiction may follow from the coastal State's exclusive sovereign rights or from nationality.

4.   It must be borne in mind that although objects and persons aboard platforms are subject to the jurisdiction of the flag State or State of registration, they may also be subject to the jurisdiction of other States. Consider the example of an individual from State A who conducts cyber operations from a ship registered in State B. State A and State B both enjoy jurisdiction over the individual, the former based on active personality, the latter on this Rule. Alternatively, consider a transponder that is owned and operated by a company registered in State A, but located on a satellite registered in State B. Both States enjoy concurrent jurisdiction pursuant to this Rule.

5.   The fact that a State other than the flag State or State of registration is technically capable of taking remote control of particular cyber infrastructure has no bearing on enforcement jurisdiction. For example, a State may not exercise jurisdiction over cyber infrastructure aboard a commercial drone registered in another State that is operating in international airspace by taking control of that drone. This conclusion, of course, assumes the absence of a specific international law basis for doing so, such as exercise of coastal State enforcement authority over vessels in the exclusive economic zone and contiguous zone.[17]

---

[15] 'Ships shall sail under the flag of one State only and, save in exceptional cases expressly provided for in international treaties or in this Convention, shall be subject to its exclusive jurisdiction on the high seas.' Law of the Sea Convention, Art. 92(1).

[16] Chicago Convention, Art. 17 (regarding aircraft); Convention on Registration of Objects Launched into Outer Space, Art. II, 14 January 1975, 1023 U.N.T.S. 15 (regarding space objects). Note that State aircraft need not be registered since the Chicago Convention does not encompass them (Art. 3(a)). The mere fact that a satellite is launched into outer space does not deprive the State of registry of jurisdiction over the satellite and its activities. Outer Space Treaty, Art. VIII.

[17] It might be asserted that Arts. IV and IX of the Outer Space Treaty provide an additional legal basis for the prohibition on exercise of enforcement jurisdiction by States other than the State of registration by barring interference with the activities of other States in the peaceful exploration and use of outer space. However, these provisions are generally interpreted as limited to interference that rises to the level of a violation of Art. 2(4) of the UN Charter.

6.   If an aircraft or satellite has not been registered in accordance with applicable internationally recognized procedures, the nationality thereof will be that of the respective owner. With regard to ownership by corporations (juridical persons), it is a well-established rule of public international law that nationality is determined by either the place of incorporation 'or from other various links including the centre of administration'.[18] During an international armed conflict, the nationality of a corporation may also be determined by the so-called 'control test'.[19]

7.   Submarine cables located on the continental shelf may constitute cyber infrastructure because data is transmitted through them. They are governed by traditional rules of jurisdiction deriving from their owner-ship, as well as by other aspects of international law, such as the Law of the Sea Convention[20] and Article 54 of the Hague Regulations.

Rule 4 – Sovereign immunity and inviolability

Any interference by a State with cyber infrastructure aboard a plat-form, wherever located, that enjoys sovereign immunity constitutes a violation of sovereignty.

1.   This Rule must be distinguished from Rule 3. The latter refers to cyber infrastructure located aboard platforms on the high seas, in inter-national airspace, or in outer space. This Rule applies only to those platforms that enjoy sovereign immunity. Their location is irrelevant.

2.   'Sovereign immunity' provides that a sovereign platform or object, and all objects or persons thereon, are immune from the exercise of jurisdiction aboard that platform by another State. International law clearly accords sovereign immunity to certain objects used for non-commercial governmental purposes, regardless of their location.[21] It is generally accepted that warships and 'ships owned or operated by a State and used only for government non-commercial service' enjoy immunity

---

[18] IAN BROWNLIE, PRINCIPLES OF PUBLIC INTERNATIONAL LAW 420 (7th ed. 2008).

[19] Corporations controlled by enemy nationals, even though not incorporated (or other-wise registered) in enemy territory, may be deemed to have enemy character if they are under the actual control of a person or of persons residing, or carrying on business, in enemy territory. See, e.g., Daimler Co. Ltd v. Continental Tyre and Rubber Co. [1916] 2 A.C. 307 (Eng.).

[20] Law of the Sea Convention, Arts. 86, 87(1)(c).

[21] Note that the present Manual does not deal with diplomatic immunity or with the immunity of government officials.

from the jurisdiction of any State other than the flag State.[22] Further, State aircraft enjoy sovereign immunity.[23] The International Group of Experts agreed that space objects operated for non-commercial governmental purposes also have sovereign immunity.[24]

3.   In order to enjoy sovereign immunity and inviolability, the cyber infrastructure aboard the platform in question must be devoted exclusively to government purposes. For example, government institutions that operate as market participants *vis-à-vis* the Internet cannot claim that the cyber infrastructure involved enjoys sovereign immunity, because that infrastructure does not serve exclusively governmental purposes. Likewise, a satellite used for both governmental and commercial purposes will lack sovereign immunity. Some satellites have multiple transponders, each exclusively dedicated to a different user. If some of them are used for commercial purposes, the satellite will not have sovereign immunity. The International Group of Experts agreed that a satellite owned or operated by a consortium of States does not have sovereign immunity unless used for strictly non-commercial purposes. In such a case, it is arguable that the satellite would be covered by the joint sovereign immunity of the States and would thus enjoy a form of cumulative sovereign immunity.

4.   Sovereign immunity entails inviolability; any interference with an object enjoying sovereign immunity constitutes a violation of international law.[25] Interference includes, but is not limited to, activities that damage the object or significantly impair its operation. For instance, a denial of service attack against a State's military satellite would constitute a violation of its sovereign immunity. Similarly, taking control of the object would violate sovereign immunity. This was the case with regard to a 2007 incident involving the takeover and reprogramming of a British military communications satellite.

5.   Despite enjoying sovereign immunity, sovereign platforms and structures must comply with the rules and principles of international

---

[22] Law of the Sea Convention, Arts. 95, 96; US COMMANDER'S HANDBOOK, para. 2.1.

[23] UK MANUAL, para. 12.6.1; AMW MANUAL, commentary accompanying Rule 1(cc).

[24] *See* Convention on Jurisdictional Immunities, Art. 3(3) (acknowledging the sovereign immunity of space objects).

[25] *See, e.g., Owners of the Jessie, the Thomas F. Bayard, and the Pescawha (UK v. US)*, 6 R.I. A.A. 57 (1926) (Anglo American Claims Commission 1921); *Player Larga (Owners of Cargo Lately Laden on Board) Appellants v. I Congreso del Partido (Owners) Respondents, Marble Islands (Owners of Cargo Lately Laden on Board) Appellants v. same Respondents, I Congreso del Partido* [1983] 1 A.C. 244 (H.L.).

law, such as the obligation to respect the sovereignty of other States. For instance, a military aircraft non-consensually entering the national airspace of another State to conduct cyber operations can, despite its sovereign status, trigger the State's right to take necessary measures against the intruding aircraft, including, in certain circumstances, the use of force. The same would be true of a warship that conducts cyber activities in a nation's territorial sea. If the activities are inconsistent with the innocent passage regime, the coastal nation may take enforcement steps to prevent the non-innocent passage, despite the warship's sovereign immunity.[26] In both cases, the platforms retain their sovereign immunity, but that immunity does not prevent the other States from taking those actions which are lawful, appropriate, and necessary in the circumstances to safeguard their legally recognized interests.

6.   While there is no treaty rule explicitly according sovereign immunity to any objects used for non-commercial governmental purposes, it is of importance that according to Article 5 of the Convention on Jurisdictional Immunity a State enjoys immunity from the jurisdiction of the courts of another State with regard to its property.[27] It could be suggested that this provision, as well as the points made in the previous paragraph, evidence a general principle of public international law by which objects owned or used by a State for non-commercial governmental purposes are covered by the State's sovereignty. Accordingly, they are subject to that State's exclusive jurisdiction even if located outside its territory. The International Group of Experts could achieve no consensus on this point.

7.   In times of international armed conflict, the principles of sovereign immunity and inviolability cease to apply in relations between the parties to the conflict (subject to any specific rule of international law to the contrary, such as Article 45 of the Vienna Convention on Diplomatic Relations). Objects enjoying sovereign immunity and inviolability may be destroyed if they qualify as military objectives (Rule 38), or may be seized as booty of war by the respective enemy armed forces.[28] It should be noted that governmental cyber infrastructure of neutral States may qualify as a military objective in certain circumstances (Rule 91).

8.   Locations and objects may enjoy special protection affording inviolability by virtue of bilateral or multilateral agreements, such as Status of Forces Agreements. It must be borne in mind that diplomatic archives

---

[26] Law of the Sea Convention, Arts. 19, 25(1), 32.
[27] Convention on Jurisdictional Immunities, Art. 5.
[28] AMW MANUAL, Rule 136(a) and accompanying commentary.

and means of communication enjoy special protection under the Vienna Convention on Diplomatic Relations.[29] Such protection applies at all times, including periods of armed conflict (Rule 84).

Rule 5 – Control of cyber infrastructure

A State shall not knowingly allow the cyber infrastructure located in its territory or under its exclusive governmental control to be used for acts that adversely and unlawfully affect other States.

1. This Rule establishes a standard of behaviour for States in relation to two categories of cyber infrastructure: (i) any cyber infrastructure (governmental or not in nature) located on their territory; and (ii) cyber infrastructure located elsewhere but over which the State in question has either de jure or de facto exclusive control. It applies irrespective of the attributability of the acts in question to a State (Rules 6 and 7).

2. The principle of sovereign equality entails an obligation of all States to respect the territorial sovereignty of other States. As the International Court of Justice held in the *Nicaragua* judgment, 'Between independent States, respect for territorial sovereignty is an essential foundation of international relations.'[30]

3. The obligation to respect the sovereignty of another State, as noted in the International Court of Justice's *Corfu Channel* judgment, implies that a State may not 'allow knowingly its territory to be used for acts contrary to the rights of other States'.[31] Accordingly, States are required under international law to take appropriate steps to protect those rights.[32] This obligation applies not only to criminal acts harmful to other States, but also, for example, to activities that inflict serious damage, or have the potential to inflict such damage, on persons and objects protected by the territorial sovereignty of the target State.[33]

---

[29] Vienna Convention on Diplomatic Relations, Arts. 24, 27.

[30] *Nicaragua* judgment, para. 202.   [31] *Corfu Channel* case at 22.

[32] *Tehran Hostages* case, paras. 67–8.

[33] In the *Trail Smelter* case, the Tribunal, citing the Federal Court of Switzerland, noted: 'This right (sovereignty) excludes ... not only the usurpation and exercise of sovereign rights ... but also an actual encroachment which might prejudice the natural use of the territory and the free movement of its inhabitants.' *Trail Smelter* case (*US* v. *Can.*), 3 R.I. A.A. 1905, 1963 (1941). According to the Tribunal, 'under the principles of international law ... no State has the right to use or permit the use of its territory in such a manner as to cause injury ... in or to the territory of another or the properties or persons therein, when the case is of serious consequence ...' *Trail Smelter* case at 1965.

4.   These requirements are complicated by the nature of harmful cyber acts, especially time and space compression, and their often-unprecedented character. There may be circumstances in which it is not feasible for a State to prevent injury to another State. For example, State A may know that a harmful cyber attack is being prepared and will be launched from its territory against State B. However, because it has not identified the attack's exact signature and timing, the only effective option may be to isolate the network that will be used in the attack from the Internet. Doing so will often result in a 'self-denial' of service to State A. The nature, scale, and scope of the (potential) harm to both States must be assessed to determine whether this remedial measure is required. The test in such circumstances is one of reasonableness.

5.   As to scope of application, this Rule covers all acts that are unlawful and that have detrimental effects on another State (whether those effects occur on another State's territory or on objects protected under international law). The term 'unlawful' is used in this Rule to denote an activity that is contrary to the legal rights of the affected State. The International Group of Experts deliberately chose not to limit the prohibition to narrower concepts, such as use of force (Rule 11) or armed attack (Rule 13), in order to emphasize that the prohibition extends to all cyber activities from one State's territory that affect the rights of other States and have detrimental effects on another State's territory. In particular, there is no requirement that the cyber operation in question result in physical damage to objects or injuries to individuals; it need only produce a negative effect.

6.   The Rule addresses a situation in which the relevant acts are underway. For instance, a State that allows cyber infrastructure on its territory to be used by a terrorist group to undertake an attack against another State would be in violation of this Rule, as would a State that, upon notification by another State that this activity is being carried out, fails to take reasonably feasible measures to terminate the conduct.

7.   The International Group of Experts could not agree whether situations in which the relevant acts are merely prospective are covered by this Rule. Some of the Experts took the position that States must take reasonable measures to prevent them. Others suggested that no duty of prevention exists, particularly not in the cyber context given the difficulty of mounting comprehensive and effective defences against all possible threats.

8.   This Rule also applies with regard to acts contrary to international law launched from cyber infrastructure that is under the exclusive control

of a government. It refers to situations where the infrastructure is located outside the respective State's territory, but that State nevertheless exercises exclusive control over it. Examples include a military installation in a foreign country subject to exclusive sending State control pursuant to a basing agreement, sovereign platforms on the high seas or in international airspace, or diplomatic premises.

9.   This Rule applies if the relevant remedial cyber operations can be undertaken by State organs or by individuals under State control. The International Group of Experts also agreed that if a remedial action could only be performed by a private entity, such as a private Internet service provider, the State would be obliged to use all means at its disposal to require that entity to take the action necessary to terminate the activity.

10.   This Rule applies if the State has actual knowledge of the acts in question. A State will be regarded as having actual knowledge if, for example, State organs such as its intelligence agencies have detected a cyber attack originating from its territory or if the State has received credible information (perhaps from the victim State) that a cyber attack is underway from its territory.

11.   The International Group of Experts could not achieve consensus as to whether this Rule also applies if the respective State has only constructive ('should have known') knowledge. In other words, it is unclear whether a State violates this Rule if it fails to use due care in policing cyber activities on its territory and is therefore unaware of the acts in question. Even if constructive knowledge suffices, the threshold of due care is uncertain in the cyber context because of such factors as the difficulty of attribution, the challenges of correlating separate sets of events as part of a coordinated and distributed attack on one or more targets, and the ease with which deception can be mounted through cyber infrastructure.

12.   Nor could the International Group of Experts achieve consensus as to whether this Rule applies to States through which cyber operations are routed. Some Experts took the position that to the extent that a State of transit knows of an offending operation and has the ability to put an end to it, the State must do so. These Experts took notice, however, of the unique routing processes of cyber transmissions. For instance, should a transmission be blocked at one node of a network, it will usually be rerouted along a different transmission path, often through a different State. In such a case, these Experts agreed that the State of transit has no obligation to act, because doing so would have no meaningful effect on the outcome of the operation. Other Experts took the position that the

Rule applied only to the territory of the State from which the operation is launched or to territory under its exclusive control. They either argued that the legal principle did not extend to other territory *in abstracto* or justified their view on the basis of the unique difficulties of applying the Rule in the cyber context.

13.   If a State fails to take appropriate steps in accordance with this Rule, the victim State may be entitled to respond to that violation of international law by resorting to proportionate responses. These may include, where appropriate in the circumstances, countermeasures (Rule 9) or the use of force in self-defence (Rule 13).

14.   With regard to such situations during an international armed conflict, see Rule 94.

SECTION 2:   STATE RESPONSIBILITY

Rule 6 – Legal responsibility of States

A State bears international legal responsibility for a cyber operation attributable to it and which constitutes a breach of an international obligation.

1.   This Rule is based on the customary international law of State responsibility, which is largely reflected in the International Law Commission's Articles on State Responsibility. It must be noted, however, that the law of armed conflict contains a number of specific rules on State responsibility for violation thereof. In particular, Articles 3 of Hague Convention IV and 91 of Additional Protocol I provide for compensation in the case of a violation of certain rules of the law of armed conflict.[34]

2.   It is a quintessential principle of international law that States bear responsibility for an act when: (i) the act in question is attributable to the State under international law; and (ii) it constitutes a breach of an international legal obligation applicable to that State (whether by treaty or customary international law).[35] Such a breach can consist of either an act or omission.[36]

3.   In the realm of cyberspace, an internationally wrongful act can consist, inter alia, of a violation of the United Nations Charter (e.g., a use of force committed through cyber means, Rule 10) or a violation of a law of armed conflict obligation (e.g., a cyber attack against civilian

---

[34] *See also* ICRC Customary IHL Study, Rules 149, 150.
[35] Articles on State Responsibility, Arts. 1–2.   [36] Articles on State Responsibility, Art. 2

objects, Rule 37) attributable to the State in question. A breach of peacetime rules not involving conflict (e.g., a violation of the law of the sea or the non-intervention principle) also constitutes an internationally wrongful act. As an example, a warship of one State is prohibited from conducting cyber operations that are adverse to the coastal nation's interests while in innocent passage.[37]

4.   The law of State responsibility extends only to an act, or failure to act, that violates international law. In other words, an act committed by a State's organ, or otherwise attributable to it, can only amount to an 'internationally wrongful act' if it is contrary to international law.[38] The law of State responsibility is not implicated when States engage in other acts that are either permitted or unregulated by international law.[39] For instance, international law does not address espionage *per se*. Thus, a State's responsibility for an act of cyber espionage conducted by an organ of the State in cyberspace is not be engaged as a matter of international law unless particular aspects of the espionage violate specific international legal prohibitions (as in the case of cyber espionage involving diplomatic communications, Rule 84).

5.   The causation of damage is not a precondition to the characterization of a cyber operation as an internationally wrongful act under the law of State responsibility.[40] However, the rule in question may include damage as an essential element. In such cases, damage is a *conditio sine qua non* of the attachment of State responsibility. For instance, under a customary rule of international law, States are prohibited from inflicting significant damage on another State through activities on their own territory (Rule 5). In the absence of such damage, no responsibility attaches unless another rule not containing an element of damage has been violated.

6.   In addition to being internationally wrongful, an act must be attributable to a State to fall within the ambit of this Rule. All acts or omissions of organs of a State are automatically and necessarily attributable to that State.[41] The concept of 'organs of a State' in the law of State responsibility is broad. Every person or entity that has that status under the State's

---

[37] Law of the Sea Convention, Art. 19.

[38] This is a stringent requirement since, as formulated by the ICJ, 'it is entirely possible for a particular act ... not to be in violation of international law without necessarily constituting the exercise of a right conferred by it'. *Kosovo* Advisory Opinion, para. 56.

[39] *Kosovo* Advisory Opinion, para. 84; *Lotus* case at 18.

[40] Articles on State Responsibility, commentary accompanying Art. 2.

[41] Articles on State Responsibility, Art. 4(1).

internal legislation will be an organ of the State regardless of their function or place in the governmental hierarchy.[42] Any cyber activity undertaken by the intelligence, military, internal security, customs, or other State agencies will engage State responsibility under international law if it violates an international legal obligation applicable to that State.

7.   It does not matter whether the organ in question acted in compliance with, beyond, or without any instructions. When committed by an organ of the State, and provided that organ is acting in an apparently official capacity,[43] even so-called ultra vires acts trigger a State's international legal responsibility if they breach international obligations.[44]

8.   For the purposes of the law of State responsibility, persons or entities that, while not organs of that State, are specifically empowered by its domestic law to exercise 'governmental authority' are equated to State organs.[45] When acting in such a capacity, their actions, as with State organs, are attributable to that State. Examples include a private corporation that has been granted the authority by the government to conduct offensive computer network operations against another State, as well as a private entity empowered to engage in cyber intelligence gathering. It is important to emphasize that State responsibility is only engaged when the entity in question is exercising elements of governmental authority. For example, States might have legislation authorizing private sector Computer Emergency Response Teams (CERTs) to conduct cyber defence of governmental networks. While so acting, their activities automatically engage the responsibility of their sponsoring State. However, there are no State responsibility implications when a private sector CERT is performing information security services for private companies.

---

[42] Articles on State Responsibility, Art. 4(2).
[43] Articles on State Responsibility, para. 13 of commentary accompanying Art. 4: 'A particular problem is to determine whether a person who is a State organ acts in that capacity. It is irrelevant for this purpose that the person concerned may have had ulterior or improper motives or may be abusing public power. Where such a person acts in an apparently official capacity, or under colour of authority, the actions in question will be attributable to the State. The distinction between unauthorized conduct of a State organ and purely private conduct has been clearly drawn in international arbitral decisions … The case of purely private conduct should not be confused with that of an organ functioning as such but acting *ultra vires* or in breach of the rules governing its operation. In this latter case, the organ is nevertheless acting in the name of the State.'
[44] Articles on State Responsibility, Art. 7.
[45] Articles on State Responsibility, Art. 5, and accompanying commentary.

9. In certain circumstances, the conduct of non-State actors may be attributable to a State and give rise to the State's international legal responsibility.[46] Article 8 of the Articles on State Responsibility, which restates customary international law, notes 'the conduct of a person or group of persons shall be considered an act of a State under international law if the person or group of persons is in fact acting on the instructions of, or under the direction or control of, that State in carrying out the conduct'.[47] This norm is particularly relevant in the cyber context. For example, States may contract with a private company to conduct cyber operations. Similarly, States have reportedly called upon private citizens to conduct cyber operations against other States or targets abroad (in a sense, 'cyber volunteers').

10. The International Court of Justice has held, in the context of military operations, that a State is responsible for the acts of non-State actors where it has 'effective control' over such actors.[48] For instance, the provision by a State of cyber expertise during the planning of specific cyber attacks may, depending on how deep the involvement goes, give rise to State responsibility for any internationally wrongful acts committed by such non-State actors. It is sometimes asserted that uncertainty surrounds the degree of 'control' required for a non-State actor's conduct to be attributable to the State. In *Tadić*, the International Criminal Tribunal for the Former Yugoslavia adopted an 'overall control' test – a less stringent threshold – in the context of individual criminal responsibility and for the purpose of determining the nature of the armed conflict.[49] However, in the *Genocide* judgment, the International Court of Justice distinguished such an evaluation from that conducted for the

---

[46] Articles on State Responsibility, Arts. 9, 10. The International Group of Experts reached the conclusion that it is currently difficult to imagine scenarios in which Art. 9 results in State responsibility given its requirement that the conduct be carried out in the absence or default of the official authorities. The International Group of Experts was uncertain whether Art. 10, which addresses the conduct of an insurrectional or other movement that becomes a government, accurately reflects customary international law.

[47] Articles on State Responsibility, Art. 8. 'In the text of article 8, the three terms "instructions", "direction" and "control" are disjunctive; it is sufficient to establish any one of them. At the same time it is made clear that the instructions, direction or control must relate to the conduct which is said to have amounted to an internationally wrongful act.' Articles on State Responsibility, para. 7 of commentary accompanying Art. 8.

[48] The Court articulated the effective control standard for the first time in the *Nicaragua* judgment, para. 115. *See also Genocide* judgment, paras. 399–401.

[49] *Tadić* Appeals Chamber judgment, paras. 131, 145.

purpose of establishing State responsibility.[50] Nevertheless, even by an 'overall control' test, the requisite control would need to go beyond 'the mere financing and equipping of such forces and involv[e] also participation in the planning and supervision of military operations'.[51] Moreover, as noted below, even if the lower 'overall control' test were to be adopted, it would not apply to individuals or unorganized groups.[52]

11.   These situations must be distinguished from those in which private citizens, on their own initiative, conduct cyber operations (so-called 'hacktivists' or 'patriotic hackers'). The material scope of applicability of Article 8 is relatively stringent in that it is limited to instructions, direction, or control. The State needs to have issued specific instructions or directed or controlled a particular operation to engage State responsibility.[53] Merely encouraging or otherwise expressing support for the independent acts of non-State actors does not meet the Article 8 threshold.

12.   The place where the act in question takes place, or where the actors involved are located, does not affect the determination of whether State responsibility attaches. For instance, consider a group in State A that assimilates computers located in State B into its botnet. The group uses the botnet to overload computer systems in State C based on instructions received from State D. The conduct is attributable under the law of State responsibility to State D. Note that State A cannot be presumed responsible solely based on the fact that the group was located there, nor can it be presumed that State B bears responsibility for the group's acts merely because of the location of the bots on its territory.

13.   This rule applies only to attribution for the purposes of State responsibility. However, a State's involvement with non-State actors may itself constitute a violation of international law, even in cases where the actions of the non-State actors involved cannot be attributed to the State. For

---

[50] *Genocide* judgment, paras. 403–405.

[51] *Tadić* Appeals Chamber judgment, para. 145.

[52] The *Tadić* Appeals Chamber judgment noted, at para. 132, that: 'It should be added that courts have taken a different approach with regard to *individuals or groups not organised into military structures*. With regard to such individuals or groups, courts have not considered an overall or general level of control to be sufficient, but have instead insisted upon specific instructions or directives aimed at the commission of specific acts, or have required public approval of those acts following their commission.'

[53] 'On the other hand, where persons or groups have committed acts under the effective control of a State, the condition for attribution will still be met even if particular instructions may have been ignored. The conduct will have been committed under the control of the State and it will be attributable to the State in accordance with article 8.' Articles on State Responsibility, para. 8 of commentary accompanying Art. 8.

instance, if State A provides hacking tools that are subsequently employed by an insurgent group on its own initiative against State B (i.e., the group is not acting under the control of State A), the mere provision of these tools is insufficient to attribute the group's attack to State A. Nevertheless, such assistance can itself constitute a violation of international law.[54]

14.   Even when the conditions of Article 8 are not initially met, acts may be retroactively attributed to the State.[55] Pursuant to Article 11 of the Articles on State Responsibility, 'Conduct which is not attributable to a State under the preceding articles shall nevertheless be considered an act of that State under international law if and to the extent that the State acknowledges and adopts the conduct in question as its own.'[56] For instance, consider computer operations conducted by non-State actors against a State. If another State later expresses support for them and uses its cyber capabilities to protect the non-State actors against counter-cyber operations, State responsibility will attach for those operations and any related subsequent acts of the group. Note that this provision is narrowly applied. Not only are the conditions of 'acknowledgement' and 'adoption' cumulative, they also require more than mere endorsement or tacit approval.[57]

Rule 7 – Cyber operations launched from governmental cyber infrastructure

The mere fact that a cyber operation has been launched or otherwise originates from governmental cyber infrastructure is not sufficient evidence for attributing the operation to that State, but is an indication that the State in question is associated with the operation.

1.   It must be emphasized that this Rule only relates to operations launched or originating from governmental cyber infrastructure. It does not address operations routed through such infrastructure (Rule 8). Additionally, it does not apply to operations launched or otherwise initiated

---

[54] *See Nicaragua* judgment, para. 242.
[55] *Tehran Hostages* case, para. 74: 'The approval given to these facts by the Ayatollah Khomeini and other organs of the Iranian State, and the decision to perpetuate them, translated continuing occupation of the Embassy and detention of the hostages into acts of that State. The militants, authors of the invasion and jailers of the hostages, had now become agents of the Iranian State for whose acts the State itself was internationally responsible.'
[56] Articles on State Responsibility, Art. 11.
[57] Articles on State Responsibility, commentary accompanying Art. 11.

from cyber infrastructure that does not qualify as governmental cyber infrastructure, even if located on the State's territory. This Rule should not be understood as predetermining the evidentiary conclusions that States may draw as to the attribution of cyber events.

2. With regard to its governmental character, it is immaterial whether the respective cyber infrastructure is owned by the government or remains the property of a private entity, as in the case of items leased by the government. Provided the use is non-commercial, it does not matter which governmental purposes the respective equipment serves. Furthermore, all branches of government are covered by the term. Accordingly, the infrastructure may be used for military, police, customs, or any other governmental purposes.

3. Rule 7 merely denotes that the fact that a cyber operation has been mounted from government cyber infrastructure is an indication of that State's involvement. In and of itself, the Rule does not serve as a legal basis for taking any action against the State involved or otherwise holding it responsible for the acts in question. Prior to the advent of cyber operations, the use of governmental assets, in particular military equipment, would typically have been attributed to the State without question because of the unlikelihood of their use by persons other than State organs or individuals or groups authorized to exercise governmental functions. This traditional approach cannot be followed in the cyber context. It may well be that government cyber infrastructure has come under the control of non-State actors who then use it to conduct cyber operations.

4. Note that each situation must be considered in context. For instance, a regular pattern of taking control of governmental cyber infrastructure by a non-State group in order to launch cyber operations may serve as a counter-indication that a State is associated with a particular operation. Similarly, reliable human intelligence that indicates governmental computers will be, or have been, employed by non-State actors to conduct operations might also suffice. Indeed, spoofing is a widely used cyber technique, designed to feign the identity of another individual or organization. Its particular relevance in this context was demonstrated by the incidents involving Estonia (2007) and Georgia (2008).

5. Operation of the Rule is not limited to a State's own territory. Examples would include cyber operations launched from ships on the high seas, aircraft in international airspace, and satellites in outer space over which a State exercises exclusive control.

Rule 8 – Cyber operations routed through a State

The fact that a cyber operation has been routed via the cyber infrastructure located in a State is not sufficient evidence for attributing the operation to that State.

1. This Rule addresses cyber operations launched from the cyber infrastructure located in one State that are routed through government or non-government cyber infrastructure located in another. In such a situation, the latter cannot be presumed to be associated with the cyber operation. This is because the characteristics of cyberspace are such that the mere passage of data through the infrastructure located in a State does not presuppose any involvement by that State in the associated cyber operation.

2. Recall that pursuant to Rule 5 a State must not knowingly allow its cyber infrastructure to be used for acts adverse to the rights of other States.[58] However, the International Group of Experts was unable to achieve consensus as to whether that Rule applies to States through which cyber operations are routed. To the extent that it does, the State of transit will bear responsibility for failing to take reasonable measures to prevent the transit.

3. There may be other criteria according to which the respective act can be attributed to a State (Rule 6). For instance, this Rule is without prejudice to the rights and obligations of neutral States during an international armed conflict (Rules 91 to 95).

Rule 9 – Countermeasures

A State injured by an internationally wrongful act may resort to proportionate countermeasures, including cyber countermeasures, against the responsible State.

1. Rule 9 and its accompanying Commentary are derived from Articles 22 and 49 to 53 of the International Law Commission's Articles on State Responsibility. It must be noted that certain provisions of the Articles are controversial and may not reflect customary international law. These are discussed below.

2. Countermeasures are necessary and proportionate actions that a 'victim State' takes in response to a violation of international law by an 'offending State'. The acts comprising the countermeasures would be

---

[58] On the nature of these rights, see Rule 5 and accompanying Commentary.

unlawful were it not for the offending State's conduct. Such counter-measures must be intended to induce compliance with international law by the offending State. For example, suppose State B launches a cyber operation against an electrical generating facility at a dam in State A in order to coerce A into increasing the flow of water into a river running through the two States. State A may lawfully respond with proportionate countermeasures, such as cyber operations against State B's irrigation control system.

3.   Pursuant to Article 49(1) of the Articles on State Responsibility, the sole permissible purpose of countermeasures is, as noted, to induce the responsible State to resume compliance with its international legal obligations (or to achieve compliance directly). The majority of the International Group of Experts accordingly agreed that if the internation-ally wrongful act in question has ceased, the victim State is no longer entitled to initiate, or to persist in, countermeasures, including cyber countermeasures.[59] The Experts noted that State practice is not fully in accord, leaving the law on countermeasures ambiguous. States sometimes appear to be motivated by punitive considerations when resorting to countermeasures, especially when imposed after the other State's violation of international law has ended. It is therefore far from settled whether the restrictive approach adopted by the International Law Commission reflects customary international law.

4.   In general, countermeasures, including cyber countermeasures, can only be resorted to by the injured State after having called upon the State in question to cease its internationally wrongful act.[60] This requirement is not absolute, in that a State is entitled to take 'urgent countermeasures' which are necessary for the preservation of its rights, even in advance of the injury.[61] While the term 'urgent countermeasures' is not authoritatively defined in international law, the International Group of Experts agreed that these procedural requirements largely reflect customary international law.

5.   Uncertainty resides, however, in the substantive requirements that apply to the implementation of countermeasures. It is generally accepted that 'Countermeasures shall not affect: (a) the obligation to

---

[59] Articles on State Responsibility, Art. 53.

[60] Art. 52(1)(b) of the Articles on State Responsibility requires the State taking the measures to 'notify the responsible State of any decision to take countermeasures and offer to negotiate with that State'.

[61] Articles on State Responsibility, Art. 52(2).

refrain from the threat or use of force as embodied in the United Nations Charter; (b) obligations for the protection of fundamental human rights; (c) obligations of a humanitarian character prohibiting reprisals; [or] (d) other obligations under peremptory norms of general international law'.[62] While points (b)–(d) are relevant in the cyber context, the critical issue is point (a). The majority of the International Group of Experts agreed that it implies that cyber countermeasures may not involve the threat or use of force (Rule 11); the legality of threats or uses of force is exclusively regulated by the United Nations Charter and corresponding norms of customary international law. A minority of Experts favoured the approach articulated by Judge Simma in the International Court of Justice's *Oil Platforms* judgment. He took the position that proportionate countermeasures could involve a limited degree of military force in response to circumstances below the Article 51 threshold of 'armed attack'.[63] However, all Experts agreed that cyber countermeasures may not rise to the level of an 'armed attack' (Rule 13).

6. Cyber countermeasures 'shall, as far as possible, be taken in such a way as to permit the resumption of performance of the obligations in question'.[64] In short, they should, to the extent feasible, consist of measures that have temporary or reversible effects. In the realm of cyberspace, this requirement implies that actions involving the permanent disruption of cyber functions should not be undertaken in circumstances where their temporary disruption is technically feasible and would achieve the necessary effect. As indicated by the phrase 'as far as possible', the requirement that the effects of the cyber countermeasures be temporary or reversible is not of an absolute nature.

7. Although the Articles on State Responsibility impose no requirement for countermeasures to be quantitatively or qualitatively similar to the violation of international law that justified them, widespread agreement exists that countermeasures must be 'proportionate' to be lawful. Two tests of proportionality have been advanced. The first, articulated in the *Naulilaa* arbitral award, requires that countermeasures be proportionate to the gravity of the initiating breach.[65] The objective of this test is to avoid escalation. The second test, drawn from the International Court of Justice's *Gabčíkovo-Nagymoros*

---

[62] Articles on State Responsibility, Art. 50.

[63] *Oil Platforms* judgment, paras. 12–13 (separate opinion of Judge Simma).

[64] Articles on State Responsibility, Art. 49(3).   [65] *Naulilaa* arbitration at 1028.

judgment and reflected in Article 51 of the Articles on State Responsibility, requires that countermeasures must be commensurate with the
injury suffered, taking into account the gravity of the internationally
wrongful act and the rights in question.[66] While the International
Group of Experts concluded that neither test had achieved a degree
of acceptance such as to exclude the other, it was agreed that the
availability of countermeasures by cyber means expands the options
available to the victim State for a proportionate response.

8.   Article 48 of the Articles on State Responsibility provides that a
'State other than an injured State is entitled to invoke the responsibility
of another State ... if: (a) the obligation breached is owed to a group of
States including that State and is established for the protection of a
collective interest of the group; or (b) the obligation breached is owed
to the international community as a whole'. The International Group
of Experts agreed that Article 48 accurately reflects customary international law. However, it is often difficult to determine when obligations are owed to a particular group of States as distinct from
obligations owed to an individual State. Additionally, disagreement
exists among international law experts as to which norms and obligations have *erga omnes* character.

9.   Countermeasures may not be directed against individuals or
violate peremptory norms of international law.

10.   It is important to distinguish countermeasures from actions
taken based on the 'plea of necessity'. Under certain circumstances,
States may invoke the plea of necessity in order to justify protective
(cyber) measures that violate the interests of other States. According to
Article 25 of the Articles on State Responsibility, 'necessity' is an
accepted ground precluding wrongfulness under international law.
The threshold for the invocation of necessity is high; the plea of
necessity may only be invoked in exceptional cases,[67] and the precise
scope and limits of this plea remain the subject of some debate.[68]
Whether a State may use force in accordance with the plea of necessity
is highly uncertain.[69]

11.   Necessity is not dependent on the prior unlawful conduct of
another State. Moreover, it may justify such measures as are necessary

---

[66] *Gabčíkovo-Nagymoros Project* (*Hung.* v. *Slovak.*), 1997 I.C.J. 7, para. 85 (25 September).
[67] Articles on State Responsibility, Art. 25(1) and accompanying commentary.
[68] Articles on State Responsibility, commentary accompanying Art. 25.
[69] Articles on State Responsibility, commentary accompanying Art. 25.

to protect essential interests of a State against a grave and imminent peril even though those measures affect the interests of other States (or even the international community as a whole) which are not necessarily responsible for creating the condition of necessity. The measures, however, may not 'seriously impair' the 'essential' interests of States affected by them.[70] Ultimately, the determination of whether actions may be taken based on a plea of necessity requires a balancing of interests between the State invoking the plea and those of the affected States (or whole international community).

12.   In cases where the exact nature and, in particular, origin of a cyber incident are unclear, certain protective (cyber) measures may be justified on the basis of the plea of necessity. For example, if a State is faced with a cyber incident that endangers its essential interests and there is no other way to address the situation, it may in some cases temporarily shut off certain cyber infrastructure, even if doing so affects cyber systems in other States. Similarly, if faced with significant cyber operations against a State's critical infrastructure, the plea of necessity could justify a State's resort to counter-hacking. Nevertheless, as the International Law Commission has pointed out, the course of action selected must be the 'only way' available to safeguard the interest in question and it must not seriously impair the essential interests of other States or those of the international community as a whole.[71]

13.   The term 'countermeasures' is used in this Rule as a legal term of art that must be distinguished from the military term 'countermeasures', which refers to activities designed to defeat the operation of a weapon. Countermeasures must also be differentiated from acts of retorsion. Acts of retorsion are so-called 'unfriendly', although lawful, measures that a State takes *vis-à-vis* one or more other States.[72] Unlike countermeasures, acts of retorsion do not require a preceding unlawful act and they may be undertaken with retaliatory or coercive motives. For example, during the 2007 Estonian cyber incidents, banks and other businesses, in consultation with the Estonian CERT and government ministries, suspended some services to Internet protocol (IP) addresses from Russia. In this regard, note that since the ITU

---

[70] Articles on State Responsibility, Art. 25(1)(b) and accompanying commentary.

[71] Articles on State Responsibility, Art. 25 and accompanying commentary. *See also* *Gabčíkovo-Nagymaros Project*, para. 55.

[72] Articles on State Responsibility, chapeau commentary accompanying Chapter II of pt 3.

Constitution allows States to stop or suspend international telecommunications when appropriate, the action did not qualify as a countermeasure.[73] Finally, countermeasures as dealt with here must be distinguished from belligerent reprisals, which are available only during an armed conflict, subject to special rules (Rule 46).

---

[73] Art. 34 permits stoppage of individual private telecommunications on the basis of security concerns. Art. 35 allows a State to suspend international telecommunications, provided immediate notification is given to other States Parties to the Convention.

2

The use of force

1.   The International Court of Justice has stated that Articles 2(4) (Rules 10 to 12) and 51 (Rule 13 to 17) of the United Nations Charter, regarding the prohibition of the use of force and self-defence respectively, apply to 'any use of force, regardless of the weapons employed'.[1] The International Group of Experts unanimously agreed that this statement is an accurate reflection of customary international law. Therefore, the mere fact that a computer (rather than a more traditional weapon, weapon system, or platform) is used during an operation has no bearing on whether that operation amounts to a 'use of force'. Similarly, it has no bearing on whether a State may use force in self-defence.

2.   State practice is only beginning to clarify the application to cyber operations of the *jus ad bellum*, the body of international law that governs a State's resort to force as an instrument of its national policy. In particular, the lack of agreed-upon definitions, criteria, and thresholds for application, creates uncertainty when applying the *jus ad bellum* to the rapidly changing realities of cyber operations. The International Group of Experts acknowledged that as cyber threats and opportunities continue to emerge and evolve, State practice may alter contemporary interpretations and applications of the *jus ad bellum* in the cyber context. The analysis set forth in this chapter examines the norms resident in the *jus ad bellum* as they exist at the time of the Manual's adoption by the International Group of Experts in July 2012.

SECTION 1:   PROHIBITION OF THE USE OF FORCE

Rule 10 – Prohibition of threat or use of force

A cyber operation that constitutes a threat or use of force against the territorial integrity or political independence of any State, or that

---

[1] *Nuclear Weapons* Advisory Opinion, para. 39.

is in any other manner inconsistent with the purposes of the United Nations, is unlawful.

1.   Article 2(4) of the United Nations Charter provides that 'All Members [of the United Nations] shall refrain in their international relations from the threat or use of force against the territorial integrity or political independence of any State, or in any other manner inconsistent with the Purposes of the United Nations.' The prohibition is undoubtedly a norm of customary international law.[2]

2.   In addition to the specific prohibition of threats or uses of force against the territorial integrity or political independence of any State, the United Nations Charter's *travaux préparatoires* suggest that the reference in Article 2(4) to threats or uses of force inconsistent with the 'purposes of the United Nations' (laid down in Article 1 of the Charter) was intended to create a presumption of illegality for any threat or use of force.[3] In other words, even acts that are not directed against either the territorial integrity or political independence of a State may nevertheless violate the prohibition if they are inconsistent with the purposes of the United Nations. There are two widely acknowledged exceptions to the prohibition on the use of force – uses of force authorized by the Security Council under Chapter VII (Rule 18) and self-defence pursuant to Article 51 and customary international law (Rule 13). The International Group of Experts did not take a position as to the lawfulness of other uses of force, such as humanitarian intervention.

3.   The terms 'use of force' and 'threat of the use of force' are defined in Rules 11 and 12 respectively.

4.   An action qualifying as a 'use of force' need not necessarily be undertaken by a State's armed forces. For example, it is clear that a cyber operation that would qualify as a 'use of force' if conducted by the armed forces would equally be a 'use of force' if undertaken by a State's intelligence agencies or by a private contractor whose conduct is attributable to the State based upon the law of State responsibility. With regard to those entities whose actions may be attributed to States, see Rules 6 to 8.

5.   Although, by its own express terms, Article 2(4) applies solely to Members of the United Nations, the prohibition also extends to non-Member States by virtue of customary international law. However, Article 2(4) and its customary international law counterpart do not apply to the

---

[2] *Nicaragua* judgment, paras. 188–90.
[3] *See* Doc. 1123, I/8, 6 U.N.C.I.O. Docs. 65 (1945); Doc. 784, I/1/27, 6 U.N.C.I.O. Docs. 336 (1945); Doc. 885, I/1/34, 6 U.N.C.I.O. Docs. 387 (1945).

acts of non-State actors, including individuals, organized groups, and terrorist organizations, unless they are attributable to a State pursuant to the law of State responsibility (Rule 6). In such a case, it would be the State, not the non-State actor, which is deemed to be in violation. The actions of non-State actors may be unlawful under international and domestic law, but not as a violation of the prohibition on the use of force.

6. The fact that a cyber operation does not rise to the level of a use of force does not necessarily render it lawful under international law. In particular, a cyber operation may constitute a violation of the prohibition on intervention. Although not expressly set out in the United Nations Charter, the prohibition of intervention is implicit in the principle of the sovereign equality of States laid out in Article 2(1) of the United Nations Charter. It is mentioned in a number of treaties and United Nations resolutions, the most significant of which is the Declaration on Friendly Relations. According to the International Court of Justice, the principle is 'part and parcel of customary international law'.[4]

7. The precise scope and content of the non-intervention principle remains the subject of some debate. In the *Nicaragua* case, the International Court of Justice held that 'the principle forbids all States or groups of States to intervene directly or indirectly in the internal or external affairs of other States'.[5] Therefore, 'a prohibited intervention must accordingly be one bearing on matters in which each State is permitted, by the principle of State sovereignty, to decide freely. One of these is the choice of a political, economic, social and cultural system, and the formulation of foreign policy'.[6] For instance, the Court held that supplying funds to insurgents was 'undoubtedly an act of intervention in the internal affairs of Nicaragua', although not a use of force.[7]

8. It is clear that not all cyber interference automatically violates the international law prohibition on intervention; 'interference pure and simple is not intervention'.[8] As noted by the Court in *Nicaragua*, 'intervention is wrongful when it uses methods of coercion'.[9] It follows that cyber espionage and cyber exploitation operations lacking a coercive element do not *per se* violate the non-intervention principle. Mere intrusion into another State's systems does not violate the non-intervention

---

[4] *Nicaragua* judgment, para. 202. [5] *Nicaragua* judgment, para. 205.
[6] *Nicaragua* judgment, para. 205. [7] *Nicaragua* judgment, para. 228.
[8] I OPPENHEIM'S INTERNATIONAL LAW: PEACE 432 (Robert Jennings and Arthur Watts eds., 9th ed. 1992).
[9] *Nicaragua* judgment, para. 205.

principle. In the view of the International Group of Experts, this holds true even where such intrusion requires the breaching of protective virtual barriers (e.g., the breaching of firewalls or the cracking of passwords).

9. The assessment, however, becomes complex when it comes to other operations along the broad spectrum of cyber operations. In these cases, the determination of whether the principle of non-intervention has been violated, particularly the determination of whether there has been an element of coercion, depends on the circumstances of each individual case. The clearest cases are those cyber operations, such as the employment of the Stuxnet worm, that amount to a use of force. Such operations are also acts of intervention because all uses of force are coercive *per se*.

10. Cyber operations falling below the use of force threshold are more difficult to characterize as a violation of the principle of non-intervention. Acts meant to achieve regime change are often described as a clear violation. So too is coercive 'political interference'. When such actions are taken or facilitated by cyber means, they constitute prohibited intervention. Cases in point are the manipulation by cyber means of elections or of public opinion on the eve of elections, as when online news services are altered in favour of a particular party, false news is spread, or the online services of one party are shut off. As always, the decisive test remains coercion. Thus, it is clear that not every form of political or economic interference violates the non-intervention principle.

Rule 11 – Definition of use of force

A cyber operation constitutes a use of force when its scale and effects are comparable to non-cyber operations rising to the level of a use of force.

1. This Rule examines the term 'use of force' found in Rule 10. The United Nations Charter offers no criteria by which to determine when an act amounts to a use of force. In discussions regarding the appropriate threshold for a use of force, the International Group of Experts took notice of the *Nicaragua* judgment. In that case, the International Court of Justice stated that 'scale and effects' are to be considered when determining whether particular actions amount to an 'armed attack' (Rule 13).[10] The Experts found the focus on scale and effects to be an equally useful approach when distinguishing acts that qualify as uses of

---

[10] *Nicaragua* judgment, para. 195.

force from those that do not. In other words, 'scale and effects' is a shorthand term that captures the quantitative and qualitative factors to be analysed in determining whether a cyber operation qualifies as a use of force.

2.   There is no authoritative definition of, or criteria for, 'threat' or 'use of force'. However, certain categories of coercive operations are not uses of force. At the 1945 Charter drafting conference in San Francisco, States considered and rejected a proposal to include economic coercion as a use of force.[11] The issue arose again a quarter of a century later during the proceedings leading to the General Assembly's Declaration on Friendly Relations. The question of whether 'force' included 'all forms of pressure, including those of a political or economic character, which have the effect of threatening the territorial integrity or political independence of any State' was answered in the negative.[12] Accordingly, whatever 'force' may be, it is not mere economic or political coercion. Cyber operations that involve, or are otherwise analogous to, these coercive activities are definitely not prohibited uses of force.

3.   As an example, non-destructive cyber psychological operations intended solely to undermine confidence in a government or economy do not qualify as uses of force. Additionally, the International Court of Justice held in the *Nicaragua* case that merely funding guerrillas engaged in operations against another State did not reach the use of force threshold.[13] Thus, for instance, merely funding a hacktivist group conducting cyber operations as part of an insurgency would not be a use of force.

4.   A use of force need not involve the employment of military or other armed forces by the State in question. In *Nicaragua*, the International Court of Justice found that arming and training a guerrilla force that is engaged in hostilities against another State qualified as a use of force.[14] Therefore, providing an organized group with malware and the training necessary to use it to carry out cyber attacks against another State would also qualify.

5.   This conclusion raises the question of whether affording sanctuary (safe haven) to those mounting cyber operations of the requisite severity

---

[11] 6 U.N.C.I.O. Docs. 334, 609 (1945); Doc. 2, 617(e)(4), 3 U.N.C.I.O. Docs. 251, 253–4 (1945).
[12] UN GAOR Special Comm. on Friendly Relations, UN Doc. A/AC.125/SR.110 to 114 (1970). *See also* Rep. of the Special Comm. on Friendly Relations and Cooperation Among States, 1969, UN GAOR, 24th Sess., Supp. No. 19, at 12, UN Doc. A/7619 (1969). The draft declaration contained text tracking that of UN Charter Art. 2(4).
[13] *Nicaragua* judgment, para. 228.   [14] *Nicaragua* judgment, para. 228.

amounts to a 'use of force' (or 'armed attack').[15] The majority of the International Group of Experts took the position that in most cases simply granting sanctuary is insufficient to attribute the actions of non-State actors to the State for the purpose of finding a use of force by that State. Similarly, they did not deem the failure of a State to police its territory in order to prevent the launch of cyber operations to be a use of force (but see Rule 5 on the obligations of States *vis-à-vis* control over cyber infrastructure). That said, the majority agreed that the provision of sanctuary coupled with other acts, such as substantial support or providing cyber defences for the non-State group, could, in certain circumstances, be a use of force.

6.   In determining whether an act constitutes a 'use of force', it is useful to consider the notion of 'armed attack', which is the threshold at which a State may lawfully use force in self-defence (Rule 13). In the *Nicaragua* judgment, the International Court of Justice distinguished the 'most grave' forms of the 'use of force' (those constituting an 'armed attack' for the purposes of the law of self-defence) from other less grave forms.[16] The International Group of Experts agreed, therefore, that any cyber operation which rises to the level of an 'armed attack' in terms of scale and effects pursuant to Rule 13, and which is conducted by or otherwise attributable to a State, qualifies as a 'use of force'.

7.   The International Group of Experts acknowledged a contrary view whereby the distinction between the two concepts is either so narrow as to be insignificant or non-existent. This position, articulated by the United States after the *Nicaragua* judgment, asserts that any illegal use of force can qualify as an armed attack triggering the right of self-defence; there is no gravity threshold distinguishing illegal uses of force from armed attacks.[17] On this view, no gap exists between an unlawful use of force and an armed attack, although the principles of necessity and proportionality that apply to actions in self-defence may limit the responses available to a State that has been attacked.

8.   To summarize, some cyber actions are undeniably not uses of force, uses of force need not involve a State's direct use of armed force,

---

[15] *See* Declaration on Friendly Relations (addressing the issue of State acquiescence to organized activities on its territory).

[16] *Nicaragua* judgment, para. 191. The Court pointed to the Declaration on Friendly Relations, noting that while certain of the actions referred to therein constituted armed attacks, others only qualified as uses of force.

[17] *See, e.g.,* Abraham D. Sofaer, *International Law and the Use of Force*, 82 AMERICAN SOCIETY OF INTERNATIONAL LAW PROCEEDINGS 420, 422 (1988).

and all armed attacks are uses of force. This leaves unresolved the question as to what actions short of an armed attack constitute a use of force. Acts that injure or kill persons or damage or destroy objects are unambiguously uses of force (see the Commentary to Rule 13 expressing an analogous conclusion, but requiring the harm to be 'significant'). Since other cases are less clear, the International Group of Experts took notice of an approach that seeks to assess the likelihood that States will characterize a cyber operation as a use of force.[18] The method expounded operates on the premise that in the absence of a conclusive definitional threshold, States contemplating cyber operations, or that are the target thereof, must be highly sensitive to the international community's probable assessment of whether the operations violate the prohibition on the use of force.

9. The approach focuses on both the level of harm inflicted and certain qualitative elements of a particular cyber operation. In great part, it is intended to identify cyber operations that are analogous to other non-kinetic or kinetic actions that the international community would describe as uses of force. To the extent such operations would be assessed as reaching the use of force threshold, so too would cyber operations of the same scale and effects. The approach suggests that States are likely to consider and place great weight on the following factors, inter alia, when deciding whether to characterize any operation, including a cyber operation, as a use of force. It must be emphasized that they are merely factors that influence States making use of force assessments; they are not formal legal criteria.

(a) *Severity.* Subject to a *de minimis* rule, consequences involving physical harm to individuals or property will in and of themselves qualify the act as a use of force. Those generating mere inconvenience or irritation will never do so. Between the extremes, the more consequences impinge on critical national interests, the more they will contribute to the depiction of a cyber operation as a use of force. In this regard, the scope, duration, and intensity of the consequences will have great bearing on the appraisal of their severity. A cyber operation, like any operation, resulting in damage, destruction, injury, or death is highly likely to be considered a use of force. Severity is self-evidently the most significant factor in the analysis.

---

[18] This approach was originally proposed in Michael N. Schmitt, *Computer Network and the Use of Force in International Law: Thought on a Normative Framework*, 37 COLUMBIA JOURNAL OF TRANSNATIONAL LAW 885, 914 (1999).

(b) Immediacy. The sooner consequences manifest, the less opportunity
States have to seek peaceful accommodation of a dispute or to
otherwise forestall their harmful effects. Therefore, States harbour a
greater concern about immediate consequences than those that are
delayed or build slowly over time, and are more likely to characterize
a cyber operation that produces immediate results as a use of force
than cyber actions that take weeks or months to achieve their
intended effects.

(c) Directness. The greater the attenuation between the initial act and
its consequences, the less likely States will be to deem the actor in
violation of the prohibition on the use of force. Whereas the immediacy factor focuses on the temporal aspect of the consequences in
question, directness examines the chain of causation. For instance,
market forces, access to markets, and the like determine the eventual
consequences of economic coercion (*e.g.*, economic downturn). The
causal connection between the initial acts and their effects tends to
be indirect – economic sanctions may take weeks or even months to
have a significant effect. In armed actions, by contrast, cause and
effect are closely related. An explosion, for example, directly harms
people or objects. Cyber operations in which the cause and effect
are clearly linked are more likely to be characterized as uses of force.

(d) Invasiveness. Invasiveness refers to the degree to which cyber operations intrude into the target State or its cyber systems contrary to
the interests of that State. As a rule, the more secure a targeted
cyber system, the greater the concern as to its penetration. For
example, intrusion into a military system that has been accredited
at Evaluation Assurance Level 7 (EAL7) of the *Common Criteria*
is more invasive than merely exploiting vulnerabilities of an openly
accessible non-accredited system at a civilian university or small
business.[19] Additionally, the degree to which the intended effects
of a cyber operation are limited to a particular State increases the
perceived invasiveness of those operations.

Domain name is a highly visible indicator in cyberspace and for
that reason may carry significance in assessing the extent of invasiveness of an operation. Cyber operations that specifically target
the domain name of a particular State (e.g., 'mil.ee') or of a
particular State organ may, for this reason, be considered more

---

[19] Common Criteria for Information Technology Security Evaluation, International Standard ISO/IEC 15408, ver. 3.1 (July 2009).

invasive than those operations directed at non-State specific domain name extensions such as '.com'.

This factor must be cautiously applied in the cyber context. In particular, computer network exploitation is a pervasive tool of modern espionage. Though highly invasive, cyber espionage does not rise to the level of a use of force due to the absence of a direct prohibition in international law on espionage *per se* (Rule 66). Thus, actions such as disabling cyber security mechanisms in order to monitor keystrokes would, despite their invasiveness, be unlikely to be seen as a use of force. This does not mean that acts undertaken in order to enable cyber espionage will not constitute a use of force. For example, a non-consensual penetration of national airspace by a military aircraft serving as a platform for cyber espionage can sometimes qualify as a use of force.

(e) *Measurability of effects.* This factor derives from the greater willingness of States to characterize actions as a use of force when the consequences are apparent. Traditionally, the armed forces carried out operations that qualified as uses of force and the effects of the operations were generally measurable (as in the case of battle damage assessments). In the cyber realm, consequences may be less apparent. Therefore, the more quantifiable and identifiable a set of consequences, the easier it will be for a State to assess the situation when determining whether the cyber operation in question has reached the level of a use of force. Accordingly, a cyber operation that can be evaluated in very specific terms (e.g., amount of data corrupted, percentage of servers disabled, number of confidential files exfiltrated) is more likely to be characterized as a use of force than one with difficult to measure or subjective consequences.

(f) *Military character.* A nexus between the cyber operation in question and military operations heightens the likelihood of characterization as a use of force. This contention is supported by the fact that the United Nations Charter is particularly concerned with military actions. Its preamble provides that 'armed force shall not be used, save in the common interest',[20] while Article 44 uses the term 'force' without the qualifier 'armed' in a situation that clearly refers to the use of military force. Further, the use of force has

---

[20] UN Charter, Preamble.

traditionally been understood to imply force employed by the military or other armed forces.

(g) State involvement. The extent of State involvement in a cyber operation lies along a continuum from operations conducted by a State itself (e.g., the activities of its armed forces or intelligence agencies) to those in which its involvement is peripheral. The clearer and closer a nexus between a State and cyber operations, the more likely it is that other States will characterize them as uses of force by that State.

(h) Presumptive legality. International law is generally prohibitive in nature.[21] Acts that are not forbidden are permitted; absent an express treaty or accepted customary law prohibition, an act is presumptively legal. For instance, international law does not prohibit propaganda, psychological operations, espionage, or mere economic pressure *per se.* Therefore, acts falling into these and other such categories are presumptively legal (although in a particular situation they may in fact violate an international law norm). This being so, they are less likely to be considered by States as uses of force.[22]

10. These factors are not exhaustive. Depending on the attendant circumstances, States may look to others, such as the prevailing political environment, whether the cyber operation portends the future use of

---

[21] *Lotus* case at 19.

[22] The criteria of the analysis may be evaluated in light of questions such as the following:

  (a) Severity: How many people were killed? How large an area was attacked? How much damage was done within this area?
  (b) Immediacy: How soon were the effects of the cyber operation felt? How quickly did its effects abate?
  (c) Directness: Was the action the proximate cause of the effects? Were there contributing causes giving rise to those effects?
  (d) Invasiveness: Did the action involve penetrating a cyber network intended to be secure? Was the locus of the action within the target country?
  (e) Measurability: How can the effects of the action be quantified? Are the effects of the action distinct from the results of parallel or competing actions? How certain is the calculation of the effects?
  (f) Military character: Did the military conduct the cyber operation? Were the armed forces the target of the cyber operation?
  (g) State involvement: Is the State directly or indirectly involved in the act in question? But for the acting State's sake, would the action have occurred?
  (h) Presumptive legality: Has this category of action been generally characterized as a use of force, or characterized as one that is not? Are the means qualitatively similar to others presumed legitimate under international law?

military force, the identity of the attacker, any record of cyber operations by the attacker, and the nature of the target (such as critical infrastructure). Moreover, the factors operate in concert. As an example, a highly invasive operation that causes only inconvenience such as temporary denial of service is unlikely to be classified as a use of force. By contrast, some may categorize massive cyber operations that cripple an economy as a use of force, even though economic coercion is presumptively lawful.

11.   Finally, it must be understood that 'use of force' as used in this Rule and 'armed attack' (Rule 13) are standards that serve different normative purposes. The 'use of force' standard is employed to determine whether a State has violated Article 2(4) of the United Nations Charter and the related customary international law prohibition. By contrast, the notion of 'armed attack' has to do with whether the target State may respond to an act with a use of force without itself violating the prohibition on using force. This distinction is critical in that the mere fact that a use of force has occurred does not alone justify a use of force in response.[23] States facing a use of force not amounting to an armed attack will, in the view of the International Group of Experts, have to resort to other measures if they wish to respond lawfully, such as countermeasures (Rule 9) or actions consistent with the plea of necessity (Commentary accompanying Rule 9).

Rule 12 – Definition of threat of force

A cyber operation, or threatened cyber operation, constitutes an unlawful threat of force when the threatened action, if carried out, would be an unlawful use of force.

1.   This Rule examines the term 'threat' as used in Rule 10.

2.   The phrase 'cyber operation, or threatened cyber operation' in this Rule applies to two situations. The first is a cyber operation that is used to communicate a threat to use force (whether kinetic or cyber). The second is a threat conveyed by any means (e.g., public pronouncements) to carry out cyber operations qualifying as a use of force.

3.   It is generally accepted that threats by States and officials in a position to make good those threats are lawful if the threatened action

---

[23] *But see* discussion of countermeasures rising to the level of use of force in the Commentary accompanying Rule 9 (noting a minority view allowing countermeasures at this level).

is itself lawful.[24] There are two recognized exceptions to the international law prohibition on the use of force: the exercise of the right of self-defence and actions implementing a United Nations Security Council resolution under Chapter VII of the United Nations Charter (Rules 13 and 18). For instance, it would be lawful to threaten that a State will defend itself forcefully if attacked. Threatening other actions that do not violate international law would likewise be lawful.

4. Although threats are usually intended to be coercive in effect, there is no requirement that a specific 'demand' accompany the threat. The essence of a threat is that it is explicitly or impliedly communicative in nature. Actions which simply threaten the security of the target State, but which are not communicative in nature, do not qualify. For example, consider the case in which tensions between State A and State B are high. State A begins aggressively to develop the capability to conduct massive malicious cyber operations against State B. The mere acquisition of such capabilities that can be used to conduct uses of force does not constitute a threat. However, if the leader of State A announces, either on a conditional basis or otherwise, that the capabilities will be used for that purpose against State B, State A will be in violation of this Rule.

5. The International Group of Experts was divided as to whether a State manifestly lacking any capability to make good its threat, can violate this Rule. Despite the difference of opinion, it must be noted that cyber capability is not as dependent on a State's size, population, or economic and military capacity as is the capacity to use conventional force. This means that it may be more difficult for a State to evaluate the capacity of another State to make good on its threat to use force by cyber means. Therefore, this issue plays a diminished role in evaluating cyber threats.

6. Similarly, no consensus could be achieved regarding a State that possesses the capability to carry out the threat but which clearly has no intention of doing so. An example would be that of a State that possesses an offensive cyber capability and whose leader utters threats against other States for purely domestic political reasons.

---

[24] By distinguishing lawful from unlawful threats, the International Court of Justice conceded the existence of the former: '[I]f it is to be lawful, the declared readiness of a State to use force must be a use of force that is in conformity with the Charter.' *Nuclear Weapons* Advisory Opinion, para. 47.

SECTION 2:   SELF-DEFENCE

Rule 13 – Self-defence against armed attack

A State that is the target of a cyber operation that rises to the level of an armed attack may exercise its inherent right of self-defence. Whether a cyber operation constitutes an armed attack depends on its scale and effects.

1.   According to Article 51 of the United Nations Charter, '[n]othing in the present Charter shall impair the inherent right of individual or collective self-defence if an armed attack occurs against a Member of the United Nations, until the Security Council has taken the measures necessary to maintain international peace and security'. This Article recognizes and reflects the customary right of self-defence.

2.   An armed attack must have a trans-border element. This criterion is always met when one State engages in a cyber operation otherwise qualifying as an armed attack against another State, or directs non-State actors, wherever they may be, to do so. The more difficult case involves cyber operations by non-State actors against one State that are not conducted on behalf of another State. The issue of whether non-State actors not acting on behalf of a State can initiate an armed attack is dealt with below. With regard to acts organized, conducted, and directed solely from within a State's own territory, States may use force in accordance with their own domestic laws (informed by international law standards such as human rights law and, in situations of non-international armed conflict, the law of armed conflict).

3.   The right to employ force in self-defence extends beyond kinetic armed attacks to those that are perpetrated entirely through cyber operations. The International Group of Experts unanimously concluded that some cyber operations may be sufficiently grave to warrant classifying them as an 'armed attack' within the meaning of the Charter. This conclusion is in accord with the International Court of Justice's insistence in its *Nuclear Weapons* Advisory Opinion that the choice of means of attack is immaterial to the issue of whether an operation qualifies as an armed attack.[25] Moreover, the position is consistent with State practice.[26] For example, it is universally accepted that chemical,

---

[25] *Nuclear Weapons* Advisory Opinion, para. 39.
[26] *See, e.g., White House Cyber Strategy*, at 10, 13.

biological, and radiological attacks of the requisite scale and effects to constitute armed attacks trigger the right of self-defence. This is so, despite their non-kinetic nature, because the ensuing consequences can include serious suffering or death. Identical reasoning would apply to cyber operations.

4. The International Group of Experts was divided as to whether the notion of armed attack, because of the term 'armed', necessarily involves the employment of 'weapons' (Rule 41). The majority took the position that it did not and that instead the critical factor was whether the effects of a cyber operation, as distinct from the means used to achieve those effects, were analogous to those that would result from an action otherwise qualifying as a kinetic armed attack.

5. In the view of the International Group of Experts, the term 'armed attack' is not to be equated with the term 'use of force' appearing in Rule 11.[27] An armed attack presupposes at least a use of force in the sense of Article 2(4). However, as noted by the International Court of Justice, not every use of force rises to the level of an armed attack.[28] The scale and effects required for an act to be characterized as an armed attack necessarily exceed those qualifying the act as a use of force. Only in the event that the use of force reaches the threshold of an armed attack is a State entitled to respond using force in self-defence.

6. The phrase 'scale and effects' is drawn from the *Nicaragua* judgment.[29] In that case, the Court identified scale and effects as the criteria that distinguish actions qualifying as an armed attack from those that do not. It noted the need to 'distinguish the most grave forms of the use of force (those constituting an armed attack) from other less grave forms', but provided no further guidance in this regard.[30] Therefore, the parameters of the scale and effects criteria remain unsettled beyond the indication that they need to be grave. That said, some cases are clear. The International Group of Experts agreed that any use of force that injures or kills persons or damages or destroys property would satisfy the scale and effects requirement. They also agreed that acts of cyber intelligence gathering and cyber theft, as well as cyber operations that involve brief or periodic interruption of non-essential cyber services, do not qualify as armed attacks.

---

[27] However, not all States accept this view. *See* discussion in Commentary accompanying Rule 11.

[28] *Nicaragua* judgment, para. 191.   [29] *Nicaragua* judgment, para. 195.

[30] *Nicaragua* judgment, para. 191.

7.   The Experts took the view that the law is unclear as to the precise point at which the extent of death, injury, damage, destruction, or suffering caused by a cyber operation fails to qualify as an armed attack. In the *Nicaragua* judgment, the International Court of Justice distinguished between an armed attack and a 'mere frontier incident'.[31] This distinction has been criticized by numerous commentators who adopt the view that only inconsequential actions are to be excluded.[32] In this regard, the International Court of Justice has itself indicated that an attack on a single military platform or installation might qualify as an armed attack.[33]

8.   An important issue is whether a State may exercise the right of self-defence in response to a series of cyber incidents that individually fall below the threshold of an armed attack. In other words, can they constitute an armed attack when aggregated? The determinative factor is whether the same originator (or originators acting in concert) has carried out smaller-scale incidents that are related and that taken together have the requisite scale. If there is convincing evidence that this is the case, the International Group of Experts agreed that there are grounds for treating the incidents as a composite armed attack.[34]

9.   The case of actions that do not result in injury, death, damage, or destruction, but which otherwise have extensive negative effects, is unsettled. Some of the Experts took the position that harm to persons or physical damage to property is a condition precedent to the characterization of an incident as an armed attack. Others took the view that it is not the nature (injurious or destructive) of the consequences that matters, but rather the extent of the ensuing effects. The classic scenario illustrating this division of opinion is a cyber incident directed against a major international stock exchange that causes the market to crash. The International Group of Experts was divided over the characterization of such an event. Some of the Experts were unprepared to label it as an armed attack, because they were not satisfied that mere financial loss constitutes damage for this purpose. Others emphasized the catastrophic effects such a crash would occasion and therefore regarded them as

---

[31] *Nicaragua* judgment, para. 195.

[32] *See, e.g.,* Yoram Dinstein, WAR, AGGRESSION AND SELF DEFENCE 210–11 (5th ed. 2011); William H. Taft, *Self Defense and the Oil Platforms Decision,* 29 YALE JOURNAL OF INTERNATIONAL LAW 295, 300 (2004).

[33] *Oil Platforms* judgment, paras. 57, 61.

[34] This approach has been labelled the 'pin-prick' theory, the 'accumulation of effects' theory, and 'Nadelstichtaktik'.

sufficient to characterize the cyber operation as an armed attack. By the same approach, a cyber operation directed against major components (systems) of a State's critical infrastructure that causes severe, albeit not destructive, effects would qualify as an armed attack.

10.   A further challenging issue in the cyber context involves determining which effects to consider in assessing whether an action qualifies as an armed attack. The International Group of Experts agreed that all reasonably foreseeable consequences of the cyber operation so qualify. Consider, for example, the case of a cyber operation targeting a water purification plant. Sickness and death caused by drinking contaminated water are foreseeable and should therefore be taken into account.

11.   The International Group of Experts was divided over the issue of whether the effects in question must have been intended. For instance, consider the example of cyber espionage by State A against State B that unexpectedly results in significant damage to State B's cyber infrastructure. Some Experts were not willing to characterize the operation as an armed attack, although they acknowledged that measures could be taken to counteract the negative effects of the operation (especially in accordance with the principle of necessity discussed in the Commentary to Rule 9). The majority of the International Group of Experts took the view that intention is irrelevant in qualifying an operation as an armed attack and that only the scale and effects matter. However, any response thereto would have to comport with the necessity and proportionality criteria (Rule 14); the former would prove a significant hurdle in this respect. All the Experts agreed that the lawfulness of the response would be determined by the reasonableness of State B's assessment as to whether an armed attack was underway.

12.   A cyber armed attack by State A against State B may have bleed-over effects in State C. If those effects meet the scale and effects criteria for an armed attack, the majority of the International Group of Experts would conclude that State C is entitled to resort to the use of force in self-defence, so long as the defensive action complied with the necessity and proportionality criteria. Indeed, even if the cyber operations against State B do not qualify as an armed attack, this would not preclude the bleed-over effects from amounting to an armed attack against State C. As to the issue of unintended bleed-over effects, see the discussion of intent above.

13.   No international cyber incidents have, as of 2012, been unambiguously and publicly characterized by the international community as reaching the threshold of an armed attack. In particular, the 2007 cyber operations against Estonia, which were widely referred to as 'cyber war',

were not publicly characterized by either Estonia or the international community as an armed attack. The International Group of Experts agreed with this assessment on the basis that the scale and effects threshold was not reached. A closer case is the 2010 Stuxnet operations. In light of the damage they caused to Iranian centrifuges, some members of the International Group of Experts were of the view that the operations had reached the armed attack threshold (unless justifiable on the basis of anticipatory self-defence (Rule 15)).

14.   It is also necessary to consider the issue of the 'originator' in determining whether an act qualifies as an armed attack. It is incontrovertible that an act conducted by organs of a State may so qualify. It is equally indisputable that the actions of non-State actors may sometimes be attributed to a State for the purpose of finding an armed attack. In the *Nicaragua* judgment, the International Court of Justice stated that

> An armed attack must be understood as including not merely action by regular forces across an international border, but also 'the sending by or on behalf of a State of armed bands, groups, irregulars or mercenaries, which carry out acts of armed force against another State of such gravity as to amount to' (*inter alia*) an actual armed attack conducted by regular forces, 'or its substantial involvement therein'.[35]

15.   For instance, if a group of private individuals under the direction of State A undertakes cyber operations directed against State B, and the consequence of those actions reaches the requisite scale and effects, State A will have committed an armed attack. This same conclusion would apply to cyber operations conducted by a single individual at the direction of a State.

16.   The issue of whether acts of non-State actors can constitute an armed attack absent direction by a State is controversial. Traditionally, Article 51 and the customary international law of self-defence were characterized as applicable solely to armed attacks undertaken by one State against another. Violent acts by non-State actors fell within the law enforcement paradigm. However, the international community characterized the 9/11 attacks by Al Qaeda on the United States as an armed attack triggering the inherent right of self-defence.[36] Such State practice

---

[35] *Nicaragua* judgment, para. 195.
[36] The Security Council adopted numerous resolutions recognizing the applicability of the right of self-defence. *See, e.g.,* S.C. Res 1368 (12 September 2001); S.C. Res. 1373 (28 September 2001). International organizations such as NATO and many individual States took the same approach. *See, e.g.,* Press Release, NATO, Statement by the North Atlantic

appears to signal a willingness of States to apply the right of self-defence to attacks conducted by non-State actors. Moreover, while Article 2(4) addresses the actions of States, Article 51 contains no such limitation *vis-à-vis* armed attacks (although the text does make it clear that only States enjoy the right of self-defence). For its part, the International Court of Justice does not seem to have been prepared to adopt this approach.[37]

17.   The majority of the International Group of Experts concluded that State practice established a right of self-defence in the face of armed attacks by non-State actors, such as terrorist or rebel groups. They would extend this right to self-defence against cyber operations conducted by information technology corporations or Internet service providers if the operations reached the armed attack threshold. As an example, the majority of the International Group of Experts would consider a devastating cyber operation undertaken by a group of terrorists from within State A against critical infrastructure located in State B as an armed attack by those cyber terrorists against State B. A minority of the Group did not accept this premise.

18.   The members of the International Group of Experts acknowledged the significant uncertainty that exists within the international law community regarding such matters as the degree of requisite organization a group must have (if any) to be capable of mounting an armed attack as a matter of law and any geographical limitations that may bear on this issue. Additionally, those Experts who took the position that a non-State group unaffiliated with a State could conduct an armed attack were split over the issue of whether a single individual mounting an operation that meets the scale and effects threshold could do so.

19.   The object of an action meeting the scale and effects requirement may also determine whether it qualifies as an armed attack. If the object of action satisfying the trans-border and scale and effects criteria consists of property or persons within the affected State's territory, the action is an armed attack against that State. It must be noted that the International Group of Experts did not achieve consensus on whether further criteria must be met in order to bring into operation the right of self-defence.

Council (12 September 2001); Terrorist Threat to the Americas, Res. 1, Twenty-Fourth Meeting of Consultation of Ministers of Foreign Affairs, Terrorist Threat to the Americas, OAS Doc. RC.24/RES.1/01 (21 September 2001); Brendan Pearson, *PM Commits to Mutual Defence*, AUSTRALIAN FINANCIAL REVIEW, 15 September 2001, at 9.

[37] *Wall* Advisory Opinion, para. 139; *Armed Activities in Congo* judgment, paras. 146–7.

While some took the position that attacks solely motivated by purely private interests would not trigger the right of self-defence, others were of the view that motives are irrelevant. This issue is likely to be resolved through State practice.

20.   If the object in question consists of property or citizens situated outside the State's territory, it is sometimes uncertain in international law whether the cyber operation can qualify as an armed attack. Attacks against non-commercial government facilities or equipment, and government personnel, certainly qualify as armed attacks so long as the above-mentioned criteria are met. For instance, a cyber operation undertaken by State A to kill State B's head of State while abroad would amount to an armed attack. The determination of whether other operations are armed attacks depends on, but is not limited to, such factors as: the extent of damage caused by the operation; whether the property involved is State or private in character; the status of the individuals who have been targeted; and whether the operations were politically motivated, that is, conducted against the property or individuals because of their nationality. No bright-line rule exists in such cases. Consider a cyber operation conducted by State A to kill the CEO of one of State B's State-owned corporations abroad. Opinions among the members of the International Group of Experts were divided as to whether the operation amounted to an armed attack.

21.   The exercise of the right of self-defence is subject to the requirements of necessity, proportionality, imminence, and immediacy (Rules 14 and 15). Of course, the exercise of self-defence is also subject to the existence of a reasonable determination that an armed attack is about to occur or has occurred, as well as to the identity of the attacker. This determination is made *ex ante*, not *ex post facto*.

22.   Self-defence measures may be conducted from, and directed against entities on or in, the territory of the originator State, the victim State's territory, the high seas, international airspace, or outer space (subject to applicable space law).

23.   When defensive cyber operations are initiated from, or employ assets located in, a State to which the attack cannot be attributed, the principle of sovereignty must be carefully considered. It is indisputable that self-defence actions may be taken on foreign territory with that State's consent without violating its sovereignty. Therefore, the key issue with regard to defensive action on another State's territory is how to characterize non-consensual actions. The International Group of Experts was divided. The majority concluded that self-defence against a cyber

armed attack in these circumstances is permissible when the territorial State is unable (e.g., because it lacks the expertise or technology) or unwilling to take effective actions to repress the relevant elements of the cyber armed attack. In particular, they emphasized that States have a duty to ensure their territory is not used for acts contrary to international law (Rule 5). By contrast, a minority of the Group took the position that using force in self-defence on the territory of a State to which the armed attack is not attributable is impermissible, although other responses, such as an action based on the plea of necessity (Rule 9), might be appropriate. This, of course, presumes the absence of either the consent of that State or an authorization by the United Nations Security Council (Rule 18).

23. Those Experts who accepted the legality of cross-border defensive actions emphasized that the victim State must first demand that the territorial State put an end to the activities comprising the armed attack. The victim State must also afford the territorial State an opportunity to address the situation. These requirements derive from an international law obligation to respect (to the greatest extent possible) the sovereignty of the State on which the defensive actions are to take place. Additionally, they are procedural safeguards against a mistaken (or premature) conclusion as to the unwillingness or inability of the territorial State to address the situation. There may be exceptional situations where there is no time to convey a demand to the latter or for the latter to resolve the situation. If immediate action to repel a cyber armed attack is required to defeat the attack or minimize its consequences, the targeted State may act immediately in self-defence. Thus, these requirements are context-specific.

Rule 14 – Necessity and proportionality

A use of force involving cyber operations undertaken by a State in the exercise of its right of self-defence must be necessary and proportionate.

1. Actions in self-defence must meet two criteria – necessity and proportionality. The International Court of Justice acknowledged both in the *Nicaragua* judgment and later confirmed them in its *Oil Platforms* judgment.[38] The Nuremberg Tribunal also recognized the criteria.[39]

---

[38] *Nicaragua* judgment, paras. 176, 194; *Nuclear Weapons* Advisory Opinion, para. 41; *Oil Platforms* judgment, paras. 43, 73–4, 76.

[39] *Nuremburg Tribunal* judgment at 435 (referring to the *Caroline* formula).

As illustrated by these decisions, they undoubtedly reflect customary international law. It is important to note that the concepts of necessity and proportionality in the *jus ad bellum* are distinct from the concept of military necessity and the rule of proportionality in the *jus in bello*.

2.   Necessity requires that a use of force, including cyber operations that amount to a use of force (Rule 11), be needed to successfully repel an imminent armed attack or defeat one that is underway. This does not mean that force has to be the only available response to an armed attack. It merely requires that non-forceful measures be insufficient to address the situation. Of course, the forceful actions may be combined with non-forceful measures such as diplomacy, economic sanctions, or law enforcement.

3.   The key to the necessity analysis in the cyber context is, therefore, the existence, or lack, of alternative courses of action that do not rise to the level of a use of force. Should passive (as distinct from active) cyber defences like firewalls be adequate to reliably and completely thwart a cyber armed attack, other measures, whether cyber or kinetic, at the level of a use of force are impermissible. Similarly, if active cyber operations not rising to the level of use of force are adequate to deter or repel armed attacks (imminent or on-going), forceful cyber or kinetic alternatives would be barred by the necessity criterion. However, when measures falling short of a use of force cannot alone reasonably be expected to defeat an armed attack and prevent subsequent ones, cyber and kinetic operations at the level of a use of force are permissible under the law of self-defence.

4.   Necessity is judged from the perspective of the victim State. The determination of necessity must be reasonable in the attendant circumstances. For example, consider a case in which State A is conducting cyber attacks against State B's cyber infrastructure resulting in significant physical destruction and the loss of life. Previous attempts to negotiate have been unsuccessful. State B launches cyber operations of its own to defend itself. Unbeknownst to State B, State A had already decided to stop its attacks. This fact does not deprive State B's defensive cyber operations of their quality as lawful uses of cyber force in self-defence.

5.   Proportionality addresses the issue of how much force, including uses of cyber force, is permissible once force is deemed necessary. The criterion limits the scale, scope, duration, and intensity of the defensive response to that required to end the situation that has given rise to the right to act in self-defence. It does not restrict the amount of force used to that employed in the armed attack since the level of force needed

to successfully mount a defence is context-dependent; more force may be necessary, or less force may be sufficient, to repel the attack or defeat one that is imminent. In addition, there is no requirement that the defensive force be of the same nature as that constituting the armed attack. Therefore, a cyber use of force may be resorted to in response to a kinetic armed attack, and vice versa.

6.   The proportionality requirement should not be overstated. It may be that the originator of the cyber armed attack is relatively invulnerable to cyber operations. This would not preclude kinetic operations in an effort to compel the attacker to desist, although they must be scaled to that purpose.

Rule 15 – Imminence and immediacy

The right to use force in self-defence arises if a cyber armed attack occurs or is imminent. It is further subject to a requirement of immediacy.

1.   Textually, Article 51 of the United Nations Charter refers to a situation in which 'an armed attack occurs'. Clearly, this covers incidents in which the effects of the armed attack have already materialized, that is, when the cyber armed attack has caused, or is in the process of causing, damage or injury. It also encompasses situations in which a cyber operation is the first step in the launch of an armed attack. The paradigmatic case involves cyber operations directed against another State's air defences to 'prepare the battlefield' for an air campaign.

2.   The majority of the International Group of Experts took the position that even though Article 51 does not expressly provide for defensive action in anticipation of an armed attack, a State need not wait idly as the enemy prepares to attack. Instead, a State may defend itself once the armed attack is 'imminent'. Such action is labelled 'anticipatory self-defence'.[40] This position is based on the standard of imminence articulated in the nineteenth century by US Secretary of State Webster following the *Caroline* incident. In correspondence with his British counterpart, Lord Ashburton, regarding a British incursion into American territory to attack Canadian rebels during the Mackenzie Rebellion, Webster opined that

---

[40] For support regarding the notion, *see* Derek W. Bowett, SELF-DEFENCE IN INTER-NATIONAL LAW 188–9 (1958). Bowett finds support for this in the *travaux* of the Charter's drafting committee. *Ibid.* at 182 (quoting Report of the Rapporteur of Committee I to Commission I, 6 U.N.C.I.O. 459 (13 June 1945)).

the right of self-defence applied only when '[the] necessity of self-defence [was] instant, overwhelming, leaving no choice of means, and no moment for deliberation'.[41] Although the incident actually had nothing to do with actions taken in anticipation of attack (the attacks in question were on-going), Webster's formulation has survived as the classic expression of the temporal threshold for anticipatory defensive actions; indeed, the Nuremberg Tribunal cited the *Caroline* correspondence with approval.[42]

3. The International Group of Experts acknowledged the view held by some commentators that acts in self-defence are permissible only once an attack has actually been launched; anticipatory self-defence is prohibited.[43] A nuanced version of this approach asserts that action in self-defence is permissible in the face of an incipient attack that has not reached its destination.[44] The speed of cyber operations would usually preclude them from falling into this category. No member of the International Group of Experts shared these views.

4. There are variations among approaches to anticipatory self-defence.[45] One approach requires that the armed attack be about to be launched, thereby imposing a temporal limitation on anticipatory actions.[46] The majority of the International Group of Experts rejected this strict temporal analysis. They took particular note of the 'last feasible window of opportunity' standard.[47] By this standard, a State may act in anticipatory self-defence against an armed attack, whether cyber or kinetic, when the attacker is clearly committed to launching an armed attack and the victim State will lose its opportunity to effectively defend itself unless it acts. In other words, it may act anticipatorily only during

---

[41] Letter from Daniel Webster to Lord Ashburton (6 August 1842), *reprinted in* 2 INTERNATIONAL LAW DIGEST 412 (John Bassett Moore ed., 1906).

[42] *Nuremburg Tribunal* judgment at 435.

[43] *See, e.g.,* Ian Brownlie, INTERNATIONAL LAW AND THE USE OF FORCE BETWEEN STATES 275–8 (1963).

[44] *See, e.g.,* Yoram Dinstein, WAR, AGGRESSION AND SELF DEFENCE 203–4 (5th ed. 2011).

[45] *See* discussion of the variations in Terry D. Gill, *The Temporal Dimension of Self-Defence: Anticipation, Pre-emption, Prevention and Immediacy, in* INTERNATIONAL LAW AND ARMED CONFLICT: EXPLORING THE FAULTLINES 113 (Michael N. Schmitt and Jelena Pejic eds., 2007).

[46] *See, e.g.,* Derek W. Bowett, SELF-DEFENCE IN INTERNATIONAL LAW 187–92 (1958).

[47] *See, e.g.,* Michael. N. Schmitt, *Cyber Operations in International Law: The Use of Force, Collective Security, Self-Defense, and Armed Conflicts, in* NATIONAL RESEARCH COUNCIL OF THE NATIONAL ACADEMIES, PROCEEDINGS OF A WORKSHOP ON DETERRING CYBERATTACKS: INFORMING STRATEGIES AND DEVELOPING OPTIONS FOR US POLICY 166 (2010).

the last window of opportunity to defend itself against an armed attack that is forthcoming. This window may present itself immediately before the attack in question, or, in some cases, long before it occurs. The critical question is not the temporal proximity of the anticipatory defensive action to the prospective armed attack, but whether a failure to act at that moment would reasonably be expected to result in the State being unable to defend itself effectively when that attack actually starts.

5.   Consider a situation in which the intelligence service of State A receives incontrovertible information that State B is preparing to launch a cyber attack that will destroy State A's primary oil pipeline within the next two weeks. The attack involves causing the microcontrollers along the pipeline to increase the pressure in the pipeline, resulting in a series of explosions. Intelligence services have no information on the specific vulnerability to be exploited, thereby preventing effective cyber defence of the microcontrollers. However, they do have information that those involved in conducting the attack will be gathered at a particular location and time. State A would be justified in concluding that the necessity of self-defence is imminent, and strikes against those individuals would be lawful as proportionate anticipatory self-defence should lesser means be inadequate.

6.   In assessing such cases, a distinction must be drawn between preparatory actions and those that constitute the initial phase of an attack. Take the case of the insertion of a logic bomb. The insertion will qualify as an imminent armed attack if the specified conditions for activation are likely to occur. The situation is analogous to the laying of naval mines in shipping routes passing through the territorial sea of the target State. This situation must be distinguished from that of emplacing remotely activated malware. If the initiator is merely acquiring the capability to initiate an armed attack in the future, the criterion of imminence is not met. However, if the initiator has actually decided to conduct an armed attack using the malware, an armed attack becomes imminent at the point that the victim State must act lest it lose the opportunity to defend itself effectively. Of course, it will often be difficult to make the distinction in practice. The lawfulness of any defensive response will be determined by the reasonableness of the victim State's assessment of the situation.

7.   Preventive strikes, that is, those against a prospective attacker who lacks either the means or the intent to carry out an armed attack, do not qualify as lawful anticipatory self-defence. Accordingly, the fact that an overtly hostile State is capable of launching cyber attacks – even

devastating ones – does not alone entitle a potential victim State to act defensively with force. The potential victim State must first reasonably conclude that the hostility has matured into an actual decision to attack. Until arriving at this conclusion, the victim State's response would be limited to non-forceful measures and referral of the matter to the Security Council (Rule 18). Of course, even if one State has the intent and opportunity to conduct an armed attack against another, the right of the victim State to take defensive measures at the use of force level does not mature until such time as failure to act would deprive the victim of its ability to defend itself effectively when the attack does come.

8. The requirement of immediacy (as distinct from the requirement of imminence discussed above) distinguishes an act of self-defence from mere retaliation. It refers to the period following the execution of an armed attack within which the victim State may reasonably respond in self-defence. Factors such as the temporal proximity between attack and response, the period necessary to identify the attacker, and the time required to prepare a response are relevant in this regard.

9. A further issue in this regard is how to assess the length of time within which a self-defence situation continues following the completion of the particular incident forming the basis for the right of self-defence. For instance, a cyber armed attack may commence with a wave of cyber operations against the victim State. The self-defence situation does not necessarily conclude with the termination of those cyber operations. If it is reasonable to conclude that further cyber operations are likely to follow, the victim State may treat those operations as a 'cyber campaign' and continue to act in self-defence. However, if such a conclusion is not reasonable, any further use of force, whether kinetic or cyber, is liable to be characterized as mere retaliation. In the final analysis, the requirement of immediacy boils down to a test of reasonableness in light of the circumstances prevailing at the time.

10. In some cases, the fact that a cyber armed attack has occurred or is occurring may not be apparent for some time. This may be so because the cause of the damage or injury has not been identified. Similarly, it may be that the initiator of the attack is not identified until well after the attack. The classic example of both situations is employment of a worm such as Stuxnet. In such cases, the criterion of immediacy is not met unless the conditions described in the previous paragraph apply.

Rule 16 – Collective self-defence

The right of self-defence may be exercised collectively. Collective self-defence against a cyber operation amounting to an armed attack may only be exercised at the request of the victim State and within the scope of the request.

1. The right to collective self-defence authorizes a State or multiple States to come to the assistance of another State that is the victim of an armed attack.[48] This right, explicitly set forth in Article 51 of the United Nations Charter, reflects customary international law.

2. Before a State may come to the assistance of another State in collective self-defence, it must have received a request for such assistance from the victim of the armed attack.[49] Both the victim State and the State providing assistance must be satisfied that there is an imminent (Rule 15) or on-going armed attack. There is no rule in customary international law permitting one State to engage in collective self-defence of another State solely on the basis of the former's own assessment of the situation.

3. When a State exercises collective self-defence on behalf of another State, it must do so within the scope of the other's request and consent. In other words, the right to engage in collective self-defence is subject to the conditions and limitations set by the victim State. That State may, for instance, limit the assistance to non-kinetic measures or to passive rather than active cyber defences.

4. Collective self-defence may be exercised either on the basis of a previously concluded collective defence treaty or an ad hoc arrangement. As an example, NATO Allies have agreed 'that an armed attack against one or more of them in Europe or North America shall be considered an attack against them all and consequently they agree that, if such an armed attack occurs, each of them, in exercise of the right of individual or collective self-defence recognized by Article 51 of the Charter of the United Nations, will assist the Party or Parties so attacked'.[50] An example of an ad hoc arrangement is

---

[48] For the different modalities of collective self defence, see Yoram Dinstein, WAR, AGGRESSION AND SELF-DEFENCE, 278–80 (5th ed. 2011).

[49] *Nicaragua* judgment, para. 199. In *Nicaragua*, the International Court of Justice articulated a requirement for a 'declaration' by the State that has been the victim of the armed attack. *Ibid.* paras. 232–4. The International Group of Experts concluded that this requirement is satisfied by the request for assistance.

[50] North Atlantic Treaty (Washington Treaty), Art. 5, 34 U.N.T.S. 234.

the assistance provided to Kuwait by a coalition of States in 1990–1 in response to the armed attack by Iraq.

5.   The requirements of necessity, proportionality, imminence, and immediacy (Rules 14 and 15) apply to collective self-defence.

Rule 17 – Reporting measures of self-defence

Measures involving cyber operations undertaken by States in the exercise of the right of self-defence pursuant to Article 51 of the United Nations Charter shall be immediately reported to the United Nations Security Council.

1.   The requirement to report exercises of self-defence to the United Nations Security Council is found in Article 51 of the United Nations Charter. The failure of a Member of the United Nations to report actions that it takes in self-defence to the Security Council is a violation of its obligations under Article 51.[51] However, the reporting requirement should not be interpreted as customary international law. In *Nicaragua*, the International Court of Justice specifically addressed this question. It held that 'it is clear that in customary international law it is not a condition of the lawfulness of the use of force in self-defence that a procedure so closely dependent on the content of a treaty commitment and of the institutions established by it should have been followed'.[52] Therefore, the failure does not divest the State in question of the right to act in self-defence.

2.   According to Article 51, the right to act in self-defence continues until the Security Council 'has taken measures necessary to maintain international peace and security'. The nature and scope of the measures encompassed in this provision are a matter of controversy. The majority of the International Group of Experts took the position that the Council must expressly divest the State of its right of self-defence under Article 51. All Experts agreed that only the Security Council enjoys such authority, although it has never exercised it.

3.   The fact that a State is lawfully conducting actions in the exercise of its right of self-defence, or has elected not to do so, does not deprive the Security Council of its authority in relation to the maintenance of international peace and security under Chapter VII of the Charter.

---

[51] *Nicaragua* judgment, para. 235.   [52] *Nicaragua* judgment, para. 200.

SECTION 3:   ACTIONS OF INTERNATIONAL GOVERNMENTAL ORGANIZATIONS

Rule 18 – United Nations Security Council

Should the United Nations Security Council determine that an act constitutes a threat to the peace, breach of the peace, or act of aggression, it may authorize non-forceful measures, including cyber operations. If the Security Council considers such measures to be inadequate, it may decide upon forceful measures, including cyber measures.

1.   This Rule is based on Chapter VII of the United Nations Charter. Article 39 of the Charter empowers the Security Council to 'determine the existence of any threat to the peace, breach of the peace, or act of aggression and [to] make recommendations, or decide what measures shall be taken in accordance with Articles 41 and 42, to maintain or restore international peace and security'. To date, the Security Council has never determined that a cyber operation constitutes a threat to the peace, breach of the peace, or act of aggression. However, it is incontrovertible that the Security Council has the authority to do so.

2.   Although the Security Council typically exercises its authority under Article 39 with regard to specific incidents or situations, it has labelled two significant phenomena as threats to the peace – international terrorism[53] and the proliferation of weapons of mass destruction.[54] The Security Council could equally decide that particular types of cyber operations amount to a threat to the peace, breach of the peace, or act of aggression *in abstracto*, that is, without reference to particular acts that have or are about to occur. For instance, it is within the authority of the Security Council to determine that cyber operations directed at national banking systems or critical national infrastructure qualify as such.

3.   Once it has made the determination under Article 39, the Security Council may consider taking measures pursuant to Article 41. That Article provides that the Council 'may decide what measures not involving the use of armed force are to be employed to give effect to its decisions, and it may call upon the Members of the United Nations to apply such measures. These may include complete or partial interruption of economic relations and of rail, sea, air, postal, telegraphic, radio, and other means of communication, and the severance of diplomatic

---

[53] *See, e.g.,* S.C. Res. 1373 (28 September 2001).   [54] *See, e.g.,* S.C. Res. 1540 (28 April 2004).

relations.' Non-forceful measures are those that do not rise to the level of a use of force (Rule 11). The list of measures referred to in Article 41 of the Charter is non-exhaustive.[55]

4. The reference to 'complete or partial interruption of … postal, telegraphic, radio and other means of communication' in Article 41 is especially important in the cyber context. This provision, in light of the Council's wide margin of discretion, confirms that the Security Council may decide upon a complete or partial interruption of cyber communications with a State or non-State actor.[56]

5. All United Nations Member States are obliged to implement Security Council decisions (as distinct from recommendations) under Chapter VII of the Charter. Generally, Security Council resolutions leave it to States to decide upon the specific means by which they fulfil their obligation to implement the Council's decisions at the domestic level. In the case of sanctions involving cyber communications, domestic implementation would be indispensable. For instance, it may be necessary to require Internet service providers (government and private alike) to adopt restrictive measures. Accordingly, States might have to adopt domestic legislation or regulations that compel Internet service providers subject to their jurisdiction to comply with the terms of the particular resolution (Rules 2 and 3).

6. The last sentence of Rule 18 is based on Article 42 of the Charter.[57] Once the Security Council determines that a threat to the peace, breach of the peace, or act of aggression exists and that non-forceful measures would be inadequate or have proved to be inadequate to maintain or restore international peace or security,[58] it may authorize the use

---

[55] *Tadić*, Decision on the Defence Motion for Interlocutory Appeal, para. 35.

[56] For example, in 2001, the Monitoring Mechanism on Sanctions against UNITA raised the possibility of measures being taken to interrupt Internet connections with UNITA. Monitoring Mechanism on Sanctions against UNITA Report, appended to Letter from the Chairman of the Security Council Committee established pursuant to Resolution 864 to the President of the Security Council (12 October 2001), paras. 64–9, UN Doc. S/2001/966.

[57] Art. 42 of the United Nations Charter provides: 'Should the Security Council consider that measures provided for in Article 41 would be inadequate or have proved to be inadequate, it may take such action by air, sea, or land forces as may be necessary to maintain or restore international peace and security. Such action may include demonstrations, blockade, and other operations by air, sea, or land forces of Members of the United Nations.'

[58] As the wording of this Rule makes clear, 'measures not involving the use of armed force' do not need to have been actually taken, i.e., the United Nations Security Council may immediately resort to the measures envisioned under the second sentence of this Rule.

of force. Consider a situation in which State A is developing a nuclear weapons capability. That State has ignored demands by the Security Council to put an end to its activities and has weathered economic sanctions authorized pursuant to Article 41. The Security Council could authorize Member States to conduct cyber operations against State A designed to disrupt the weapons programme.

7. In the context of this Rule, the Security Council often provides that 'all necessary measures' (or similar language) may be taken to implement a resolution.[59] The phrase implies the authority to employ cyber operations against the State or entity that is the object of the resolution in question. It also encompasses taking kinetic action against the cyber capabilities of that State or entity. Of course, any measures taken must fall within the scope of the resolution's mandate or authorization.

8. It is uncertain whether other rules of international law limit the authority of the Security Council to authorize or mandate action. For instance, a mandate specifically to conduct cyber attacks against civilians or civilian objects would generally violate international humanitarian law (Rule 32). It is unsettled whether a Security Council authorization to conduct such attacks would as a matter of law override the prohibition. Whatever the case, it is clear that a decision by the Security Council to disregard rules of international law should not be taken lightly. Under no circumstances may the Security Council deviate from rules of a *jus cogens* nature.

9. While Article 42 indicates that enforcement measures may be taken by 'air, sea or land forces of Members of the United Nations', the International Group of Experts agreed that any action undertaken on the basis of this Rule may be implemented by, or against, cyberspace capabilities.

Rule 19 – Regional organizations

International organizations, arrangements, or agencies of a regional character may conduct enforcement actions, involving or in response

---

[59] An example can be found in S.C. Res. 678, para. 2 (1991) (Iraq–Kuwait): 'Authorizes Member States co-operating with the Government of Kuwait, unless Iraq on or before 15 January 1991 fully implements ... the above-mentioned resolutions, to use all necessary means to uphold and implement resolution 660 (1990) and all subsequent relevant resolutions and to restore international peace and security in the area'.

to cyber operations, pursuant to a mandate from, or authorization by, the United Nations Security Council.

1. This Rule is based on Chapters VII and VIII of the United Nations Charter whereby the Security Council may turn to regional arrangements or agencies for enforcement action under its authority. It is a point of contention in international law as to whether the regional arrangement or agency may engage in enforcement action in the absence of an express authorization to do so by the Security Council.

2. The term 'regional' is drawn from Article 52(1) of the United Nations Charter, according to which the arrangements or agencies addressed in Chapter VIII of the Charter are regional systems of collective security 'appropriate for regional action'. Qualification as a regional arrangement or agency is not clear-cut. For instance, NATO has always taken the position that it is not such an organization because its purpose is primarily one of collective defence as opposed to collective security. With respect to Rule 19, technical qualification as a regional organization is irrelevant because the Security Council may authorize the taking of enforcement measures by any grouping of States, whether organized in advance or on an ad hoc basis, under Chapter VII.

3. The phrase 'enforcement actions' in this Rule derives from Article 53(1) of the Charter.[60] It refers to the power conferred on the Security Council under Articles 41 and 42, that is, to authorize or mandate non-forceful or forceful measures in order to maintain or restore international peace and security. Enforcement action must be distinguished from action (including cyber operations) taken by regional arrangements or agencies on the basis of collective self-defence (Rule 16).

4. The text of the Rule makes clear that enforcement actions by regional arrangements or agencies may include cyber operations. It also recognizes that enforcement actions may be taken in response to situations consisting in part or in whole of cyber activities.

5. The terms 'mandate' and 'authorization' are included to distinguish situations in which the Security Council specifically designates a particular entity to conduct operations from those in which individual States or regional entities act pursuant to a broader authorization by the Security Council that has not specifically designated it (e.g., an ad hoc coalition). Rule 19 includes both situations.

---

[60] This phrase or equivalent phrases were also used in UN Charter Arts. 2(5), 2(7), 5, 11(2), 45, 48, 49, and 50. None of these provisions contains a definition.

PART II

The law of cyber armed conflict

3

The law of armed conflict generally

Rule 20 – Applicability of the law of armed conflict

Cyber operations executed in the context of an armed conflict are subject to the law of armed conflict.

1.   The law of armed conflict applies to cyber operations as it would to any other operations undertaken in the context of an armed conflict. Despite the novelty of cyber operations and the absence of specific rules within the law of armed conflict explicitly dealing with them, the International Group of Experts was unanimous in finding that the law of armed conflict applies to such activities in both international and non-international armed conflicts (Rules 22 and 23).[1]

2.   A condition precedent to the application of the law of armed conflict is the existence of an armed conflict. The term 'armed conflict' was first used in a law of war codification in the 1949 Geneva Conventions,[2] but has never been authoritatively defined as a matter of treaty law. It has today replaced the term 'war' for law of armed conflict purposes. As used in this Manual, armed conflict refers to a situation involving hostilities, including those conducted using cyber means.[3] The term takes on a different meaning for the purposes of characterizing international and non-international armed conflict. Rules 22 and 23 discuss the extent of hostilities required to reach those thresholds.

3.   To illustrate, in 2007 Estonia was the target of persistent cyber operations. However, the law of armed conflict did not apply to those cyber operations because the situation did not rise to the level of an armed conflict. By contrast, the law of armed conflict governed the cyber operations that occurred during the international armed conflict between

---

[1]   For a State position on this issue, *see, e.g.*, US Department of Defense, Cyberspace Policy Report – A Report to Congress Pursuant to the National Defense Authorization Act for Fiscal Year 2011, Section 934, at 7, 9 (November 2011).

[2]   Geneva Conventions I–IV, Art. 2.

[3]   Occupations that meet no armed resistance also qualify as armed conflicts despite the absence of hostilities. Geneva Conventions I–IV, Art. 2.

Georgia and Russia in 2008 because they were undertaken in furtherance of that conflict. The latter case illustrates that in a situation of on-going kinetic hostilities amounting to an armed conflict, the applicable law of international or non-international armed conflict will govern cyber operations undertaken in relation to that conflict. The precise aspects of the law of armed conflict that apply depend on whether the conflict is international or non-international in character.

4.   The term 'cyber operations' includes, but is not limited to, 'cyber attacks' (Rule 30). As used in this Manual, cyber attacks is a term of art referring to a specific category of cyber operations. Certain cyber operations, such as those affecting the delivery of humanitarian assistance (Rule 86), are governed by the law of armed conflict even when those operations do not rise to the level of an 'attack'.

5.   The International Group of Experts adopted the phrase 'in the context of an armed conflict' as a compromise formula with respect to the scope of the law of armed conflict. All members of the International Group of Experts agreed that there must be a nexus between the cyber activity and the armed conflict for the law of armed conflict to apply to the activity in question. However, they differed as to the nature of that nexus. According to one view, the law of armed conflict governs any cyber activity conducted by a party to an armed conflict against its opponent (note, in this regard, the discussion on attributability in the Commentary to Rule 22). According to the second view, the cyber activity must have been undertaken in furtherance of the hostilities, that is, in order to contribute to the originator's military effort. Consider a cyber operation conducted by State A's Ministry of Trade against a private corporation in enemy State B in order to acquire commercial secrets during an armed conflict. According to the first view, the law of armed conflict would govern that operation because it is being conducted by a party to the armed conflict against a corporation of the enemy State. Those Experts adopting the second view considered that the law of armed conflict does not apply because the link between the activity and the hostilities is insufficient.

6.   The International Group of Experts noted that the precise parameters of the phrase 'in the context of' are less clear in a non-international armed conflict. This is because a State retains certain law enforcement obligations and rights with respect to its territory in which the hostilities are taking place, notwithstanding the armed conflict.[4] To the extent that

---

[4] Of course a State may also have law enforcement responsibilities during an international armed conflict. However, such responsibilities tend to be more pronounced during a non-international armed conflict.

it is involved in purely law enforcement activities, domestic and human rights law, not the law of armed conflict, apply.

7.   The law of armed conflict does not embrace activities of private individuals or entities that are unrelated to the armed conflict. Take, for example, the case of a private corporation that is engaging in theft of intellectual property to achieve a market advantage over a competitor in the enemy State. In principle, the law of armed conflict does not govern such activity.

8.   The applicability of the law of armed conflict does not depend upon the qualification of the situation under the *jus ad bellum* (Chapter 2). Pursuant to the principle of equal application of the law of armed conflict, even a resort to armed force that is unlawful from the perspective of *jus ad bellum* is subject to the law of armed conflict.[5]

9.   It should be noted that the application of the law of armed conflict to cyber operations can prove problematic. It is often difficult to identify the existence of a cyber operation, its originator, its intended object of attack, and its precise effects. Still, these questions of fact do not prejudice the application of the law of armed conflict.

10.   To the extent an express rule of the law of armed conflict does not regulate cyber activities, regard should be had to the Martens Clause, found in Hague Convention IV,[6] the 1949 Geneva Conventions,[7] and Additional Protocol I.[8] The text in Hague Convention IV provides that:

> Until a more complete code of the laws of war has been issued, the High Contracting Parties deem it expedient to declare that, in cases not included in the Regulations adopted by them, the inhabitants and the belligerents remain under the protection and the rule of the principles of the law of nations, as they result from the usages established among civilized peoples, from the laws of humanity, and the dictates of the public conscience.

To the extent that cyber activities are conducted in the course of an armed conflict, the Martens Clause, which reflects customary international law,

---

[5] Paragraph 5 of the preamble to Additional Protocol I provides that its provisions, as well as those of the four 1949 Geneva Conventions, 'must be fully applied in all circumstances to all persons who are protected by those instruments, without any adverse distinction based on the nature or origin of the armed conflict or on the causes espoused by or attributed to the Parties to the conflict'. *See also* UK MANUAL, paras. 3.12, 3.12.1; CANADIAN MANUAL, para. 204.

[6] Hague Convention IV, preamble.

[7] Geneva Convention I, Art. 63; Geneva Convention II, Art. 62; Geneva Convention III, Art. 142; Geneva Convention IV, Art. 158.

[8] Additional Protocol I, Art. 1(2).

functions to ensure that such activities are not conducted in a legal vacuum. This point is without prejudice to the disputed question of the applicability of human rights law during armed conflict.

Rule 21 – Geographical limitations

Cyber operations are subject to geographical limitations imposed by the relevant provisions of international law applicable during an armed conflict.

1. The law of armed conflict (which includes the law of neutrality), in conjunction with other fields of international law (e.g., the law of the sea, air law, and space law, where applicable in armed conflict[9]), prescribes the geographic space in which cyber operations may be conducted. Relevant legal issues include the place from which cyber operations are launched, the location of any necessary instrumentalities, and the location of target cyber systems. As a rule, cyber operations may be conducted from, on, or with effects in the entire territory of the parties to the conflict, international waters or airspace, and, subject to certain limitations, outer space. Cyber operations are generally prohibited elsewhere. Of particular importance in this regard is the law of neutrality, because cyber operations can transit neutral territory and may have unintended effects therein. Neutrality is discussed in Chapter 7.

2. Restrictions based on geographical limitations may be particularly difficult to implement in the context of cyber warfare. For instance, consider a cyber attack using cloud computing techniques. Data used to prosecute the attack from one State may be replicated across servers in a number of other States, including neutral States, but only observably reflected on the systems where the attack is initiated and completed. As discussed in Rules 8 and 92, there is no general prohibition on the mere transit of data through areas where the conduct of cyber operations is otherwise prohibited during an armed conflict.

3. According to the traditional view of the law of armed conflict, military operations during a non-international armed conflict must be limited to the territory (including the territorial sea) and national airspace of the State in which the conflict is taking place. However, events over the past decade such as the conflict in Afghanistan and transnational counter-terrorist operations have caused this bright line to

---

[9] For instance, Art. 88 of the Law of the Sea Convention is inapplicable during armed conflict.

become blurred. Today the exact geographical scope of non-international armed conflict raises a number of complex issues. Many States and commentators now take the view that a non-international armed conflict may extend to areas beyond the borders of the State in question, arguing that it is the status of the actors, not geography, which is the determinative factor in classification of conflict (Rule 23).[10] Others maintain the traditional view, although they generally accept the notion of 'spill over' of that conflict into neighbouring States.

Rule 22 – Characterization as international armed conflict

An international armed conflict exists whenever there are hostilities, which may include or be limited to cyber operations, occurring between two or more States.

1. The generally accepted criteria for the existence of an international armed conflict, which reflect customary international law, are derived from Common Article 2 of the 1949 Geneva Conventions.[11] The Article provides:

> The present Convention shall apply to all cases of declared war or of any other armed conflict which may arise between two or more of the High Contracting Parties even if the state of war is not recognized by one of them. The Convention shall also apply to all cases of partial or total occupation of the territory of a High Contracting Party, even if the said occupation meets with no armed resistance.[12]

Reduced to basics, an armed conflict under this Rule requires both 'international' and 'armed' components.

2. The International Group of Experts agreed that a conflict is international if two or more States are involved as parties on opposing sides. It also agreed that a conflict is international when non-State actors under the 'overall control' of one State engage in hostilities against another State (see discussion below). As a practical matter, it may be difficult to ascertain whether a State is controlling a non-State actor's cyber activities.

---

[10] Harold Hongju Koh, *The Obama Administration and International Law,* Address at the Annual Meeting of the American Society of International Law (25 March 2010).

[11] UK MANUAL, para. 3.2; US COMMANDER'S HANDBOOK, para. 5.1.2.1; CANADIAN MANUAL at GL-9; GERMAN MANUAL, para. 202; AMW MANUAL, Rule 1(r).

[12] Geneva Conventions I–IV, Art. 2.

3.   The question of whether the actions of a non-State organized armed group against one State may be attributed to another State such that a conflict is international was explicitly addressed in the International Criminal Tribunal for the Former Yugoslavia's *Tadić* Appeals Chamber judgment.[13] The Appeals Chamber articulated an 'overall control' test in determining that Bosnian Serb units were sufficiently directed by the Federal Republic of Yugoslavia to conclude that an international armed conflict existed.[14] As the Chamber explained,

> control by a State over subordinate armed forces or militias or paramilitary units may be of an overall character (and must comprise more than the mere provision of financial assistance or military equipment or training). This requirement, however, does not go so far as to include the issuing of specific orders by the State, or its direction of each individual operation. Under international law it is by no means necessary that the controlling authorities should plan all the operations of the units dependent on them, choose their targets, or give specific instructions concerning the conduct of military operations and any alleged violations of international humanitarian law. The control required by international law may be deemed to exist when a State (or, in the context of an armed conflict, the Party to the conflict) has a role in organising, coordinating or planning the military actions of the military group, in addition to financing, training and equipping or providing operational support to that group.[15]

4.   The International Court of Justice has observed that the overall control test 'may well be ... applicable and suitable'[16] for classification purposes; the International Criminal Court has also adopted it.[17] Applying the test, if State A exercises overall control over an organized group of computer hackers that penetrate State B's cyber infrastructure and cause significant physical damage, the armed conflict qualifies as 'international' in nature. State A need not have instructed the group to attack particular

---

[13] *Tadić*, Appeals Chamber judgment, paras. 131–40, 145.

[14] *Tadić*, Appeals Chamber judgment, paras. 131, 145, 162.

[15] *Tadić*, Appeals Chamber judgment, para. 137.

[16] *Genocide* judgment, para. 404. Note that the Court also addressed the issue of the attribution of the genocide by Bosnian Serb armed forces at Srebrenica to the Federal Republic of Yugoslavia. It usefully distinguished between the degree of control necessary to classify a conflict as international and that required in order to hold a State internationally responsible for the acts of non-State actors. With regard to the latter situation, it adopted Art. 8 of the Articles on State Responsibility as an accurate reflection of customary international law. *Genocide* judgment, paras. 398–401, 413–14.

[17] *Lubanga* judgment, para. 541.

aspects of the infrastructure, but, instead, only needs to have exerted sufficient control over the group to instruct it to mount a campaign against cyber infrastructure cyber targets.

5.   Mere support for a group of non-State actors involved in a non-international armed conflict does not 'internationalize' the conflict. In other words, support alone does not transform a non-international armed conflict into an international armed conflict between the supporting State and the State in whose territory the conflict is occurring. As noted above, the *Tadić* Appeals Chamber found that financing, training, equipping, and providing operational support by a State to a non-State group was not, without more, sufficient to characterize the situation between the two States concerned as international.[18] If the State's support does not rise to the level of overall control over the group, it may nevertheless be unlawful as an intervention in the domestic affairs of the State concerned (Commentary accompanying Rule 10).[19]

6.   Despite the absence of a definitive bright-line test regarding support, the International Group of Experts did agree that the threshold for internationalization is a high one. For example, merely taking measures to maintain rebel access to the national cyber infrastructure was not considered by the Experts to suffice. Similarly, the provision of cyber attack tools for rebel use would not reach the threshold. By contrast, providing specific intelligence on cyber vulnerabilities that renders particular rebel cyber attacks possible would, in their view, suffice.

7.   Some cases are more difficult to assess. Consider a cyber operation conducted by State A to assist rebels in State B. The operation is designed to shut down State B's cyber communications capabilities. It might be argued that the operation internationalizes the conflict if State B relies upon the system for military communications. If it does not so rely, it may be less easy to characterize the operation as sufficient to internationalize the conflict. Of course, if State A actually participates in the conflict on behalf of the non-State group, and its actions reach the 'armed' level (see below), an international armed conflict between the two States would exist irrespective of the degree of control exercised over the group.

8.   The overall control test is inapplicable to the conduct of individuals, or insufficiently organized groups. According to the International Criminal Tribunal for the Former Yugoslavia, such individuals or groups must receive specific instructions (or subsequent public approval) from

---

[18] *Tadić*, Appeals Chamber judgment, para. 137.   [19] UN Charter Art. 2(1).

a State before their conduct can be attributed to that State for the purpose of determining the existence of an international armed conflict.[20] As an example, there is no definitive evidence that the hacktivists involved in the cyber operations against Estonia in 2007 operated pursuant to instructions from any State, nor did any State endorse and adopt the conduct. For these reasons (besides the issue of whether the conflict was 'armed'), the situation cannot be characterized as an international armed conflict.

9.   Some members of the International Group of Experts took the position that an international armed conflict can also exist between a State and a non-State organized armed group operating transnationally even if the group's conduct cannot be attributed to a State. They point out that such conflicts are not confined within the borders of a single State, and therefore have an international element.[21] The majority of the Experts rejected this view on the ground that such conflicts are non-international in character (Rule 23).

10.   For States Party to Additional Protocol I, armed conflicts in which peoples are fighting against colonial domination, alien occupation, or racist regimes in the exercise of their right of self-determination are to be considered international armed conflicts.[22]

11.   In addition to being international, an international armed conflict must be 'armed'. The law of armed conflict does not directly address the meaning of the term 'armed conflict', but the notion clearly requires the existence of hostilities. Therefore, the International Group of Experts included the concept of hostilities in this Rule. Hostilities presuppose the collective application of means and methods of warfare (Rule 41). The constituent hostilities may involve any combination of kinetic and cyber operations, or cyber operations alone. Of course, hostilities exist whenever one State engages in 'cyber attacks' (Rule 30) against another.

12.   Although hostilities are, for the International Group of Experts, undeniably a condition precedent to the armed component of international armed conflict, controversy exists as to the threshold of the requisite violence. According to the ICRC commentary to the 1949 Geneva Conventions, 'Any difference arising between two States and

---

[20] *Tadić*, Appeals Chamber judgment, paras. 132, 137, 141, 145. Adoption or endorsement of conduct of a non-State group was first addressed in the *Tehran Hostages* case, para. 74.

[21] *See* discussion in HCJ 769/02, *The Public Committee against Torture in Israel* v. *The Government of Israel*, para. 18 [2006] (Isr.).

[22] Additional Protocol I, Art. 1(4).

leading to the intervention of armed forces is an armed conflict ... It makes no difference how long the conflict lasts, or how much slaughter takes place.'[23] For example, a cyber operation that causes a fire to break out at a small military installation would suffice to initiate an international armed conflict. The competing view requires greater extent, duration, or intensity of hostilities, although proponents of this view have not agreed on any particular threshold.[24] Its advocates point out that State practice demonstrates that there have been a number of isolated incidents such as sporadic border clashes or naval incidents that were not treated as international armed conflicts. By analogy, a single cyber incident that causes only limited damage, destruction, injury, or death would not necessarily initiate an international armed conflict for these Experts. Notwithstanding this difference of opinion, it would be prudent to treat the threshold of international armed conflict as relatively low. In all likelihood, such incidents will be evaluated on a case-by-case basis in light of the attendant circumstances.

13.   To be 'armed', a conflict need not involve the employment of the armed forces. Nor is the involvement of the armed forces determinative. For example, should entities such as civilian intelligence agencies engage in cyber operations otherwise meeting the armed criterion, an armed conflict may be triggered. Similarly, using the armed forces to conduct tasks that are normally the responsibility of non-military agencies does not alone initiate an armed conflict. For example, the fact that the armed forces undertake cyber espionage directed at another State does not in itself result in an armed conflict, even if it is typically performed by civilian intelligence agencies.

14.   The 2010 Stuxnet operation against SCADA systems in Iran, as a result of which centrifuges at a nuclear fuel processing plant were physically damaged, illustrates the difficulty of making the armed determination. The International Group of Experts was divided as to whether the damage sufficed to meet the armed criterion. Characterization was further complicated by the fact that questions remain as to whether the Stuxnet operation was conducted by a State or by

---

[23] ICRC Geneva Convention I Commentary at 32; ICRC Geneva Convention II Commentary at 28; ICRC Geneva Convention III Commentary at 23; ICRC Geneva Convention IV Commentary at 20.

[24] Christopher Greenwood, *Scope of Application of Humanitarian Law, in* The Handbook of International Humanitarian Law 45, 57 (Dieter Fleck ed., 2nd ed. 2008); Howard S. Levie, *The Status of Belligerent Personnel 'Splashed' and Rescued by a Neutral in the Persian Gulf Area*, 31 Virginia Journal of International Law 611, 613–14 (1991).

individuals whose conduct is attributable to a State for the purposes of finding an international armed conflict.

15.   As illustrated by the Stuxnet incident, significant legal and practical challenges stand in the way of definitively concluding that a cyber operation has initiated an international armed conflict. To date, no international armed conflict has been publicly characterized as having been solely precipitated in cyberspace. Nevertheless, the International Group of Experts unanimously concluded that cyber operations alone might have the potential to cross the threshold of international armed conflict.

16.   So long as the armed and international criteria have been met, an international armed conflict exists. This is so even if a party does not recognize the conflict as such.[25] The determination is a factual one.

17.   In certain cases, the law of international armed conflict applies despite the absence of hostilities. In particular, a belligerent occupation meeting with no armed resistance will, as a matter of law, trigger application of that body of law.[26] Additionally, an international armed conflict can come into existence merely by virtue of a declaration of war.[27] Finally, it is generally accepted that the establishment of a naval or aerial blockade initiates an international armed conflict. However the international armed conflict arises, the law of armed conflict will govern all cyber operations conducted in the context of that conflict.

Rule 23 – Characterization as non-international armed conflict

A non-international armed conflict exists whenever there is protracted armed violence, which may include or be limited to cyber operations, occurring between governmental armed forces and the forces of one or more armed groups, or between such groups. The confrontation must reach a minimum level of intensity and the parties involved in the conflict must show a minimum degree of organization.

1.   This Rule is a general restatement of the customary international law of armed conflict regarding the threshold for the existence of a non-international armed conflict. The first sentence is based on Common Article 3 of the 1949 Geneva Conventions, which reflects customary international law.[28] That Article applies to 'armed conflicts not of an

---

[25] Geneva Conventions I–IV, Art. 2.   [26] Geneva Conventions I–IV, Art. 2.
[27] Geneva Conventions I–IV, Art. 2.
[28] Note that Art. 8(c) of the Rome Statute adopts the Common Article 3 threshold with regard to war crimes committed during a non-international armed conflict. *See also* UK

international character occurring in the territory of one of the High Contracting Parties', that is, to situations in which hostilities occur between governmental armed forces and non-governmental organized armed groups or between such groups.[29] The second sentence is based on case law development of the issues of intensity and organization.

2.   Application of the law of armed conflict does not depend on the type of military operation or on the specific means and methods of warfare employed. Therefore, cyber operations alone, in the absence of kinetic operations, can bring a non-international armed conflict into existence. Given the requisite threshold of violence and the degree of organization of the armed groups required for a non-international armed conflict (discussed below), cyber operations in and of themselves will only in exceptional cases amount to a non-international armed conflict. Of course, if a conflict qualifies as a non-international armed conflict by virtue of on-going kinetic operations, the law of non-international armed conflict would govern any associated cyber operations.

3.   By Common Article 3, a non-international armed conflict occurs 'in the territory of one of the High Contracting Parties'. This text has generated a debate over the geographical scope of non-international armed conflict. One school of thought holds that the word 'one' in the quoted phrase signifies that non-international armed conflicts are confined to those that take place within the territorial boundaries of a single State. By this interpretation, an armed conflict that crosses a border would generally qualify as an international armed conflict. A second school of thought, adopted by the majority of the International Group of Experts, holds that the 'one' is a reference to the territory of any of the Contracting Parties. Accordingly, the phrase imposes no territorial limitations so long as the relevant States are Party to the 1949 Geneva Conventions.[30] Thus, if cyber attacks are undertaken during a non-international armed conflict from outside the territory of the State, that fact alone will not cause the conflict to be international in character.[31] It must also be borne in mind that the transit of data through cyber

MANUAL, para. 3.3; AMW MANUAL, commentary accompanying Rule 1(f); NIAC MANUAL, para. 1.1.1 (limiting the geographical scope of such conflicts).
[29] Tadić, Decision on the Defence Motion for Interlocutory Appeal, paras. 67, 70; UK MANUAL, para. 3.5 (as amended). See generally US COMMANDER'S HANDBOOK para. 5.1.2.2; CANADIAN MANUAL at GL-13; GERMAN MANUAL, paras. 201–11.
[30] See, e.g., Hamdan v. Rumsfeld, 548 US 557, 630–1 (2006) (applying Common Article 3 to conflict occurring across multiple States' political boundaries).
[31] See, e.g., AMW MANUAL, commentary accompanying Rule 2(a).

infrastructure located outside a State in which a non-international armed conflict is occurring does not render the conflict international.

4.   The law of armed conflict applies to all activities undertaken in pursuit of the armed conflict, and all associated effects (e.g., collateral damage), wherever they occur in the territory of a State involved in a non-international armed conflict. This means that in that State there is no 'zone of conflict' to which applicability of law of armed conflict is confined. Moreover, the International Group of Experts agreed that the law of armed conflict applies to activities conducted in the context of the conflict that occur outside the State in question. This is of particular importance because cyber activities in furtherance of a non-international armed conflict may well be launched remotely, far from the location of the conventional hostilities. Some States have weak regulatory regimes governing cyber activities or are technically incapable of effectively policing cyber activities occurring on their territory. They offer an appealing base of operations for those engaged in cyber attacks against the government during a non-international armed conflict. The International Group of Experts acknowledged the existence of a narrower approach that accepts the possibility of a non-international armed conflict which crosses borders, but that imposes a requirement of geographical proximity to the State involved in the conflict.

5.   The term 'armed conflict' is not expressly defined in the law of armed conflict for the purposes of finding that a conflict is non-international in character. However, it is clear that 'situations of internal disturbances and tensions, such as riots, isolated and sporadic acts of violence, and other acts of a similar nature' are not included. This standard is set forth in Article 1(2) of Additional Protocol II and is today acknowledged as reflecting the customary international law distinction between non-international armed conflicts and hostilities not meeting the threshold for such conflicts.[32] Sporadic cyber incidents, including those that directly cause physical damage or injury, do not, therefore, constitute non-international armed conflict. Similarly, cyber operations that incite incidents such as civil unrest or domestic terrorism do not qualify. For instance, the calls that appeared on the Internet for riots by the Russian minority in Estonia in 2007 cannot be regarded as meeting that threshold.

---

[32] Art. 8(f) of the Rome Statute excludes such situations from the ambit of 'armed conflicts not of an international character'. See also UK MANUAL, para. 15.2.1; CANADIAN MANUAL, para. 1709; AMW MANUAL, commentary accompanying Rule 2(a).

6. The threshold for non-international armed conflict has been further developed in case law. In *Tadić*, the International Criminal Tribunal for the Former Yugoslavia affirmed that a non-international armed conflict exists when there is protracted armed violence between organized armed groups within a State.[33] This holding is widely accepted as setting forth the two key criteria for qualification as a non-international armed conflict – intensity of the hostilities and the involvement of an organized armed group.[34] Subsequent judgments of the International Criminal Tribunal for the Former Yugoslavia have de-emphasized the importance of other factors, such as geographical scope and temporal duration, subordinating these concepts within the concept of intensity.[35]

7. Various indicative criteria have been suggested to facilitate the determination whether a given situation has met the required intensity threshold.[36] The International Criminal Tribunal for the Former Yugoslavia has looked to such factors as the gravity of attacks and their recurrence;[37] the temporal and territorial expansion of violence and the collective character of hostilities;[38] whether various parties were able to operate from a territory under their control;[39] an increase in the number of government forces;[40] the mobilization of volunteers and the distribution and type of weapons among both parties to the conflict;[41] the fact that the conflict led to a large displacement of people;[42] and whether the conflict is the subject of any relevant scrutiny or action by the Security Council.[43] In view of the intensity threshold, cyber operations alone can trigger a non-international armed conflict in only rare cases.

8. The development of further State practice notwithstanding, network intrusions, the deletion or destruction of data (even on a large scale),

---

[33] *Tadić*, Decision on the Defence Motion for Interlocutory Appeal, para. 70.

[34] *See, e.g., Milošević* decision, paras. 16–17; *Prosecutor v. Furundžija*, Case No. IT-95-17/1-T, Trial Chamber judgment, para. 59 (Int'l Crim. Trib. for the Former Yugoslavia, 10 December 1998); *Delalić* judgment, para. 183; UK Manual, para. 15.3.1.

[35] *Haradinaj* judgment, para. 49.

[36] *See, e.g., Haradinaj* judgment, paras. 40–9; *Lubanga* judgment, para. 538; ICRC Geneva Convention I Commentary at 49–50; ICRC Geneva Convention IIII Commentary at 35–6; ICRC Geneva Convention IV Commentary at 35–6.

[37] *Mrkšić* judgment, para. 419; *Hadžihasanović* judgment, para. 22; *Limaj* judgment, paras. 135–67.

[38] *Hadžihasanović* judgment, para. 22; *Milošević* decision, paras. 28–9;

[39] *Milošević* decision, para. 29; *Delalić* judgment, para. 187;

[40] *Limaj* judgment, paras. 146, 159, 164–5; *Milošević* decision, para. 30.

[41] *Mrkšić* judgment, paras. 39–40, 407–8; *Milošević* decision, paras. 31.

[42] *Haradinaj* judgment, para. 49.   [43] *Mrkšić* judgment, paras. 420–1.

computer network exploitation, and data theft do not amount to a non-international armed conflict. The blocking of certain Internet functions and services would not, for example, suffice to trigger a non-international armed conflict, nor would defacing governmental or other official websites.

9.   As noted in the *Tadić* Appeals Chamber judgment, the violence that qualifies an armed conflict as non-international must be protracted, although the term 'protracted' has not been quantified in the law.[44] It is clear, however, that the qualifying violence need not be continuous in nature.[45] Frequent, albeit not continuous, cyber attacks occurring within a relatively defined period may be characterized as protracted.

10.   The International Group of Experts struggled with the question of whether non-destructive cyber operations conducted during civil disturbances or in connection with other acts of violence not qualifying as a non-international armed conflict can tip the scale and cause the hostilities to rise to the level of an armed conflict. For instance, assume an organized armed group has orchestrated civil disturbances. Although destruction of property is involved, such destruction is insufficiently severe to meet the intensity criterion for non-international armed conflict. The International Group of Experts achieved no consensus as to whether non-destructive but severe cyber operations satisfy the intensity criterion.

11.   For a non-international armed conflict to exist, there must be at least one non-State organized armed group involved in the hostilities.[46] Such a group is 'armed' if it has the capacity of undertaking cyber attacks (Rule 30). It is 'organized' if it is under an established command structure and has the capacity to sustain military operations.[47] The extent of organization does not have to reach the level of a conventional militarily disciplined unit.[48] However, cyber operations and computer attacks by

---

[44] *Tadić*, Decision on the Defence Motion for Interlocutory Appeal, para. 70. In *Abella*, the Inter-American Commission on Human Rights characterized a 30-hour clash between dissident armed forces and the Argentinian military as non-international armed conflict. *Abella* v. *Argentina*, Case 11.137, Inter-Am. C.H.R., Report No. 55/97, OEA\Ser.L\V \II.98, doc. 6 rev. (1998).

[45] In *Limaj*, the International Criminal Tribunal for the Former Yugoslavia concluded that the conflict in Kosovo in 1998 could be described as 'periodic armed clashes occurring virtually continuously at intervals averaging three to seven days over a widespread and expanding geographic area'. *Limaj* judgment, paras. 168, 171–3.

[46] AMW MANUAL, commentary accompanying Rule 2(a).

[47] *Limaj* judgment, para. 129.   [48] *Limaj* judgment, paras. 132–4.

private individuals do not suffice. Even small groups of hackers are unlikely to fulfil the requirement of organization. Whether or not a given group is organized must be determined on a case-by-case basis.

12.   To assess organization, the International Criminal Tribunal for the Former Yugoslavia has taken into account numerous factors. For instance, in *Limaj*, the Tribunal considered, inter alia: the organization and structure of the Kosovo Liberation Army (KLA), which had a general staff and created eleven zones with a commander for each; the adoption of internal regulations; the nomination of a spokesperson; the issuance of orders, political statements and communiqués; the establishment of headquarters; the capacity to launch coordinated action between KLA units; the establishment of a military police and disciplinary rules; the ability of the KLA to recruit new members and its capacity to provide military training; the creation of weapons distribution channels; the use of uniforms and various other equipment; and the participation by the KLA in political negotiations to resolve the Kosovo crisis.[49]

13.   This raises the question of 'virtual' organization in which all activities that bear on the criterion occur online. At one end of the spectrum are hackers who operate wholly autonomously. The mere fact that many hackers are attacking a State, for example, would not render them organized. At the other is a distinct online group with a leadership structure that coordinates its activities by, for instance, allocating speci-fied cyber targets amongst themselves, sharing attack tools, conducting cyber vulnerability assessments, and doing cyber damage assessment to determine whether 'reattack' is required. The group is operating 'cooperatively'. The majority of the International Group of Experts agreed that the failure of members of the group physically to meet does not alone preclude it from having the requisite degree of organization.

14.   It has been asserted that the organization must be of a nature to allow implementation of the law of armed conflict.[50] If so, the require-ment would be difficult to comply with in the case of a virtual armed group since there would be no means to implement the law with regard to individuals with whom there is no physical contact. The International

---

[49] *Limaj* judgment, paras. 94–129. The International Criminal Tribunal for Rwanda uses the same test as the International Criminal Tribunal for Former Yugoslavia to evaluate both the intensity and organization of the parties to the conflict for each of their cases. *Akayesu* judgment, paras. 619–21.

[50] ICRC ADDITIONAL PROTOCOLS COMMENTARY, para. 4470. This requirement is express with regard to Additional Protocol II conflicts (Art. 1(1)), but it is unclear whether it applies as well to Common Article 3 type conflicts.

Group of Experts was divided as to whether such difficulty would bar qualification as an organized armed group.

15. The more difficult case is that of an informal grouping of individuals who operate not cooperatively, but rather 'collectively', that is simultaneously but without any coordination. For instance, acting with a shared purpose, they access a common website which contains tools and vulnerable targets, but do not organize their cyber attacks in any fashion. The majority of the International Group of Experts took the position that an informal grouping of individuals acting in a collective but otherwise uncoordinated fashion cannot comprise an organized armed group; there must be a distinct group with sufficient organizational structure that operates as a unit. Others suggested that whether an informal group meets the organization criterion would depend upon a variety of context-specific factors, such as the existence of an informal leadership entity directing the group's activities in a general sense, identifying potential targets, and maintaining an inventory of effective hacker tools. All the Experts agreed that the mere fact that individuals are acting toward a collective goal does not satisfy the organization criterion. For example, if a website offers malware and a list of potential cyber targets, those who independently use the site to conduct attacks would not constitute an organized armed group.

16. Although Common Article 3 specifically provides that its application does not affect the legal status of the parties to a conflict, States have often been reluctant to admit the existence of a non-international armed conflict. Whether a non-international armed conflict exists is a question of fact that depends on the level of violence taking place and the parties' degree of organization. It is therefore an objective test that is unaffected by the subjective views of those engaged in the hostilities.[51]

17. Additional Protocol II governs certain non-international armed conflicts for Parties thereto. An Additional Protocol II conflict is one which takes place between the armed forces of a State and dissident armed forces or other organized armed groups that control sufficient territory so 'as to enable them to carry out sustained and concerted military operations'.[52] Unlike Common Article 3, the Protocol does not apply to armed conflicts occurring only between non-State armed groups and requires physical control of territory. Control over cyber activities alone is insufficient to constitute control of territory for Additional

---

[51] *Akayesu* judgment, para. 603.   [52] Additional Protocol II, Art. 1(1).

Protocol II purposes (although control over cyber activities may be indicative of the degree of territorial control a group enjoys).

Rule 24 – Criminal responsibility of commanders and superiors

(a) Commanders and other superiors are criminally responsible for ordering cyber operations that constitute war crimes.

(b) Commanders are also criminally responsible if they knew or, owing to the circumstances at the time, should have known their subordinates were committing, were about to commit, or had committed war crimes and failed to take all reasonable and available measures to prevent their commission or to punish those responsible.

1. This Rule emphasizes that commanders and other superiors do not escape criminal responsibility by virtue of the fact that they did not personally commit an act that constitutes a war crime. It is found in treaty and case law.[53] Applicable in both international and non-international armed conflict, Rule 24 reflects customary international law.[54] No basis exists for excluding the application of the Rule to cyber operations that constitute war crimes.

2. Related Articles in Geneva Conventions I to IV set forth the principle expressed in *lit.* (a).[55] They stipulate that Parties to the instrument must enact domestic legislation that provides 'effective penal sanctions for

---

[53] Geneva Convention I, Art. 49; Geneva Convention II, Art. 50; Geneva Convention III, Art. 129; Geneva Convention IV, Art. 146; Cultural Property Convention, Art. 28; Second Cultural Property Protocol, Art. 15(2). Additional Protocol I, Arts. 86–7; Rome Statute, Arts. 25(3)(b), 28.

[54] Rome Statute, Art. 25(3); ICTY Statute, Art. 7(1); ICTR Statute, Art. 6(1); Sierra Leone Statute, Art. 6(1); United Nations Transitional Administration in East Timor, Art. 14(3); UN Doc. UNTAET/REG/2000/15 (6 June 2000); US COMMANDER'S HANDBOOK, para. 6.1.3; UK MANUAL, paras. 16.36–16.36.6; CANADIAN MANUAL, para. 1504; ICRC CUSTOMARY IHL STUDY, Rules 152, 153. The jurisprudence of international tribunals illustrates the application of the principle of command responsibility. *See, e.g., Prosecutor v. Blaškić*, Case No. IT-95-14-T, Trial Chamber judgment, paras. 281–2 (Int'l Crim. Trib. for the Former Yugoslavia 3 March 2000); *Prosecutor v. Krstić*, Case No. IT-98-33-T, Trial Chamber judgment, para. 605 (Int'l Crim. Trib. for the Former Yugoslavia 2 August 2001); *Kayishema* judgment, para. 223; *Akayesu* judgment, paras. 472–4, 483; *Delalić*, judgment, paras. 333–4; *Martić*, Case No. IT-95-11-R61, Review of Indictment, paras. 20–1 (Int'l Crim. Trib. for the Former Yugoslavia 8 March 1996); *Prosecutor v. Rajić*, Case No. IT-95-12-R61, Review of the Indictment, paras. 1, 59, 71 (Int'l Crim. Trib. for the Former Yugoslavia 13 September 1996).

[55] Geneva Convention I, Art. 49; Geneva Convention II, Art. 50; Geneva Convention III, Art. 129; Geneva Convention IV, Art. 146.

persons committing, or ordering to be committed, any of the grave breaches' of the Conventions. The Articles further obligate Parties to search for persons alleged to have committed such offences and either to bring them before their own courts, or to hand them over to another Party for prosecution when that Party has made out a prima facie case as to the matter in question.

3.   In the context of cyber warfare, the Rule imposes criminal responsibility on any military commander or other superior (including civilians) who orders cyber operations amounting to a war crime.[56] A clear example is ordering cyber attacks to be conducted against civilians who are not directly participating in hostilities (Rule 32). Similarly, ordering indiscriminate cyber attacks to be launched would result in the criminal responsibility of the person so ordering the attack, regardless of whether that individual took any personal part in the actual conduct of the operation (Rule 49).

4.   Such responsibility extends down through the chain of command or control. For example, a subordinate commander who orders his or her troops to comply with an order from a superior to commit a particular war crime is equally responsible for ordering a war crime. Similarly, consider the case of a senior commander who orders cyber operations to be conducted to achieve a particular operational effect without specifying how those operations are to be conducted. A subordinate commander at any level who in compliance with the order directs those under his control to launch cyber attacks against protected persons or places would be individually responsible for the attacks.

5.   *Lit.* (b)'s requirement to take measures to prevent war crimes or punish those who have committed them is based on Article 87 of Additional Protocol I. A commander or other superior who becomes aware that a cyber operation may have resulted in a war crime must accordingly take steps to ensure the matter is investigated as appropriate in the circumstances and reported to appropriate investigative and judicial authorities.[57]

6.   The concept of responsibility for acts that a commander or superior may not have ordered, but which he or she should have known of, was enunciated decades before adoption of the Protocol, in the case of General Yamashita. A US military commission following the Second World War held that Yamashita had failed to exercise 'effective control'

---

[56] This extension is based on the Rome Statute, Art. 28(b).

[57] *See, e.g.*, Rome Statute, Art. 28(a)(ii), (b)(iii).

over certain of his forces that had committed atrocities, and that the nature of the offences themselves provided prima facie evidence of his knowledge thereof.[58] In the decades since the decision, this finding has matured into the standard found in *lit.* (b).

7.   Article 28(a) of the Rome Statute sets forth a contemporary articulation of the principle. It provides that a

> military commander or person effectively acting as a military commander shall be criminally responsible for crimes within the jurisdiction of the Court committed by forces under his or her effective command and control, or effective authority and control as the case may be, as a result of his or her failure to exercise control properly over such forces, where:
>
> (i) That military commander or person either knew or, owing to the circumstances at the time, should have known that the forces were committing or about to commit such crimes; and
>
> (ii) That military commander or person failed to take all necessary and reasonable measures within his or her power to prevent or repress their commission or to submit the matter to the competent authorities for investigation and prosecution.

As this extract illustrates, the key to the notion is the exercise of, or the ability to exercise, effective control over those who have committed the actual offences.[59]

8.   The extension of criminal responsibility to commanders who knew or should have known that an operation constituting a war crime has been, is being, or will be conducted is especially important in the context of cyber warfare.[60] In order to avoid criminal responsibility for the acts of their subordinates, commanders and other superiors must take appropriate steps to become aware of the operations being conducted by

---

[58] Trial of General Tomoyuki Yamashita, 4 LAW REPORTS OF TRIALS OF WAR CRIMINALS 1, sec. 12 (1948). It must be noted that the decision has sometimes been criticized on the basis that Yamashita was held responsible for acts committed in very remote areas. However, the legal principle of command responsibility enunciated in the case is uncontested.

[59] The principle also appears in the statutes of the international criminal tribunals. ICTY Statute, Art. 7(3); ICTR Statute, Art. 6(3). *See also* e.g. *Blaškić* judgment, paras. 62, 91, 218, 417, 484, 632; *Prosecutor* v. *Halilović*, Case No. IT-01-48-T, Trial Chamber judgment, paras. 38–100, 747, 751–2 (16 November 2005); *Kordić and Čerkez*, Case No. IT-95-14/2-A, Appeals Chamber judgment, para. 827 (Int'l Crim. Trib. for the Former Yugoslavia 17 December 2004); *Kayishema* judgment, paras. 209–10, 216–18, 222–5, 228–9, 231. *See also* UK MANUAL, para. 16.36.5; CANADIAN MANUAL, para. 1621.

[60] Note that Art. 28 of the Rome Statute applies to all crimes within the jurisdiction of the International Criminal Court, not just war crimes.

their units, understand those operations and their consequences, and exercise control over them. Admittedly, the technical complexity of cyber operations complicates matters. Commanders or other superiors in the chain of command cannot be expected to have a deep knowledge of cyber operations; to some extent, they are entitled to rely on the knowledge and understanding of their subordinates. Nevertheless, the fact that cyber operations may be technically complicated does not alone relieve commanders or other superiors of the responsibility for exercising control over subordinates. Of course, wilful or negligent failure to acquire an understanding of such operations is never a justification for lack of knowledge. As a matter of law, commanders and other superiors are assumed to have the same degree of understanding as a 'reasonable' commander at a comparable level of command in a similar operational context. In all cases, the knowledge must be sufficient to allow them to fulfil their legal duty to act reasonably to identify, prevent, or stop the commission of cyber war crimes.

9. Note that the individuals addressed by this Rule need not be a 'commander' or be acting as such. For example, Article 28(b) of the International Criminal Court Statute extends responsibility to 'superiors' who have 'effective responsibility and control' over their subordinates, although it appears to have set a slightly higher standard by using the phraseology knew or 'consciously disregarded information which clearly indicated' the commission of a war crime.[61] There is no requirement for military status. The Rule would encompass, for instance, civilian superiors of civilian intelligence or security agencies that conduct cyber operations during an armed conflict.

---

[61] Rome Statute, Art. 28(b). *See also Prosecutor* v. *Delalić*, Case No. IT-96-21-A, Appeals Chamber judgment, paras. 239, 254 (20 February 2001); UK MANUAL, para. 16.36.6; CANADIAN MANUAL, para. 1621.

4

Conduct of hostilities

Rule 25 – Participation generally

The law of armed conflict does not bar any category of person from participating in cyber operations. However, the legal consequences of participation differ, based on the nature of the armed conflict and the category to which an individual belongs.

1.   The customary international law of armed conflict does not prohibit any individual from participating in an armed conflict, whether international or non-international. It should be noted that Article 43(2) of Additional Protocol I provides that 'members of the armed forces of a Party to a conflict (other than medical personnel and chaplains covered by Article 33 of Geneva Convention III) are combatants, that is to say they have the right to participate directly in hostilities'. This provision, applicable in international armed conflict, confirms that combatants enjoy immunity in respect of the acts undertaken as part of the hostilities. It does not prohibit others from engaging in those hostilities.

2.   Although the law of armed conflict contains no prohibition on participation, it does set forth consequences that result from such participation. Three are of particular importance: combatant immunity, prisoner of war status, and targetability. The issue of targetability is dealt with in Rules 30 to 59 on attacks. Entitlement to combatant immunity and prisoner of war status depend on whether the individual concerned is a combatant in an international armed conflict. These issues are discussed in the following two Rules.

3.   In accordance with Rule 35, a civilian who directly participates in hostilities loses certain protections attendant to civilian status for such time as he or she so participates.

Rule 26 – Members of the armed forces

In an international armed conflict, members of the armed forces of a party to the conflict who, in the course of cyber operations, fail to comply with the requirements of combatant status lose their entitlement to combatant immunity and prisoner of war status.

1.   The generally accepted understanding of combatancy derives from the Hague Regulations.[1] Geneva Convention III adopts the standard in Article 4A with regard to the entitlement to prisoner of war status.[2] Although Article 4A(1), (2), (3), and (6) is textually applicable only to such status, it is universally understood as reflecting the customary international law criteria for combatancy. The notion of combatancy is limited to international armed conflict; there is no non-international armed conflict equivalent of either prisoner of war status or combatant immunity.

2.   According to the majority of the International Group of Experts, customary international law provides that individuals who are nationals of the capturing party are not entitled to combatant status.[3] A minority of the Experts argued that there is no basis in international law for this position.

3.   Combatants are entitled to treatment as prisoners of war in accordance with Geneva Convention III upon capture.[4] They are also entitled to combatant immunity, that is, they may not be prosecuted for having engaged in belligerent acts that are lawful under the law of armed conflict.[5] For instance, a combatant who conducts cyber operations that violate domestic criminal law may not be prosecuted for such actions so long as they are carried out in compliance with the law of armed conflict. Combatant immunity is a customary international law principle recognized in Article 43(2) of Additional Protocol I.

4.   There are two categories of combatant.[6] The first consists of 'members of the armed forces of a Party to the conflict as well as

---

[1]   Hague Regulations, Art. 1.

[2]   US COMMANDER'S HANDBOOK, para. 5.4.1.1; AMW MANUAL, Rule 10(b)(i) and accompanying commentary. *But see* ICRC INTERPRETIVE GUIDANCE at 22.

[3]   *See, e.g., Prosecutor v. Koi* [1968] A.C. 829 (P.C. 1967). *See also* Yoram Dinstein, THE CONDUCT OF HOSTILITIES UNDER THE LAW OF INTERNATIONAL ARMED CONFLICT 46 (2nd ed. 2010).

[4]   Geneva Convention III, Art. 4A. Technically, they are entitled to this status as soon as they fall 'into the power of the enemy'. *Ibid.* Arts. 4A, 5.

[5]   US COMMANDER'S HANDBOOK, para. 5.4.1.1.

[6]   *See also* Rule 27 regarding *levées en masse*.

members of militias or volunteer corps forming part of such armed forces'.[7] This category primarily includes members of a State's armed forces.

5. The second category comprises 'members of other militias and members of other volunteer corps, including those of organized resistance movements, belonging to a Party to the conflict'.[8] Such organized armed groups are assimilated to the armed forces and as a group must, pursuant to Article 4A(2) of Geneva Convention III and customary international law, fulfil four conditions:

(a) be commanded by a person responsible for his subordinates;
(b) wear a distinctive emblem or attire that is recognizable at a distance;
(c) carry arms openly; and
(d) conduct operations in accordance with the law of armed conflict.

Irregular forces that meet these conditions and belong to a party to the conflict qualify as combatants, and are entitled to combatant immunity and prisoner of war status.[9]

6. In Geneva Convention III, the four conditions are set forth with regard only to organized armed groups assimilated to the armed forces. The majority of the International Group of Experts took the position that the four requirements are implicit in the Conventions for members of the armed forces and that, therefore, only members of the armed forces who meet the four requirements qualify for combatant status, and its attendant benefits. A minority of the Experts took the position that the requirements are limited to those groups assimilated to the armed forces. By this position, the sole qualification for combatant status for members of the armed forces is status as members.

7. Every State organ meets the requirement of belonging to a party to the conflict. The issue of belonging only arises with respect to organized armed groups that are assimilated to the armed forces, that is, those groups addressed in Article 4A(2) of Geneva Convention III. The concept of 'belonging to' was examined during the meetings that resulted

---

[7] Geneva Convention III, Art. 4A(1). *See also* Geneva Convention I, Art. 13(1); Geneva Convention II, Art. 13(1).
[8] Geneva Convention III, Art. 4A(2). *See also* Geneva Convention I, Art. 13(2); Geneva Convention II, Art. 13(2).
[9] US COMMANDER'S HANDBOOK, para. 5.4.1.1. *But see* ICRC INTERPRETIVE GUIDANCE at 22 (noting that 'strictly speaking' the criteria apply only to status as a combatant with regard to prisoner of war entitlements).

in the ICRC Interpretive Guidance.[10] The International Group of Experts agreed with the approach taken in the Guidance. By this approach, 'the concept of "belonging to" requires at least a de facto relationship between an organized group and a Party to the conflict'. Such a relationship need not be officially declared; it may be 'expressed through tacit agreement or conclusive behaviour that makes clear for which party the group is fighting'.[11] As an example, a State may turn to a group of private individuals to conduct cyber operations during an armed conflict because the group possesses capability or knowledge that State organs do not. The group belongs to a party to the conflict and, so long as it meets the other requirements of combatancy, its members will enjoy combatant status. Of course, during a non-international armed conflict, an organized non-State group is the party to the conflict.

8. If a person engaged in cyber operations during an armed conflict is a member of an organized armed group not belonging to a party to the conflict, it does not matter if the group and its members comply with the four criteria of combatancy. That person will not have combatant status and therefore not be entitled to combatant immunity or to be treated as a prisoner of war. Such a person would be an 'unprivileged belligerent', as discussed below.

9. The condition of being commanded by a person responsible for subordinates is best understood as an aspect of the requirement that the group in question be 'organized'. The criterion of organization was previously discussed in the context of non-international armed conflict (Rule 23). There, the unique nature of virtual organizations was highlighted. The same considerations apply in the present context. While not normally an issue in respect of regularly constituted State armed forces, or even well-established organized armed groups, a claim of combatant status could be significantly weakened if the persons asserting that status are part of a loosely organized group or association. This could result, for example, from organizing solely over the Internet. In a similar vein, members of such a group may have difficulty establishing that they are acting under a responsible commander. Even more problematic is the requirement that the group be subject to an internal disciplinary system capable of enforcing compliance with the law of armed conflict. Cumulatively, these requirements make it highly unlikely that a purely

[10] *See also* ICRC INTERPRETIVE GUIDANCE at 23–4 (citing ICRC GENEVA CONVENTION III COMMENTARY).
[11] ICRC INTERPRETIVE GUIDANCE at 23.

virtual organization would qualify as an organized armed group for the purposes of determining combatant status.

10. Combatant status requires that the individual wear a 'fixed distinctive sign'.[12] The requirement is generally met through the wearing of uniforms. There is no basis for deviating from this general requirement for those engaged in cyber operations. Some members of the International Group of Experts suggested that individuals engaged in cyber operations, regardless of circumstances such as distance from the area of operations or clear separation from the civilian population, must always comply with this requirement to enjoy combatant status. They emphasized that the customary international law of armed conflict in relation to combatant immunity and prisoner of war status offers no exceptions to this rule. Article 44(3) of Additional Protocol I does provide for an exception.[13] However, it does not reflect customary international law.[14]

11. Other Experts took the position that an exception to the requirement to wear a distinctive sign exists as a matter of customary international law. They argued that the requirement only applies in circumstances in which the failure to have a fixed distinctive sign might reasonably cause an attacker to be unable to distinguish between civilians and combatants, thus placing civilians at greater risk of mistaken attack. Consider a situation in which a Special Forces team is tasked to identify and attack a military cyber control facility located in a cluster of similar civilian facilities. A failure of the military personnel in the facility to wear uniforms would make it more difficult for the Special Forces team to distinguish the military from civilian facilities, thereby heightening the risk that the civilian facilities will mistakenly be made the object of attack.

12. Some of these Experts limited the exception in the previous paragraph to situations in which combatants engaged in cyber operations are located within a military objective for which there is a separate

---

[12] The ICRC CUSTOMARY IHL STUDY, Rule 106, provides that 'Combatants must distinguish themselves from the civilian population while they are engaged in an attack or in a military operation preparatory to an attack. If they fail to do so, they do not have the right to prisoner-of-war status.'

[13] Some States Party to the Protocol limit its application to occupied territory and the situation referred in Art. 1(4) of the same treaty. See, e.g., UK Additional Protocol Ratification Statement, para. (g). See also UK MANUAL, paras. 4.5–4.5.3.

[14] Michael J. Matheson, Remarks in Session One: The United States Position on the Relation of Customary International Law to the Protocols Additional to the 1949 Geneva Conventions, 2 AMERICAN UNIVERSITY JOURNAL OF INTERNATIONAL LAW AND POLICY 419, 425 (1987).

requirement of marking, i.e., a warship or military aircraft. For instance, since military aircraft are required to bear an external mark signifying nationality and military status, they argued that there is no specific requirement for military personnel on board to wear a distinctive sign indicating their status.[15]

13.   The issue of whether computers and software constitute weapons is discussed in Rule 41 and its accompanying Commentary. However, even if they qualify as weapons, the requirement to carry arms openly has little application in the cyber context.

14.   The obligation to comply with the law of armed conflict attaches to the group as a whole. Individual members of a group that adopts the tactic of conducting cyber attacks against civilian cyber infrastructure do not qualify for combatant status even if they individually comply with the law. By contrast, although a group may generally comply with the law, various individual members of the group may commit war crimes. Those individual members who commit the war crimes retain their combatant status, but may be tried for them.

15.   A party to a conflict may incorporate a paramilitary or armed law enforcement agency into its armed forces.[16] The majority of the International Group of Experts took the position that this provision of the law does not extend to intelligence or other government agencies not entrusted with law enforcement functions. However, a minority of the Experts argued that the issue fell within the classic domain of State sovereignty and that therefore a State is free to incorporate any entity it wishes into the armed forces.

16.   Although Article 43(3) of Additional Protocol I provides that the other parties to a conflict shall be notified of such incorporation, failure to so notify the enemy does not imply that the individuals concerned remain civilians.[17] Once such groups have been properly incorporated into the armed forces, their members may conduct cyber operations to the same extent as members of the regular armed forces. The fact that they also continue to perform a law enforcement function has no bearing on this status. Absent incorporation, the cyber activities of such groups are governed by the rules pertaining to participation in hostilities (Rules 25 and 35).

---

[15] They will generally do so, however, in order to exhibit their status as members of the armed forces in the event that they become separated from the aircraft. AMW Manual, commentary accompanying Rule 117.

[16] Additional Protocol I, Art. 43(3).

[17] AMW Manual commentary accompanying Rule 10.

17.   Members of the armed forces or groups assimilated to the armed forces who do not qualify for combatant status (and civilians taking a direct part in hostilities, Rule 35) are unprivileged belligerents. All members of the International Group of Experts agreed that unprivileged belligerents, as defined in this rule, enjoy no combatant immunity and are not entitled to prisoner of war status.[18] Such persons are subject to prosecution under the domestic laws of the capturing State for conducting cyber operations that are unlawful under domestic law even if such acts are lawful under the law of armed conflict when committed by a combatant. The classic examples are conducting cyber attacks against military personnel or military objectives. An unprivileged belligerent, like any other individual, including a combatant, may be prosecuted for commission of a war crime.

18.   As noted above, a division of opinion exists with regard to the four conditions for combatant status that apply to groups assimilated to the armed forces. For those Experts who took the position that the conditions apply equally to the armed forces, a member of the armed forces captured while wearing no distinctive attire (or emblems) is not entitled to prisoner of war status. Those Experts taking the contrary position would conclude that the individual's membership in the armed forces suffices for entitlement to prisoner of war status, although, in certain specific circumstances, wearing civilian clothing might be perfidious (Rule 60) or subject the individual concerned to being treated as a spy (Rule 66).

19.   The International Group of Experts agreed that unprivileged belligerency as such is not a war crime.[19] However, they recognized the existence of a contrary position.

20.   In a non-international armed conflict, the notion of belligerent (combatant) immunity does not exist. Domestic law exclusively determines the question of any immunity from prosecution.[20] In this regard, it must be remembered that many cyber activities, like certain forms of hacking, have been criminalized as matters of domestic law. For instance,

---

[18] US COMMANDER'S HANDBOOK, paras. 5.4.1.2, 11.3. Some members of the International Group of Experts took the position that civilians entitled to prisoner of war status pursuant to Art. 4A(4) and (5) of Geneva Convention III enjoy no immunity if they participate in hostilities, but would not lose prisoner of war status.

[19] AMW MANUAL, commentary accompanying Rule 111(b).

[20] UK MANUAL, paras. 15.6.1, 15.6.2. The statement is not absolute. For instance, consider the case of a foreign diplomat who has taken a direct part in hostilities in a manner that violates the law of the State to which she is accredited.

if a member of either the armed forces or the opposition forces hacks into the adversary's computer systems, domestic law will determine the legality of such actions. Note that domestic law often permits members of the armed forces and law enforcement agencies to conduct activities such as the use of force that would otherwise be unlawful. Of course, any State or international tribunal with jurisdiction over the individual and the offence may prosecute someone, including a member of the State's security forces, who commits war crimes during a non-international armed conflict.

Rule 27 – *Levée en masse*

In an international armed conflict, inhabitants of unoccupied territory who engage in cyber operations as part of a *levée en masse* enjoy combatant immunity and prisoner of war status.

1.   This rule is based on Article 2 of the Hague Regulations and Article 4A(6) of Geneva Convention III. It reflects customary international law,[21] but does not apply to non-international armed conflict.

2.   A *levée en masse* consists of the inhabitants (i.e., not an individual or a small group) of non-occupied territory 'who on the approach of the enemy spontaneously take up arms to resist invading forces, without having time to form themselves into regular armed units'.[22] In light of the requirements for an invasion and for the territory to be unoccupied at the time the acts of resistance occur, the circumstances under which a *levée en masse* can exist are factually limited.[23] *Levées en masse* need not be organized, and although their members must carry arms openly and respect the laws and customs of war, they need not wear a distinctive emblem or other identifying attire.[24] The ICRC Commentary to Geneva Convention III states that the notion of a *levée en masse* is 'applicable to populations which act in response to an

---

[21] US COMMANDER's HANDBOOK, para. 5.4.1.1; UK MANUAL, paras. 4.8, 11.12; CANADIAN MANUAL, para. 306; GERMAN MANUAL, paras. 310, 501; ICRC CUSTOMARY IHL STUDY, commentary accompanying Rule 106.

[22] Geneva Convention III, Art. 4A(6). *See also* ICRC CUSTOMARY IHL STUDY, commentary accompanying Rule 5, which explains that members of a *levée en masse* are an exception to the definition of civilians in that although they are not members of the armed forces, they qualify as combatants.

[23] UK MANUAL, para. 4.8; GERMAN MANUAL, para. 310. *See also* ICRC INTERPRETIVE GUIDANCE at 25.

[24] ICRC GENEVA CONVENTION III COMMENTARY at 67.

order by their government given over the wireless'.[25] Extension to orders given by cyber means is appropriate.

3.   As applied in the cyber context, application of the concept is somewhat problematic. Consider a case in which members of the population spontaneously begin to mount cyber operations in response to an invasion of their country. If the operations involve a large segment of the population and if they target the invading force, those involved will arguably qualify as members of a *levée en masse*. However, the means and expertise necessary to engage effectively in cyber operations may be relatively limited in the population. It is unclear whether a *levée en masse* can be comprised solely of a significant portion of the cyber-capable members of the population.

4.   Moreover, a *levée en masse* was historically understood as involving a general uprising of the population to repel an invasion by an approaching force. Since it did not contemplate military operations deep into enemy territory, it is questionable whether individuals launching cyber operations against enemy military objectives other than the invading forces can be considered members of a *levée en masse*.

5.   The International Group of Experts was divided as to whether the privileges associated with the *levée en masse* concept apply to a civilian population countering a massive cyber attack, the effects of which are comparable to those of a physical invasion by enemy forces. According to a majority of the Experts, the concept of *levée en masse* is to be understood in a narrow sense, requiring the physical invasion of national territory.

Rule 28 – Mercenaries

Mercenaries involved in cyber operations do not enjoy combatant immunity or prisoner of war status.

1.   Article 47(1) of Additional Protocol I reflects a customary international law rule that mercenaries, including those engaged in cyber operations, are unprivileged belligerents.[26] As the notions of combatant status and belligerent immunity do not apply in non-international armed conflict, this Rule has no relevance to non-international armed conflict.

---

[25] ICRC GENEVA CONVENTION III COMMENTARY at 67.
[26] UK MANUAL, paras. 4.10–4.10.4 (as amended); CANADIAN MANUAL, para. 319; GERMAN MANUAL, para. 303; ICRC CUSTOMARY IHL STUDY, Rule 108.

2.   The most widely accepted definition of mercenary is found in Article 47(2) of Additional Protocol I. It sets forth six conditions that must be cumulatively fulfilled: special recruitment; direct participation in hostilities; desire for private gain as primary motivation; neither a national of a party to the conflict nor a resident of territory controlled by a party; not a member of the armed forces of a party to the conflict; and not sent by another State on official duty as a member of its armed forces. For example, consider a private company located in State A that is engaged by State B to conduct cyber operations on its behalf in its armed conflict with State C. So long as the six criteria are fully met, its employees who conduct the cyber operations are mercenaries, and thus unprivileged belligerents. The same would be true with regard to a 'hacker for hire' who meets the criteria, even if operating alone and far from the battlefield.

3.   It is clear that no person qualifying as a mercenary enjoys combatant status. This is especially important in light of the criminalization of mercenarism by many States.

Rule 29 – Civilians

Civilians are not prohibited from directly participating in cyber operations amounting to hostilities, but forfeit their protection from attacks for such time as they so participate.

1.   As noted in Rule 25, no rule of treaty or customary international law prohibits civilians from directly participating in hostilities during either international or non-international armed conflict. However, they lose their protection from attack (Rule 32) when doing so (Rule 35).[27]

2.   In accordance with customary international law, Article 50(1) of Additional Protocol I defines civilians in negative terms as being all persons who are neither members of the armed forces nor of a *levée en masse*. This approach is implicit in Geneva Conventions III and IV. As a general matter, then, during an international armed conflict, civilians are persons who are not members of the armed forces or of groups assimilated to the armed forces (e.g., organized resistance groups belonging to a party to the conflict) and who are not participants in a *levée en masse* (Rules 26 and 27).

---

[27] US COMMANDER'S HANDBOOK, para. 8.2.4; UK MANUAL, para. 5.3.2. (as amended); CANADIAN MANUAL, para. 318; NIAC MANUAL, paras. 1.1.2, 1.1.3, 2.1.1.2; AMW MANUAL, chapeau to sec. F.

3. The majority of the International Group of Experts agreed that civilians retain civilian status even if they directly participate in cyber hostilities. For instance, consider an international armed conflict in which civilian patriotic hackers independently undertake offensive cyber operations against the enemy's forces. Such individuals may be lawfully targeted, and, unless they qualify as participants in a *levée en masse*, lack combatant immunity for their actions. A minority of the Group took the position that these individuals qualify as neither combatants nor civilians, and therefore do not benefit from the protections of Geneva Conventions III or IV, respectively.

4. The fact that there is no combatant status in respect of non-international armed conflict sometimes results in differing terminology. Neither Common Article 3 to the Geneva Conventions nor Additional Protocol II defines the term 'civilian'. For the purposes of this Manual, civilians in a non-international armed conflict are those individuals who are not members of the State's armed forces, dissident armed forces, or other organized armed groups.

5. Although the law of armed conflict does not prohibit participation in a non-international armed conflict, all participants remain subject to its specific prohibitions, such as that on attacking individuals taking no active part in hostilities (Rule 32). Moreover, civilians are subject to prosecution under the domestic law of the State that captures them, which may include a prohibition on participation.

SECTION 2:   ATTACKS GENERALLY

1. The law of armed conflict applies to the targeting of any person or object during armed conflict irrespective of the means or methods of warfare employed. Consequently, basic principles such as distinction and the prohibition of unnecessary suffering will apply to cyber operations just as they do to other means and methods of warfare. The applicability of particular treaty rules is determined by such matters as whether a State is a Party to the treaty in question, its status as a party to the conflict, and the type of armed conflict (international or non-international).

2. The principles and Rules set forth in the sections regarding attacks (Rules 30 to 58) apply equally to situations in which cyber means are used to take control of enemy weapons and weapon systems, as in the case of taking control of an unmanned combat aerial system (UCAS) and using it to conduct attacks.

3.   Article 49(3) of Additional Protocol I limits the Protocol's provisions on the conduct of hostilities 'to any land, air or sea warfare which may affect the civilian population, individual civilians or civilian objects on land. They further apply to all attacks from the sea or from the air against objectives on land but do not otherwise affect the rules of international law applicable in armed conflict at sea or in the air.' The International Group of Experts agreed that despite this apparent limitation, State practice was such that the principles expressed in the section, to the extent they reflect customary international law, apply equally to attacks to or from the land, at sea, or in the air.[28] The only exception to this conclusion applies with regard to precautions in attack (see Section 7 of this chapter).

Rule 30 – Definition of cyber attack

A cyber attack is a cyber operation, whether offensive or defensive, that is reasonably expected to cause injury or death to persons or damage or destruction to objects.

1.   For the purposes of the Manual, this definition applies equally in international and non-international armed conflict.[29]

2.   The notion of 'attack' is a concept that serves as the basis for a number of specific limitations and prohibitions in the law of armed conflict. For instance, civilians and civilian objects may not be 'attacked' (Rule 32). This Rule sets forth a definition that draws on that found in Article 49(1) of Additional Protocol I: 'attacks means acts of violence against the adversary, whether in offence or defence'. By this widely accepted definition, it is the use of violence against a target that distinguishes attacks from other military operations. Non-violent operations, such as psychological cyber operations or cyber espionage, do not qualify as attacks.[30]

3.   'Acts of violence' should not be understood as limited to activities that release kinetic force. This is well settled in the law of armed conflict. In this regard, note that chemical, biological, or radiological attacks do not usually have a kinetic effect on their designated target, but it is universally agreed that they constitute attacks as a matter of law.[31] The

---

[28] Experts involved in the AMW Manual process arrived at the same conclusion. AMW MANUAL, commentary accompanying Rule 30.
[29] NIAC MANUAL, para. 1.1.6; ICRC ADDITIONAL PROTOCOLS COMMENTARY, para. 4783 and n. 19.
[30] GERMAN MANUAL, para. 474.
[31] *Tadić*, Decision on the Defence Motion for Interlocutory Appeal, paras. 120, 124 (regarding chemical weapons).

crux of the notion lies in the effects that are caused. To be characterized as an act of violence, an action must result in the consequences set forth in this Rule, which are explained below. Restated, the consequences of an operation, not its nature, are what generally determine the scope of the term 'attack'; 'violence' must be considered in the sense of violent consequences and is not limited to violent acts. For instance, a cyber operation that alters the running of a SCADA system controlling an electrical grid and results in a fire qualifies. Since the consequences are destructive, the operation is an attack.

4.   All members of the International Group of Experts agreed that the type of consequential harm set forth in this Rule qualifies an action as an attack, although, as discussed below, there are nuances to its application. The text of numerous Articles of Additional Protocol I, and the ICRC commentary thereto, supports this conclusion. For instance, Article 51(1) sets forth the general principle that the 'civilian population and individual civilians shall enjoy general protection against *dangers* arising from military operations'. Other Articles provide further support. The rules of proportionality speak of '*loss* of civilian life, *injury* to civilians, *damage* to civilian objects, or a combination thereof'.[32] Those relating to protection of the environment refer to 'widespread, long-term, and severe *damage*',[33] and the protection of dams, dykes, and nuclear electrical generating stations is framed in terms of 'severe *losses* among the civilian population'.[34] The Experts agreed that *de minimis* damage or destruction does not meet the threshold of harm required by this Rule.

5.   The word 'cause' in this Rule is not limited to effects on the targeted cyber system. Rather, it encompasses any reasonably foreseeable consequential damage, destruction, injury, or death. Cyber attacks seldom involve the release of direct physical force against the targeted cyber system; yet, they can result in great harm to individuals or objects. For example, the release of dam waters by manipulating a SCADA system could cause massive downstream destruction without damaging the system. Were this operation to be conducted using kinetic means, like bombing the dam, there is no question that it would be regarded as an attack. No rationale exists for arriving at a different conclusion in the cyber context.

6.   Although the Rule is limited to operations against individuals or physical objects, the limitation should not be understood as excluding

---

[32] Additional Protocol I, Arts. 51(5)(b), 57(2)(a)(iii), 57(2)(b).
[33] Additional Protocol I, Arts. 35(3), 55(1).   [34] Additional Protocol I, Art. 56(1).

cyber operations against data (which are non-physical entities) from the ambit of the term attack. Whenever an attack on data results in the injury or death of individuals or damage or destruction of physical objects, those individuals or objects constitute the 'object of attack' and the operation therefore qualifies as an attack. Further, as discussed below, an operation against data upon which the functionality of physical objects relies can sometimes constitute an attack.

7.   The phrase 'against the adversary' in Article 49(1) could cause confusion by suggesting that destructive operations must be directed at the enemy to qualify as attacks. The International Group of Experts agreed that such an interpretation would make little sense in light of, for instance, the prohibitions on attacking civilians and civilian objects.[35] The Experts agreed that it is not the status of an action's target that qualifies an act as an attack, but rather its consequences. Therefore, acts of violence, or those having violent effects, directed against civilians or civilian objects, or other protected persons or objects, are attacks.

8.   While the notion of attack extends to injuries and death caused to individuals, it is, in light of the law of armed conflict's underlying humanitarian purposes, reasonable to extend the definition to serious illness and severe mental suffering that are tantamount to injury. In particular, note that Article 51(2) of Additional Protocol I prohibits 'acts or threats of violence the primary purpose of which is to spread terror among the civilian population'. Since terror is a psychological condition resulting in mental suffering, inclusion of such suffering in this Rule is supportable through analogy.

9.   With regard to digital cultural property, see the Commentary accompanying Rule 82.

10.   Within the International Group of Experts, there was extensive discussion about whether interference by cyber means with the functionality of an object constitutes damage or destruction for the purposes of this Rule. Although some Experts were of the opinion that it does not, the majority of them were of the view that interference with functionality qualifies as damage if restoration of functionality requires replacement of physical components. Consider a cyber operation that is directed against the computer-based control system of an electrical distribution grid. The operation causes the grid to cease operating. In order to restore distribution, either the control system or vital components thereof must

---

[35] *See also* AMW MANUAL, commentary to Rule 1(e).

be replaced. The cyber operation is an attack. Those experts taking this position were split over the issue of whether the 'damage' requirement is met in situations where functionality can be restored by reinstalling the operating system.

11. A few Experts went so far as to suggest that interference with functionality that necessitates data restoration, while not requiring physical replacement of components or reinstallation of the operating system, qualifies as an attack. For these Experts, it is immaterial how an object is disabled; the object's loss of usability constitutes the requisite damage.

12. The International Group of Experts discussed the characterization of a cyber operation that does not cause the type of damage set forth above, but which results in large-scale adverse consequences, such as blocking email communications throughout the country (as distinct from damaging the system on which transmission relies). The majority of the Experts took the position that, although there might be logic in characterizing such activities as an attack, the law of armed conflict does not presently extend this far. A minority took the position that should an armed conflict involving such cyber operations break out, the international community would generally regard them as attack. All Experts agreed, however, that relevant provisions of the law of armed conflict that address situations other than attack, such as the prohibition on collective punishment (Rule 85), apply to these operations.

13. It should be noted that a cyber operation might not result in the requisite harm to the object of the operation, but cause foreseeable collateral damage at the level set forth in this Rule. Such an operation amounts to an attack to which the relevant law of armed conflict applies, particularly that regarding proportionality (Rule 51).

14. A cyber operation need not actually result in the intended destructive effect to qualify as an attack.[36] During the negotiation of Additional Protocol I the issue of whether laying land mines constituted an attack arose. The 'general feeling' of the negotiators was that 'there is an attack whenever a person is directly endangered by a mine laid'.[37] By analogy, the introduction of malware or production-level defects that are either time-delayed or activate on the occurrence of a particular event is an attack when the intended consequences meet the requisite threshold of harm. This is so irrespective of whether they are activated. Some members took the position that although there is no requirement that

---

[36] *See also* AMW MANUAL, commentary to Rule 1(e).
[37] ICRC ADDITIONAL PROTOCOLS COMMENTARY, para. 1881.

the cyber operation be successful, an attack only transpires once the malware is activated or the specified act occurs.

15.   An attack that is successfully intercepted and does not result in actual harm is still an attack under the law of armed conflict. Thus, a cyber operation that has been defeated by passive cyber defences such as firewalls, anti-virus software, and intrusion detection or prevention systems nevertheless still qualifies as an attack if, absent such defences, it would have been likely to cause the requisite consequences.

16.   Cyber operations may be an integral part of a wider operation that constitutes an attack. As an example, a cyber operation may be used to disable defences at a target that is subsequently kinetically attacked. In such a case, the cyber operation is one component of an operation that qualifies as an attack, much as laser designation makes possible attacks using laser-guided bombs. The law of armed conflict on attacks applies fully to such cyber operations.

17.   If an attack is conducted against civilians or civilian objects in the mistaken but reasonable belief that they constitute lawful targets, an attack has nonetheless occurred. However, if the attacker has fully complied with the requirement to verify the target (Rule 53), the attack will be lawful.

18.   It may be the case that the target of a cyber attack does not realize it has been attacked. For instance, a cyber attack directed against civilian infrastructure may be designed to appear as if the ensuing damage resulted from simple mechanical malfunction. The fact that a cyber attack is not recognized as such has no bearing on whether it qualifies as an attack and is subject to the law of armed conflict thereon.

19.   Care is required when identifying the originator of an attack. To illustrate, an individual may receive an email with an attachment containing malware. Execution of the malware, which occurs automatically upon opening, will cause the requisite level of harm. If that individual unwittingly forwards the email and it does cause such harm, he or she will not have conducted an attack; the email's originator will have done so. By contrast, if the intermediary forwards the email knowing it contains the malware, both individuals will have conducted an attack.

Rule 31 – Distinction

The principle of distinction applies to cyber attacks.

1.   The 1868 St Petersburg Declaration provides that 'the only legitimate object which States should endeavour to accomplish during war is

to weaken the military forces of the enemy'. This general principle is the foundation upon which the principle of distinction is based. The principle of distinction is one of two 'cardinal' principles of the law of armed conflict recognized by the International Court of Justice in its Advisory Opinion on the *Legality of the Threat or Use of Nuclear Weapons*.[38] The other is the prohibition of unnecessary suffering (Rule 42). According to the Court, these principles of customary international law are 'intransgressible'.[39]

2. Article 48 of Additional Protocol I codifies the customary international law principle: 'In order to ensure respect for and protection of the civilian population and civilian objects, the Parties to the conflict shall at all times distinguish between the civilian population and combatants and between civilian objects and military objectives and accordingly shall direct their operations only against military objectives.' The principle applies in both international and non-international armed conflict. It is included in virtually all military law of armed conflict manuals, is cited in unofficial compilations of the customary international law of armed conflict, and appears in the statutes of international tribunals.[40]

3. In non-international armed conflict, the principle of distinction obliges the parties to distinguish between civilians, on the one hand, and members of State armed forces and organized armed groups, including members of the regular or dissident armed forces, on the other.[41] The International Group of Experts agreed that this obligation also requires the parties to distinguish between military objectives and civilian objects despite the fact that Article 13 of Additional Protocol II was originally not meant to extend to civilian objects.[42]

---

[38] *Nuclear Weapons* Advisory Opinion, para. 78. According to the Court, 'States must never make civilians the object of attack and must consequently never use weapons that are incapable of distinguishing between civilian and military targets.'

[39] *Nuclear Weapons* Advisory Opinion, para. 79.

[40] *See, e.g.,* US COMMANDER'S HANDBOOK, para. 5.3.2; UK MANUAL, para. 2.5–2.5.3 (as amended); CANADIAN MANUAL, para. 423; AMW MANUAL, Rule 10; NIAC MANUAL, para. 1.2.2; ICRC CUSTOMARY IHL STUDY, Rules 1, 7; SAN REMO MANUAL, Rule 39; Rome Statute, Arts. 8(2)(b)(i) and (ii), 8(2)(e)(i) and (ii).

[41] NIAC MANUAL, para. 1.2.2. In *Tadić*, the International Criminal Tribunal for the Former Yugoslavia recognized distinction as applicable in non-international armed conflict. *Tadić*, Decision on the Defence Motion for Interlocutory Appeal, paras. 122, 127.

[42] ICRC ADDITIONAL PROTOCOLS COMMENTARY, para. 4759 (noting that Art. 13 of Protocol II provides no general protection for civilian objects). *But see* NIAC MANUAL, para. 1.2.2; ICRC CUSTOMARY IHL STUDY, Rule 10 (identifying general protection for civilian objects in non-international armed conflict).

4.   Articles 51 and 52 of Additional Protocol I reflect the principle of distinction by setting forth protections for the civilian population and civilian objects respectively (Rules 32 to 40). It also undergirds various Articles that extend special protection to particular protected persons and objects,[43] and is the basis from which the principle of proportionality and the requirement to take precautions in attack arise (Rules 51 to 58).

5.   Certain operations directed against the civilian population are lawful.[44] For instance, psychological operations such as dropping leaflets or making propaganda broadcasts are not prohibited even if civilians are the intended audience.[45] In the context of cyber warfare, transmitting email messages to the enemy population urging capitulation would likewise comport with the law of armed conflict.[46] Only when a cyber operation against civilians or civilian objects (or other protected persons and objects) rises to the level of an attack is it prohibited by the principle of distinction and those rules of the law of armed conflict that derive from the principle. Whether a particular cyber operation qualifies as an 'attack' is the subject of Rule 30.

6.   Since the principle of distinction is intransgressible, any rationale or justification for an attack not permitted by the law of armed conflict is irrelevant in determining whether the principle has been violated.[47] As an example, an attack against a civilian object would be unlawful even if it shortened the course of the conflict and thereby saved civilian lives. Similarly, cyber attacks against a civilian leader's private property designed to pressure him into capitulation would be unlawful if the property qualified as a civilian object irrespective of whether the conflict would likely be shortened.

7.   The principle of distinction, as used in this Rule, must not be confused with the obligation of combatants to distinguish themselves from the civilian population (Rule 26).

---

[43]   Additional Protocol I, Arts. 53–6.

[44]   ICRC ADDITIONAL PROTOCOLS COMMENTARY, para. 1875.

[45]   AMW MANUAL, commentary accompanying Rule 13(b). Of course, this is only so long as the actions do not violate the prohibition on terrorizing the civilian population set forth in Rule 36.

[46]   During the 2003 invasion of Iraq, 'Thousands of Iraqi military officers received e-mails on the Iraqi Defense Ministry e-mail system just before the war started.' They were told to place tanks and armoured vehicles in formation and abandon them, walk away, and go home. Richard A. Clarke and Robert K. Knake, CYBERWARFARE: THE NEXT THREAT TO NATIONAL SECURITY AND WHAT TO DO ABOUT IT 9–10 (2010).

[47]   Of course, if a civilian is attacking a member of the armed forces for reasons unrelated to the conflict, the member of the armed forces may defend him or herself. This principle applies in the cyber context.

SECTION 3:   ATTACKS AGAINST PERSONS

Rule 32 – Prohibition on attacking civilians

The civilian population as such, as well as individual civilians, shall not be the object of cyber attack.

1.   This rule is based on the principle of distinction, set forth in Rule 31. It has been codified in Article 51(2) of Additional Protocol I and Article 13(2) of Additional Protocol II and is undoubtedly reflective of customary international law in both international and non-international armed conflict.[48]

2.   As to the definition of 'civilian', see the Commentary to Rule 29. The 'civilian population' comprises all persons who are civilians. The presence within the civilian population of individuals who do not come within the definition of civilians does not deprive the population of its civilian character.[49]

3.   For a cyber operation to be prohibited by this Rule, it must qualify as an attack. The term attack is defined in Rule 30.

4.   Under this Rule, the 'object' of a cyber attack is the person against whom the cyber operation is directed. Although protected from being made the object of attack, civilians lose their protection for such time as they directly participate in hostilities (Rule 35).

5.   To qualify as the object of an attack, the harm to the relevant person (or object) must meet the level set forth in Rule 30. For instance, consider the case of a cyber operation intended to harm a particular individual by manipulating her medical information stored in a hospital's database. She would be the object of attack, but the database would not be if the damage thereto does not rise to the level required for an attack. By contrast, consider the case of a cyber attack against the SCADA system of a chemical plant that is designed to cause an explosion. The explosion is planned to result in the release of toxic substances that will kill the surrounding population. The chemical plant and the population are both objects of attack because the requisite level of harm is reached as to each of them.

---

[48]   US COMMANDER'S HANDBOOK, para. 8.3; UK MANUAL, paras. 2.5.2 (as amended), 5.3; CANADIAN MANUAL, paras. 312, 423; GERMAN MANUAL, paras. 404, 502; AMW MANUAL, Rule 11 and accompanying commentary; NIAC MANUAL, para. 2.1.1.1; ICRC CUSTOM-ARY IHL STUDY, Rule 1. *See also* Rome Statute, Arts. 8(2)(b)(i) and (ii), 8(2)(e)(i) and (ii); *Martić* judgment, paras. 67–9; *Galić* Appeals Chamber judgment, paras. 190–2.

[49]   Additional Protocol I, Arts. 50(2), 50(3).

6. The fact that a cyber attack directed against a military objective (Rule 38) foreseeably causes incidental damage, destruction, injury, or death to civilians or civilian objects does not make those individuals and objects the 'objects of attack'.[50] Consider a cyber operation designed to down military aircraft by attacking a military air traffic control system. The aircraft are lawful objects of attack. However, civilians on the ground who are injured or killed when the aircraft crash would not qualify as objects of attack. Instead, any protection such persons enjoy would derive from the principle of proportionality and the requirement to take precautions in attack (Rules 51 to 58).

Rule 33 – Doubt as to status of persons

In case of doubt as to whether a person is a civilian, that person shall be considered to be a civilian.

1. The International Group of Experts concluded that Rule 33 is reflective of customary international law and is applicable in international and non-international armed conflicts.[51] The presumption of civilian status in cases of doubt is codified in Article 50(1) of Additional Protocol I. Some law of armed conflict manuals recognize this Rule.[52]

2. A number of Experts were unable to accept an interpretation of the Rule whereby the attacker alone bears the burden of disproving civilian status in cases of doubt. They noted that since a defender has an obligation to take passive precautions (Rule 59), such an outcome would be inappropriate. Subject to this interpretation, they accepted inclusion of Rule 33 in this Manual.

3. The precise threshold at which the doubt is sufficient to bring this Rule into operation is unsettled. On ratification of Additional Protocol I, a number of States Party made relevant statements concerning Article 50(1). The United Kingdom, for instance, observed that the Article applies only in cases of 'substantial doubt still remaining' after 'assessment of the information from all sources which is reasonably available to them at the relevant time'.[53] In contrast to substantial doubt, the concept

---

[50] US COMMANDER'S HANDBOOK, para. 8.3.1.
[51] *See, e.g.*, AMW MANUAL, commentary accompanying Rule 12(a); ICRC CUSTOMARY IHL STUDY commentary accompanying Rule 6.
[52] UK MANUAL, para. 5.3.1; CANADIAN MANUAL, para. 429.
[53] UK Additional Protocol Ratification Statement, para. (h); UK MANUAL, para. 5.3.4 (as amended).

of 'reasonable doubt' has been used for the purposes of determining liability under international criminal law.[54] Whatever the precise threshold of doubt necessary to bring the Rule into play, it is clear that the mere existence of some doubt is insufficient to establish a breach.

4. The issue of doubt is especially important in the cyber context. In many countries, the use of computers and computer networks by civilians is pervasive, and the networks that civilians and the armed forces use may be conjoined. In such cases, computer use, or the use of a particular network, may not *per se* indicate military status. This predicament is compounded by the fact that the individuals are usually not physically visible while engaged in cyber activities.

5. The presumption as to civilian status is distinct from the issue of uncertainty as to direct participation in hostilities. In other words, the presumption set forth in this Rule applies when there is doubt as to whether the individual is a combatant or civilian. In the case of direct participation, the individual is by definition a civilian; thus, the matters about which doubt can exist relate to that individual's activities, not his or her status. On the presumption in the context of direct participation, see the Commentary accompanying Rule 35.

6. Although there is no directly equivalent rule in the law relating to non-international armed conflicts because the notion of combatancy does not exist in those conflicts (Rule 26), the customary principle of distinction applies. Consequently, during non-international armed conflicts, a presumption that an individual is a civilian protected against attack attaches whenever sufficient doubt on the matter exists.

Rule 34 – Persons as lawful objects of attack

The following persons may be made the object of cyber attacks:

(a) members of the armed forces;
(b) members of organized armed groups;
(c) civilians taking a direct part in hostilities; and
(d) in an international armed conflict, participants in a *levée en masse*.

1. This Rule applies in both international and non-international armed conflict, except as noted in *lit.* (d).[55] Its precise formulation is derived by negative implication from other Rules set forth in this

---

[54] *Galić* Trial Chamber judgment, para. 55.   [55] NIAC MANUAL, para. 2.1.1.

Manual. Rule 32 prohibits attacks against civilians, thereby suggesting that, subject to other restrictions in the law of armed conflict, those who are not civilians may be attacked. Rule 35 provides that despite being civilians, individuals who directly participate in hostilities lose their protection from attack. With regard to a *levée en masse*, the conclusion that its participants may be attacked is drawn by inference from the fact that they enjoy combatant status (Rule 27).

2.   Status or conduct may render an individual liable to attack. The targetability of the first two categories of persons is based on their status, whereas the targetability of the latter two depends on the conduct in which they engage.

3.   The term 'members of the armed forces' is defined and discussed in the Commentary accompanying Rule 26. In general, it refers to members of the regular armed forces and groups, such as certain volunteer groups or resistance movements, that are assimilated to the regular armed forces. However, members of the armed forces who are medical or religious personnel, or who are *hors de combat*, are not subject to attack.[56] Individuals are *hors de combat* if they have been wounded or are sick and they are neither engaging in hostile acts nor attempting to escape, have been captured, or have surrendered. A member of the armed forces who, despite being sick or wounded, continues to engage in cyber operations directed against the enemy, or that enhance or preserve his or her own side's military capabilities, is not *hors de combat*.[57]

4.   The International Group of Experts was divided over qualification as a member of an organized armed group (Commentary to Rule 23). Some of the Experts took the position that mere membership in such a group suffices. In other words, once it is reliably established that an individual belongs to an organized armed group, that individual may be attacked on the same basis as a member of the armed forces. Other Experts adopted the position set forth in the ICRC Interpretive Guidance, which limits membership in organized armed groups to those individuals with a 'continuous combat function'.[58]

---

[56] Geneva Convention I, Arts. 24, 25; Additional Protocol I, Art. 41; US COMMANDER'S HANDBOOK, paras. 8.2.3, 8.2.4.1, 8.2.4.2; UK MANUAL, para. 5.6; CANADIAN MANUAL, para. 309; GERMAN MANUAL, para. 601; AMW MANUAL, Rule 15(b); NIAC MANUAL, paras. 2.3.2, 3.2; ICRC CUSTOMARY IHL STUDY, Rule 87.

[57] *See, e.g.*, ICRC ADDITIONAL PROTOCOLS COMMENTARY, paras. 1621–2 (characterizing an attempt to communicate with one's own side as a 'hostile act').

[58] ICRC INTERPRETIVE GUIDANCE at 27. The notion involves an individual undertaking a 'continuous function for the group involving his or her direct participation in hostilities'. *Ibid.* at 33.

For these Experts, individuals who do not have such a function are to be treated as civilians who may only be attacked for such time as they directly participate in hostilities. The controversy over continuous combat function is relevant in both international and non-international armed conflict. All members of the International Group of Experts agreed that, with regard to a group that consists of both military and political or social wings, only the military wing qualifies as an organized armed group.

5. The International Group of Experts was also divided over whether an organized armed group involved in an international armed conflict must 'belong to a party to the conflict' to be subject to this Rule. For instance, a particular group may be involved in cyber attacks for reasons other than providing support to one of the parties, such as religious or ethnic animosity towards their opponent or a desire to take advantage of the instability generated by the armed conflict to accumulate power. The notion of 'belonging to a party' was examined in the Commentary to Rule 26. Some Experts adopted the approach taken in the ICRC Interpretive Guidance by which members of a group that does not belong to a party to the conflict are to be treated as civilians for the purposes of that conflict.[59] Accordingly, they can only be targeted for such time as they directly participate in hostilities. Other Experts took the position that for the purposes of this Rule, no such requirement exists; all members of the group may be targeted based on their status as such.

6. With regard to civilians directly participating in hostilities, see Rule 35 and the accompanying Commentary.

7. An interesting question in this regard is the qualification of private contractors. The International Group of Experts agreed that individual contractors are civilians who may only be targeted based on their direct participation in the hostilities (Rule 35). The more difficult case involves a company that has been contracted by a party to the conflict to perform specific military operations such as cyber attacks against the enemy. The majority of Experts took the position that the company qualifies as an organized armed group belonging to a party.[60] By contrast, the

---

[59] The Guidance does note that the group may be a party to a separate non-international armed conflict with its opponent if the violence reaches the required threshold. ICRC INTERPRETIVE GUIDANCE at 23–4.

[60] *See* ICRC INTERPRETIVE GUIDANCE at 38–9 (noting that contractors effectively incorporated into the armed forces of a party to the conflict by being given a continuous combat function would become members of an organized armed group and would no longer, for the purposes of the distinction principle, qualify as civilians). On qualification as an organized armed group, see Commentary accompanying Rule 23.

minority was of the view the contractual relationship would not be seen as a sufficient basis for regarding the company as belonging to a party (Rule 35). However, even according to the minority view, those members of the company directly participating in the hostilities may be attacked.

8.   Civilian government employees, such as members of intelligence agencies, sometimes conduct cyber operations during an armed conflict. In the event a particular group of such individuals qualifies as an organized armed group, its members are subject to attack in accordance with this Rule. Other civilian government employees are civilians who are targetable only for such time as they directly participate in hostilities (Rule 35).

9.   Persons who are taking part in a *levée en masse* are targetable throughout the period of their participation therein. For targeting purposes, they are not treated as civilians directly participating in hostilities, that is, the 'for such time' criterion does not apply (Rule 35). The criteria for qualification as a *levée en masse* are discussed in the Commentary accompanying Rule 27.

Rule 35 – Civilian direct participants in hostilities

Civilians enjoy protection against attack unless and for such time as they directly participate in hostilities.

1.   This Rule is drawn from Article 51(3) of Additional Protocol I and Article 13(3) of Additional Protocol II. It is customary international law in both international and non-international armed conflict.[61]

2.   Rule 35 does not apply to members of the armed forces, organized armed groups, or participants in a *levée en masse*. For the purposes of this Rule, such individuals are not civilians.[62] The Rule's application is limited to individuals who engage in hostilities without affiliation to any such group and to members of ad hoc groups that do not qualify as an 'organized armed group' (for instance, because they lack the requisite degree of organization). On the requirements for qualification

[61] US COMMANDER'S HANDBOOK, paras. 8.2.2, 8.3; UK MANUAL, paras. 5.3.2 (as amended), 15.8; CANADIAN MANUAL, paras. 318, 1720; GERMAN MANUAL, para. 517; AMW MANUAL, chapeau to sec. F; NIAC MANUAL, paras. 1.1.3, 2.1.1.2; ICRC CUSTOMARY IHL STUDY, Rule 6.

[62] The ICRC Interpretive Guidance limits its analysis of civilian status to situations involving the conduct of hostilities. ICRC INTERPRETIVE GUIDANCE at 11. That analysis, like that set forth in this Commentary, is without prejudice to the question of civilian status for other purposes, such as detention.

as an organized armed group, especially with regard to 'continuous combat function', see the Commentary accompanying Rule 34.

3. An act of direct participation in hostilities by civilians renders them liable to be attacked, by cyber or other lawful means. Additionally, harm to direct participants is not considered when assessing the proportionality of an attack (Rule 51) or determining the precautions that must be taken to avoid harming civilians during military operations (Rules 52 to 58).

4. The International Group of Experts generally agreed with the three cumulative criteria for qualification of an act as direct participation that are set forth in the ICRC Interpretive Guidance. First, the act (or a closely related series of acts) must have the intended or actual effect of negatively affecting the adversary's military operations or capabilities, or inflicting death, physical harm, or material destruction on persons or objects protected against direct attack (threshold of harm).[63] There is no requirement for physical damage to objects or harm to individuals. In other words, actions that do not qualify as a cyber attack will satisfy this criterion so long as they negatively affect the enemy militarily. An example of an operation satisfying the criterion is a cyber operation that disrupts the enemy's command and control network. Some members of the International Group of Experts took the position that acts that enhance one's own military capacity are included, as they necessarily weaken an adversary's relative position. An example is maintaining passive cyber defences of military cyber assets. Second, a direct causal link between the act in question and the harm intended or inflicted must exist (causal link).[64] In the previous example, the disruption to the enemy's command and control is directly caused by the cyber attack; the criterion is met. Finally, the acts must be directly related to the hostilities (belligerent nexus).[65] In the example, the fact that the system

---

[63] 'In order to reach the required threshold of harm, a specific act must be likely to adversely affect the military operations or military capacity of a party to an armed conflict or, alternatively, to inflict death, injury, or destruction on persons or objects protected against direct attack.' ICRC INTERPRETIVE GUIDANCE at 47. *See also* AMW MANUAL, commentary accompanying Rule 29.

[64] 'In order for the requirement of direct causation to be satisfied, there must be a direct causal link between a specific act and the harm likely to result either from that act, or from a coordinated military operation of which that act constitutes an integral part.' ICRC INTERPRETIVE GUIDANCE at 51. *See also* AMW MANUAL, commentary to Rule 29.

[65] 'In order to meet the requirement of belligerent nexus, an act must be specifically designed to directly cause the required threshold of harm in support of a party to the

is used to direct enemy military operations fulfils the condition. It must be cautioned that although the majority agreed on these criteria, differences of opinion existed as to their precise application to particular actions.[66]

5.   Clearly, conducting cyber attacks related to an armed conflict qualifies as an act of direct participation, as do any actions that make possible specific attacks, such as identifying vulnerabilities in a targeted system or designing malware in order to take advantage of particular vulnerabilities. Other unambiguous examples include gathering information on enemy operations by cyber means and passing it to one's own armed forces and conducting DDoS operations against enemy military systems. On the other hand, designing malware and making it openly available online, even if it may be used by someone involved in the conflict to conduct an attack, does not constitute direct participation. Neither would maintaining computer equipment generally, even if such equipment is subsequently used in the hostilities. A more difficult situation arises when malware is developed and provided to individuals in circumstances where it is clear that it will be used to conduct attacks, but where the precise intended target is unknown to the supplier. The International Group of Experts was divided as to whether the causal connection between the act of providing the malware and the subsequent attack is, in such a situation, sufficiently direct to qualify as direct participation.

6.   The criterion of belligerent nexus rules out acts of a purely criminal or private nature that occur during an armed conflict. For example, criminals who use cyber means to steal State funds belonging to a party to the conflict, but with a view to private gain, would not be direct participants in hostilities. Some members of the International Group of Experts, however, were of the view that if individuals use cyber means to steal funds, private or public, such theft would constitute direct participation if, for example, the operation was conducted to finance particular military operations.

7.   Any act of direct participation in hostilities by a civilian renders that person targetable for such time as he or she is engaged in the qualifying act of direct participation.[67] All of the Experts agreed that this

---

conflict and to the detriment of another.' ICRC INTERPRETIVE GUIDANCE at 58. *See also* AMW MANUAL, commentary accompanying Rule 29.

[66] For instance, there is a well-known, on-going debate over whether assembly of improvised explosive devices or acting as a voluntary human shield qualifies as direct participation.

[67] For further elaboration, *see* ICRC INTERPRETIVE GUIDANCE at 70–3.

would at least include actions immediately preceding or subsequent to the qualifying act.[68] For instance, travelling to and from the location where a computer used to mount an operation is based would be encompassed in the notion. Some of the Experts took the position that the period of participation extended as far 'upstream' and 'downstream' as a causal link existed.[69] In a cyber operation, this period might begin once an individual began probing the target system for vulnerabilities, extend throughout the duration of activities against that system, and include the period during which damage is assessed to determine whether 're-attack' is required.

8.   A particularly important issue in the cyber context is that of 'delayed effects'. An example is emplacement of a logic bomb designed to activate at some future point. Activation may occur upon lapse of a predetermined period, on command, or upon the performance of a particular action by the target system (e.g., activation of the fire control radar of a surface-to-air missile site). The majority of the International Group of Experts took the position that the duration of an individual's direct participation extends from the beginning of his involvement in mission planning to the point when he or she terminates an active role in the operation. In the example the duration of the direct participation would run from the commencement of planning how to emplace the logic bomb through activation upon command by that individual. Note that the end of the period of direct participation may not necessarily correspond with the point at which the damage occurs. This would be so in the case of emplacement of the logic bomb by one individual and later activation by another. The key with regard to targetability is ascertaining when a particular individual's participation begins and ends.

9.   A minority of the International Group of Experts would characterize emplacement and activation by the same individual as separate acts of direct participation. By their view, the completion of emplacement would end the first period of direct participation and taking steps later to activate the logic bomb would mark the commencement of a second period.

10.   A further issue regarding the period of direct participation, and thus susceptibility to attack, involves a situation in which an individual launches repeated cyber operations that qualify as direct participation. Such circumstances are highly likely to arise in the context of cyber operations, for an individual may mount repeated separate operations

[68] ICRC INTERPRETIVE GUIDANCE at 67–8.
[69] *See* Yoram Dinstein, THE CONDUCT OF HOSTILITIES UNDER THE LAW OF INTERNATIONAL ARMED CONFLICT at 147–9 (2nd ed. 2010).

over time, either against the same cyber target or different ones. The International Group of Experts was split on the consequence of repeated actions with regard to the duration issue. Some of the Experts took the position, adopted in the ICRC Interpretive Guidance, that each act must be treated separately in terms of direct participation analysis.[70] Other Experts argued that this position makes little operational sense. It would create a 'revolving door' of direct participation, and thus of targetability. For these Experts, direct participation begins with the first such cyber operation and continues throughout the period of intermittent activity.

11.   Consider the example of an individual hacktivist who has, over the course of one month, conducted seven cyber attacks against the enemy's command and control system. By the first view, the hacktivist was only targetable while conducting each attack. By the second, he was targetable for the entire month. Moreover, in the absence of a clear indication that the hacktivist was no longer engaging in such attacks, he or she would have remained targetable beyond that period.

12.   The International Group of Experts was divided over the issue of whether a presumption against direct participation applies. Some Experts took the position that in case of doubt as to whether a civilian is engaging in an act of direct participation (or as to whether a certain type of activity rises to the level of direct participation), a presumption against direct participation attaches.[71] Other Experts objected to the analogy to Rule 33 (regarding the presumption in cases of doubt as to status). They were of the view that when doubt over these issues exists, the attacker must, as a matter of law, review all of the relevant information and act reasonably in the circumstances when deciding whether to conduct the attack.

Rule 36 – Terror attacks

Cyber attacks, or the threat thereof, the primary purpose of which is to spread terror among the civilian population, are prohibited.

1.   Rule 36 is based upon Article 51(2) of Additional Protocol I and Article 13(2) of Additional Protocol II. It reflects customary international law and applies equally in non-international and international armed conflict.[72]

---

[70] ICRC INTERPRETIVE GUIDANCE at 44–5, 70–1.

[71] For the argument in favour of such a presumption, *see* ICRC INTERPRETIVE GUIDANCE at 75–6.

[72] *Galić* Appeals Chamber judgment, paras. 86–98, 101–4; US COMMANDER'S HANDBOOK, para. 8.9.1.2; UK MANUAL, paras. 5.21, 5.21.1; CANADIAN MANUAL, paras. 617, 1720;

2. To breach this Rule, a cyber operation must amount to a 'cyber attack', or threat thereof, as that term is applied and interpreted in Rule 30. The limitation to cyber attacks is supported by the ICRC Additional Protocols Commentary, which notes with respect to Article 51(2) that 'This provision is intended to prohibit *acts of violence* the primary purpose of which is to spread terror among the civilian population without offering substantial military advantage.'[73] As an example of the Rule's application, a cyber attack against a mass transit system that causes death or injury violates the Rule if the primary purpose of the attack is to terrorize the civilian population. It should be noted that such an operation would also constitute an unlawful attack against civilians and civilian objects (Rules 32 and 37).

3. The prohibition in this Rule extends to threats of cyber attacks, whether conveyed by cyber or non-cyber means. For instance, a threat to use a cyber attack to disable a city's water distribution system to contaminate drinking water and cause death or illness would violate the Rule if made with the primary purpose of spreading terror among the civilian population. On the other hand, consider the example of a false tweet (Twitter message) sent out in order to cause panic, falsely indicating that a highly contagious and deadly disease is spreading rapidly throughout the population. Because the tweet is neither an attack nor a threat thereof, it does not violate this Rule.

4. It must be emphasized that the essence of the prohibition is its focus on the purpose of a cyber attack, specifically the spreading of terror among a civilian population. While a lawful cyber attack against a military objective, including combatants, might cause terror, this is not the type of attack covered in this Rule. As noted in the ICRC Additional Protocols Commentary to Article 51(2), this provision is 'intended to prohibit acts of violence, the primary purpose of which is to spread terror, without offering substantial military advantage'. The commentary correctly points out that 'there is no doubt that acts of violence related to a state of war almost always give rise to some degree of terror among the population'.[74]

GERMAN MANUAL, para. 507; NIAC MANUAL, para. 2.3.9; ICRC CUSTOMARY IHL STUDY, Rule 2; AMW MANUAL, Rule 18 and accompanying commentary.
[73] ICRC ADDITIONAL PROTOCOLS COMMENTARY, para. 1940 (emphasis added).
[74] ICRC ADDITIONAL PROTOCOLS COMMENTARY, para. 1940. *See also* UK MANUAL, para. 5.21.1; ICRC ADDITIONAL PROTOCOLS COMMENTARY, para. 4786.

5.   A violation of Rule 36 requires an intent to spread terror amongst the population. The International Group of Experts agreed that terrifying one or only a few individuals, even if that is the primary purpose of the act or threat, does not suffice, although engaging in an act of violence against one person in order to terrorize a significant segment of the population would violate this Rule.[75] Consensus also existed that this Rule does not prohibit conducting attacks against enemy combatants in order to terrorize them.

6.   The text of Rule 36 only extends to conducting or threatening cyber terror attacks. However, employing cyber means to communicate a threat of kinetic attack with the primary purpose of terrorizing the civilian population is likewise prohibited by the law of armed conflict.

7.   It should be noted that Article 33 of Geneva Convention IV prohibits 'measures of intimidation or of terrorism'. Unlike the norm set forth in Article 51(2) of Additional Protocol I, which is reflected in this Rule, the Article 33 prohibition is not limited to attacks that have a primary purpose of terrorizing those individuals. However, it extends only to protected persons as defined in Article 4 of that treaty. A minority of the International Group of Experts took the position that the confluence of Article 33, Article 51(2), and State practice has resulted in a customary norm prohibiting any operations, including cyber operations, intended (whether the primary purpose or not) to terrorize the civilian population.

SECTION 4:   ATTACKS AGAINST OBJECTS

Rule 37 – Prohibition on attacking civilian objects

Civilian objects shall not be made the object of cyber attacks. Computers, computer networks, and cyber infrastructure may be made the object of attack if they are military objectives.

1.   The prohibition on attacking civilian objects derives historically from the 1868 St Petersburg Declaration, which provided that 'the only legitimate object which States should endeavour to accomplish during war is to weaken the military forces of the enemy'.[76] This norm has since been codified in

---

[75] *Galić* Trial Chamber judgment, para. 133.

[76] St Petersburg Declaration, preamble. *See also* Hague Regulations, Art. 25 (noting 'attack or bombardment … of towns, villages, dwellings, or buildings which are undefended is prohibited').

Article 52(1) of Additional Protocol I and applies in international and non-international armed conflict as customary international law.[77]

2. For a cyber operation to be prohibited by this Rule, it must qualify as an 'attack'. The term attack is defined in Rule 30.

3. Civilian objects are those objects that do not qualify as military objectives. Civilian objects and military objectives are defined in Rule 38.

4. The International Group of Experts agreed that the determination of whether an object is a civilian object protected from attack, and not a military objective, must be made on a case-by-case basis.

5. The mere fact that a cyber attack is directed against a civilian object is sufficient to violate this Rule; it does not matter whether the attack is unsuccessful.

6. It is important to distinguish this Rule, which prohibits directing attacks at civilian objects, from that which prohibits indiscriminate attacks (Rule 49). The present Rule prohibits attacks that make a protected object the 'object of attack'. In other words, the attacker is 'aiming' at the civilian object in question. Indiscriminate attacks, by contrast, are unlawful because they are not directed at any particular object (or person), irrespective of whether some of the targets struck qualify as military objectives. This Rule must also be distinguished from Rule 43, which prohibits the use of indiscriminate methods or means of warfare.

Rule 38 – Civilian objects and military objectives

Civilian objects are all objects that are not military objectives. Military objectives are those objects which by their nature, location, purpose, or use, make an effective contribution to military action and whose total or partial destruction, capture or neutralization, in the circumstances ruling at the time, offers a definite military advantage. Military objectives may include computers, computer networks, and cyber infrastructure.

1. Article 52(1) of Additional Protocol I defines civilian objects in the negative as 'all objects which are not military objectives'. The term 'military objective' was first defined in the 1923 Hague Draft Rules of Air Warfare as 'an objective whereof the total or partial destruction

---

[77] US COMMANDER'S HANDBOOK, para. 8.3; UK MANUAL, para. 5.24; CANADIAN MANUAL, para. 423; GERMAN MANUAL, para. 451; AMW MANUAL, Rule 11 and accompanying commentary; NIAC MANUAL, para. 2.1.1.1; ICRC CUSTOMARY IHL STUDY, Rules 7, 9, 10. *See also* Rome Statute, Arts. 8(2)(b)(ii), 8(2)(e)(iii), (xii).

would constitute an obvious military advantage for the belligerent'.[78] It has since been codified in Article 52(2) of Additional Protocol I, which defines military objectives as 'those objects which by their nature, location, purpose or use make an effective contribution to military action and whose total or partial destruction, capture or neutralization, in the circumstances ruling at the time, offers a definite military advantage'. This definition has been adopted by many States in their military manuals and is considered reflective of customary international law in both non-international and international armed conflict.[79] It also appears in numerous other treaty instruments.[80]

2.   As used in this Manual, the term 'military objectives' refers only to those objects meeting the definition set forth in this Rule. The International Group of Experts took this approach on the basis that the lawful targetability of individuals is dependent on either status (Rule 34) or conduct (Rule 35), and therefore requires a different analysis from that set forth in Article 52(2) of Additional Protocol I.

3.   The term 'military objective' is being used in this Rule, and throughout the Manual, in its legal sense. It is a term of art in the law of armed conflict. This legal term is not to be confused with the meaning of the term in operational usage, that is, to refer to a goal of a military operation. For example, an operation may be designed to neutralize particular electronic communications. The messages are military objectives in the operational sense, but they do not constitute a military objective in the legal sense for the reasons set forth below. However, the hardware necessary to transmit and receive the messages would amount to a military objective in the legal sense.

4.   The meaning of the term 'object' is essential to understanding this and other Rules found in the Manual. An 'object' is characterized in the ICRC Additional Protocols Commentary as something 'visible and tangible'.[81] This usage is not to be confused with the meaning ascribed to the term in the field of computer science, which connotes entities that can be manipulated by the commands of a programming language. For the purpose of this Manual, computers,

---

[78] Hague Air Warfare Rules, Art. 24(1).

[79] US COMMANDER'S HANDBOOK, para. 8.2; UK MANUAL, para. 5.4.1; CANADIAN MANUAL, para. 406; GERMAN MANUAL, para. 442; AMW MANUAL, Rule 1(y); NIAC MANUAL, para. 1.1.4; ICRC CUSTOMARY IHL STUDY, Rule 8; SAN REMO MANUAL, Rule 40.

[80] Mines Protocol, Art. 2(4); Protocol on Prohibitions and Restrictions on the Use of Incendiary Weapons, Art. 1(3), 10 October 1980, 1342 U.N.T.S. 137.

[81] ICRC ADDITIONAL PROTOCOLS COMMENTARY, paras. 2007–8.

computer networks, and other tangible components of cyber infra-structure constitute objects.

5. The majority of the International Group of Experts agreed that the law of armed conflict notion of object should not be interpreted as including data. Data is intangible and therefore neither falls within the 'ordinary meaning' of the term object[82] nor comports with the explanation of it offered in the ICRC Additional Protocols Commentary. Nevertheless, as noted in the Commentary to Rule 30, a cyber operation targeting data may, in the view of the majority of the Experts, sometimes qualify as an attack when the operation affects the functionality of computers or other cyber systems. A minority of the Experts was of the opinion that, for the purposes of targeting, data *per se* should be regarded as an object. In their view, failure to do so would mean that even the deletion of extremely valuable and important civilian datasets would potentially escape the regulatory reach of the law of armed conflict, thereby contradicting the customary premise of that law that the civilian population shall enjoy general protection from the effects of hostilities, as reflected in Article 48 of Additional Protocol I. For these Experts, the key factor, based on the underlying object and purpose of Article 52 of Additional Protocol I, is one of severity, not nature of harm. The majority characterized this position as *de lege ferenda*.

6. Objects may qualify as military objectives based on any of the four criteria set forth in the Rule (nature, location, purpose, or use).[83] 'Nature' involves the inherent character of an object, and typically refers to those objects that are fundamentally military and designed to contribute to military action.[84] Military computers and military cyber infrastructure are paradigmatic examples of objects that satisfy the nature criterion. Of particular importance in the cyber context are military command, control, communications, computer, intelligence, surveillance, and reconnaissance ('C⁴ISR') systems. For instance, military cyber systems, wherever located, and the facilities in which they are permanently housed, qualify as military objectives. The fact that civilians (whether government employees or contractors) may be operating these systems is irrelevant to the question of whether they qualify as military objectives.

---

[82] Vienna Convention on the Law of Treaties, Art. 31(1), 23 May 1969, 1155 U.N.T.S. 331.

[83] *See* AMW MANUAL, Rule 22 and accompanying commentary: US COMMANDER'S HAND-BOOK, para. 8.2; UK MANUAL, paras. 5.4.4(c)–(e).

[84] ICRC ADDITIONAL PROTOCOLS COMMENTARY, para. 2020 (stating 'this category comprises all objects directly used by the armed forces').

7. Objects may also qualify as military objectives by their 'location'. Location normally refers to a geographical area of particular military importance;[85] therefore, for instance, an IP address (or block of IP addresses) is not a location (although it is associated with cyber infrastructure that may qualify as a military objective). It is not the actual use of an area but the fact that by its location it makes an effective contribution to enemy military action that renders it a military objective. For instance, a cyber operation against a reservoir's SCADA system might be employed to release waters into an area in which enemy military operations are expected, thereby denying its use to the enemy (subject to Rule 83). In this case, the area of land is a military objective because of its military utility to the enemy. This characterization justifies using cyber means to release the reservoir's waters.

8. When a civilian object or facility is used for military ends, it becomes a military objective through the 'use' criterion.[86] For instance, if a party to the conflict uses a certain civilian computer network for military purposes, that network loses its civilian character and becomes a military objective. This is so even if the network also continues to be used for civilian purposes (with regard to attacking such 'dual-use' entities, see Rule 39). Further examples of civilian objects that may become military objectives by use, and which would therefore be liable to cyber attack, include civilian rail networks being used by the military, civilian television or radio stations that regularly broadcast military information, and civilian airfields used to launch and recover military aircraft. Care must be taken in applying this criterion. For example, an entire computer network does not qualify as a military objective based on the mere fact that an individual router so qualifies.

9. The issue of civilian factories occupied the particular attention of the International Group of Experts. All Experts agreed that a factory that produces computer hardware or software under contract to the enemy's armed forces is a military objective by use, even if it also produces items for other than military purposes. All Experts further agreed that a factory that produces items that the military only occasionally acquires is not a military objective. The difficult case involves a factory that produces

---

[85] ICRC ADDITIONAL PROTOCOLS COMMENTARY, para. 2021.

[86] Hague Regulations, Art. 27 (noting that civilian objects enjoy protected status unless 'used at the time for military purposes'). *See also* ICRC ADDITIONAL PROTOCOLS COMMENTARY, para. 2022.

items that are not specifically intended for the military, but which are frequently put to military use. Although all of the Experts agreed that the issue of whether such a factory qualifies as a military objective by use depends on the scale, scope, and importance of the military acquisitions, they were unable to arrive at any definitive conclusions as to precise thresholds.

10. Civilian objects that have become military objectives by use can revert to civilian status if military use is discontinued. Once that occurs, they regain their protection from attack. However, if the discontinuance is only temporary, and the civilian object will be used for military purposes in the future, the object remains a military objective through the 'purpose' criterion. It must be cautioned that the mere fact that a civilian object was once used for military purposes does not alone suffice to establish that it will be so used in the future.

11. The 'purpose' criterion refers to the intended future use of an object, that is, the object is not presently being used for military purposes, but is expected to be so used in the future.[87] It acquires the status of a military objective as soon as such a purpose becomes clear; an attacker need not await its conversion to a military objective through use if the purpose has already crystallized to a sufficient degree. For instance, if reliable information becomes available that a party to the conflict is about to purchase particular computer hardware or software for military purposes, those items immediately become military objectives. Similarly, a party that makes known its intention to appropriate civilian transponders on a communications satellite for military use renders those transponders military objectives.

12. Difficulty often arises in determining the enemy's intentions. The law of armed conflict provides no particular standard of likelihood for concluding that a civilian object will be converted to military use, nor does it set forth the required degree of reliability for the information on which such a determination is made. Instead, the law generally requires the attacker to act as a reasonable party would in the same or similar circumstances. In other words, the legal question to be asked is whether a reasonable attacker would determine that the reasonably available information is reliable enough to conclude that the civilian object is going to be converted to military use.

---

[87] ICRC Additional Protocols Commentary, para. 2022.

13. To qualify as a military objective, the object in question must, through one of the four criteria, make 'an effective contribution to military action'. This limiting clause requires that a prospective target contribute to the execution of the enemy's operations or otherwise directly support the military activities of the enemy.[88] For instance, if a factory makes computer hardware that is used by the military, the contribution qualifies. Similarly, a website passing coded messages to resistance forces behind enemy lines is making an effective contribution to military action, thereby rendering the cyber infrastructure supporting the website a military objective. One merely inspiring patriotic sentiment among the population is not making such a contribution, and therefore, as a civilian object, is not be subject to cyber attack.

14. The majority of the International Group of Experts was of the opinion that objects that satisfy the nature criterion are always targetable, subject to other applicable rules of the law of armed conflict. For these Experts, the requirements that a military objective be an object that makes an effective contribution to military action and that attacking it will yield a definite military advantage are inherently met for objects that are military in nature. Under this view, a military computer network necessarily makes an effective contribution and its destruction, damage, or neutralization always provide an attacker with a definite military advantage.

15. A minority of the Experts held the view that the definition of military advantage limits attacks on objects that might qualify by their nature to situations in which a resulting definite military advantage can be identified. In the network attack example, they would conclude that even though the network is military in nature, a determination must still be made as to whether a military advantage accrues to the attacker through the network's destruction, damage, or neutralization before it qualifies as a military objective.[89]

16. A major issue in the law of armed conflict is whether 'war-sustaining' economic objects can qualify as military objectives. The US Commander's Handbook gives an affirmative answer to this question. The

---

[88] Hague Regulations, Art. 23(g) (prohibiting destruction not 'imperatively demanded by the necessities of war').

[89] This opinion is based on the wording of Art. 52(2) of Additional Protocol I, which sets forth a two-pronged test: (1) the object 'make[s] an effective contribution to military action' and (2) its 'total or particular destruction, capture or neutralization, in the circumstances ruling at the time, offers a definite military advantage'. The majority agreed with the two-prong test, but took the position that the second prong is always met with regard to military objectives by nature.

Handbook replaces the phrase 'military action' with 'war-fighting or war-sustaining capability',[90] explaining 'economic objects of the enemy that indirectly but effectively support and sustain the enemy's war-fighting capability may also be attacked'.[91] Advocates of this approach would, as an illustration, argue that it is lawful to launch cyber attacks against the enemy State's oil export industry if the war effort depended on the revenue from oil sales. The majority of the International Group of Experts rejected this position on the ground that the connection between war-sustaining activities and military action was too remote. They would limit the notion of military objective to those objects that are war-fighting (used in combat) or war-supporting (otherwise making an effective contribution to military action, as with factories producing hardware or software for use by the military) and that otherwise fulfil the criteria of a military objective as defined above.

17.   'Military advantage' refers to that advantage accruing from an attack. Such advantage must be assessed by reference to the attack considered as a whole and not only from isolated or particular parts of an attack.[92] For instance, cyber attacks may be conducted against a military objective far from a location where a related major operation is about to be mounted in order to deceive the enemy as to the actual location of the pending operation. In itself, the military value of the cyber attack is insignificant since the operations are planned to occur elsewhere. However, the success of the ruse may determine the success of the overall operation. In this case, the military advantage is that anticipated from the operation as a whole, of which the ruse is a part. This point is also crucial with regard to the application of the principle of proportionality and the requirement to take precautions in attack (Rules 51 to 58). It must be cautioned that the notion of 'attack considered as a whole' refers to a specific operation or series of related operations, not the entire war.

18.   The term 'military advantage' is meant to exclude advantage that is not military in nature. In particular, it would exclude advantage that is exclusively economic, political, or psychological. Thus, for instance, a

[90] US COMMANDER'S HANDBOOK, para. 8.2.
[91] US COMMANDER'S HANDBOOK, para. 8.2.5. *See also* AMW MANUAL, commentary accompanying Rule 24.
[92] UK MANUAL, para. 5.4.4(j); UK Additional Protocol Ratification Statement, para. (i); GERMAN MANUAL, para. 444; ICRC CUSTOMARY IHL STUDY, commentary accompanying Rule 14.

cyber attack on a civilian business sector, while yielding an advantage to the attacker in the sense that it would generally weaken the enemy State, would not necessarily result in military advantage in the sense of affecting on-going or prospective military operations in a relatively direct fashion. Of course, the sector would also fail to qualify as a military objective because it does not make an effective contribution to military action.

19.   To qualify as a military objective, the military advantage likely to result must be 'definite'. The ICRC Additional Protocols Commentary provides:

> It is not legitimate to launch an attack which only offers potential or indeterminate advantages. Those ordering or executing the attack must have sufficient information available to take this requirement into account; in case of doubt, the safety of the civilian population, which is the aim of the Protocol, must be taken into consideration.[93]

20.   The term 'definite' does not imply any particular quantum of advantage. Of course, the degree of advantage accruing from an attack bears on the proportionality of an attack (Rule 51). Accordingly, a cyber attack is lawful only when the attacker reasonably concludes that the 'total or partial destruction, capture, or neutralisation' of the nominated target will yield an actual military advantage. Cyber attacks anticipated to produce only a speculative advantage are prohibited.[94]

21.   The assessment of advantage is made with regard to the 'circumstances ruling at the time'. For example, a civilian air traffic control system used for military purposes while a damaged military system is being repaired qualifies as a military objective and may be subjected to cyber attack. However, once the military system is restored and the civilian system is returned to exclusively civilian use, it no longer qualifies as a military objective (absent apparently reliable information that allows the attacker to reasonably conclude that the enemy will use it again in the future for military purposes). It would neither qualify on the basis of any of the four criteria, nor would an attack thereon yield any definite military advantage.

22.   The military advantage need not result from the destruction or damage of the military objective itself. The reference to capture and neutralization is especially important in this regard. For instance, attacking a server through which the transmissions of an enemy command and

---

[93] ICRC Additional Protocols Commentary, para. 2024.
[94] UK Manual, para. 5.4.4(i).

control facility pass can result in military advantage. No damage is done to the command and control facility, but its neutralization results in definite military advantage for the attacker.

23. Cyber operations create opportunities to influence civilian morale. Possibilities range from denial of service operations to cyber-facilitated psychological warfare. An effect on civilian morale may not be considered in determining whether an object of attack qualifies as a military objective since a decline in civilian morale is not a 'military advantage' as that term is used in this Rule. Of course, an attack carried out against an object that otherwise qualifies as a military objective can have an incidental negative impact on civilian morale. This fact has no bearing on the target's qualification as a military objective. It is especially important to note that a decline in civilian morale is not to be considered collateral damage in the context of either the rule of proportionality or the requirement to take precautions in attack (Rules 51 to 58).

24. When assessing whether a nominated target is a military objective in the cyber context, it must be borne in mind that the use of the Internet and other cyber infrastructure by military personnel may be for reasons unrelated (or only indirectly related) to the hostilities. For instance, military personnel in the field often use civilian phone or email services to commu-nicate with families and friends, pay bills, etc. The International Group of Experts was divided over whether such use renders that civilian cyber infrastructure subject to attack as a military objective through use. The majority took the position that the cyber infrastructure upon which the services depend does not so qualify because the services do not make an effective contribution to the enemy's military action and, by extension, their denial would not yield a definite military advantage to an attacker. The minority suggested that since the use of the cyber infrastructure contributes to the morale of the enemy forces, conducting an attack against it would confer a military advantage. They cautioned that this sort of conclusion should not be crafted so broadly as to suggest that any object qualifies as a military objective if damage to it hurts enemy morale. For the Experts taking this position, the deciding factor in this particular case was the actual use by military forces deployed to the area of operations. Moreover, they emphasized that the issues of proportionality and precautions in attack would have to be considered by an attacker. All Experts concurred that if the civilian email services are being used to transmit militarily useful information, the infrastructure used to transmit them is a military objective.

25. Another interesting case discussed by the International Group of Experts involved media reports. If such reports effectively contribute

to the enemy's operational picture, depriving the enemy of them might offer a definite military advantage (Commentary accompanying Rule 79). Some members of the International Group of Experts took the position that cyber infrastructure supporting their transmission qualifies as a military objective, although they cautioned that the infrastructure could only be attacked subject to the Rules regarding attack, especially those on proportionality and precautions in attack (Rules 51 to 58). In particular, they noted that the latter requirement would usually result in an obligation to only mount cyber operations designed to block the broadcasts in question. Other Experts argued that the nexus between the cyber infrastructure and military action is too remote to qualify the infrastructure as a military objective. All members of the International Group of Experts agreed that such assessments are necessarily contextual.

26.   An attacker's assessment that an object is a military objective is made *ex ante,* that is, in light of the facts as reasonably assessed by the attacker at the time of the decision to attack. For example, if a cyber attack is unsuccessful because effective enemy cyber defences prevent it and the attack yields no military advantage, this does not deprive the object of its character as a military objective.

Rule 39 – Objects used for civilian and military purposes

An object used for both civilian and military purposes – including computers, computer networks, and cyber infrastructure – is a military objective.

1.   The object and purpose of this Rule is to clarify the issue of 'dual-use' objects, since it is often the case that civilian and military users share computers, computer networks, and cyber infrastructure. Any use or future use contributing to military action renders an object a military objective (Rule 38).[95] As a matter of law, status as a civilian object and military objective cannot coexist; an object is either one or the other. This principle confirms that all dual-use objects and facilities are military objectives, without qualification.[96]

2.   An attack on a military objective that is also used in part for civilian purposes is subject to the principle of proportionality and the

---

[95] Hague Regulations, Art. 27 (protecting civilian buildings 'provided they are not being used at the time for military purposes').

[96] US COMMANDER'S HANDBOOK, para. 8.3; AMW MANUAL, commentary accompanying Rule 22(d); ICRC CUSTOMARY IHL STUDY, commentary accompanying Rule 8 (noting that status depends on application of the definition of military objective).

requirement to take precautions in attack (Rules 51 to 58). Accordingly, an attacker is required to consider any expected harm to protected civilians or civilian objects or to clearly distinguishable civilian components of the military objective when determining whether an attack would be lawful.[97] For instance, consider a pending attack against a server farm that contains servers used by the military. Civilian companies are using a number of servers in the farm exclusively for civilian purposes. The planned cyber attack will be conducted against the facility's cooling system in order to cause the facility to overheat, and thereby damage the servers it contains. Expected damage to the civilian servers must be factored into the proportionality calculation and be considered when assessing feasible precautions in attack.

3.   Cyber operations pose unique challenges in this regard. Consider a network that is being used for both military and civilian purposes. It may be impossible to know over which part of the network military transmissions, as distinct from civilian ones, will pass. In such cases, the entire network (or at least those aspects in which transmission is reasonably likely) qualifies as a military objective. The analogy is a road network used by both military and civilian vehicles. Although an attacker may not know with certainty which roads will be travelled by enemy military forces (or which road will be taken if another is blocked), so long as it is reasonably likely that a road in the network may be used, the network is a military objective subject to attack. There is no reason to treat computer networks differently.

4.   Recent conflicts have highlighted the use of social networks for military purposes. For example, Facebook has been used for the organization of armed resistance operations and Twitter for the transmission of information of military value. Three cautionary notes are necessary. First, it must be remembered that this Rule is without prejudice to the rule of proportionality and the requirement to take precautions in attack (Rules 51 to 58). Second, the issue of the legality of cyber operations against social networks depends on whether the operations rise to the level of an attack (Rule 30). If the operations do not, the issue of qualification as a military objective is moot. Third, their military use does not mean that Facebook or Twitter as such may be targeted; only those components thereof used for military purposes may be attacked.

---

[97] *But see* US COMMANDER'S HANDBOOK, para. 8.3.2.

5. In theory, the application of the definition of military objectives could lead to the conclusion that the entire Internet can become a military objective if used for military purposes. However, the International Group of Experts unanimously agreed that the circumstances under which the Internet in its entirety would become subject to attack are so highly unlikely as to render the possibility purely theoretical at the present time. Instead, the International Group of Experts agreed that, as a legal and practical matter, virtually any attack against the Internet would have to be limited to discrete segments thereof. In this regard, particular attention must be paid to the requirement to conduct operations in a manner designed to minimize harm to the civilian population and civilian objects (Rule 52), as well as the limitations on treating multiple military objectives as a single target (Rule 50).

6. An attack on the Internet itself, or large portions thereof, might equally run afoul of the principle of proportionality (Rule 51). The Internet is used heavily for civilian emergency response, civil defence, disaster relief, and law enforcement activities. It is also employed for medical diagnosis, access to medical records, ordering medicine, and so forth. Any damage, destruction, injury, or death resulting from disruption of such services would have to be considered in determining whether an attack on the Internet comported with the principle of proportionality.

7. A complicated case involves a system that generates imagery or location data for civilian use but that is also useful to the military during an armed conflict. For instance, the system may provide precise real-time information regarding ship, including warship, location. Similarly, a system may generate high-resolution imagery of land-based objects and locations, including military objectives. If the enemy uses the imagery, the system becomes a military objective by the use or purpose criteria. Since such systems serve civilian purposes, the rule of proportionality (Rule 51) and the requirement to take precautions in attack (Rules 52 to 58) would, depending on the effects caused, apply to any attack on them. In particular, if it is feasible to degrade, deny, disrupt, or alter the signals in question using cyber means instead of conducting an operation that rises to the level of an attack (and that causes collateral damage) doing so would be required by operation of Rule 54. If the operation contemplated does not rise to the level of an attack, very few law of armed conflict issues remain. For instance, it would clearly be lawful to alter the position data of vessels, although the requirement of 'due regard' would apply *vis-à-vis* merchant vessels and neutral warships. In the event infrastructure associated with the system is located in neutral territory,

or is of neutral character and is located outside belligerent territory, account must also be taken of the limitations set forth in Rules 91 to 94.

8.   The notion of dual-use targeting must be distinguished from the question of whether civilian objects may be requisitioned, or otherwise used, for military purposes. Consider the case of military forces requiring more network bandwidth to conduct military operations. To acquire the required bandwidth, a party to the conflict may, subject to the Rules in this Manual, engage in network throttling of civilian (or governmental) systems or block network access by civilians in its own or enemy territory. This situation is analogous to taking control of public roadways for exclusive use by the military. However, the party may not acquire network bandwidth, whether governmental or private, through actions on neutral territory or involving neutral platforms outside belligerent territory (Rules 91 and 92).

Rule 40 – Doubt as to status of objects

In case of doubt as to whether an object that is normally dedicated to civilian purposes is being used to make an effective contribution to military action, a determination that it is so being used may only be made following a careful assessment.

1.   This Rule applies in international and non-international armed conflict.[98]

2.   Rule 40 addresses the topic of doubt as to the conversion of a civilian object to a military objective through use. In the *lex scripta*, the issue of doubt is regulated in Article 52(3) of Additional Protocol I for Parties to that instrument. The Article provides: 'in case of doubt whether an object which is normally dedicated to civilian purposes ... is being used to make an effective contribution to military action, it shall be presumed not to be so used'. It establishes, in the event of doubt, a rebuttable presumption that objects ordinarily devoted exclusively to civilian use are not used for military purposes. In other words, doubt is legally resolved in favour of civilian status. Additionally, Article 3(8)(a) of the Amended Mines Protocol contains identical language.

3.   Note that the scope of the Rule is limited to the criterion of use in relation to qualification as a military objective. Further, the Rule only

---

[98] UK MANUAL, paras. 5.24.3, 5.4.2 (both as amended); CANADIAN MANUAL, para. 429; GERMAN MANUAL, para. 446; AMW MANUAL, Rule 12(b); ICRC CUSTOMARY IHL STUDY, commentary accompanying Rule 10.

applies as to the issue of whether or not the object in question is 'making an effective contribution to military action'.[99] It does not bear on the issue of whether or not destruction, damage, capture, or neutralization of the object will yield a definite military advantage. The sole issue addressed by this Rule is the standard for assessing whether or not a civilian object has been converted to military use. All other questions with regard to qualification as a military objective are addressed through application of the requirement to take precautions in attack (Rules 52 to 58).

4.   The International Group of Experts could not achieve agreement on whether Article 52(3) of Additional Protocol I reflected customary international law. The majority of the Experts argued that it did. The ICRC Customary IHL Study acknowledges a lack of clarity regarding the issue; nevertheless, the Study seems to support the position that Article 52(3), especially in light of its reaffirmation in Article 8(3)(a) of the Amended Mines Protocol, is customary international law.[100] Other Experts denied the existence of a presumption of civilian use and argued that the Article improperly shifted the burden of proof with regard to the precise use of an object from the defender to the attacker.[101] The Experts who objected to the presumption's customary status took the position that such presumptions apply only to doubt as to the status of individuals (Rule 33). Since the text of the Rules required consensus, this disagreement resulted in adoption of the phrase 'may only be made following a careful assessment', instead of the more definitive 'shall be considered' language of Rule 33.

5.   This Rule binds all who plan, approve, or execute an attack. They must do everything feasible to verify that the objectives to be attacked are neither civilian objects nor subject to special protection (Rule 53). When in doubt, the individuals involved in the operation should request additional information.[102]

6.   Rule 40 applies in the case of objects 'normally dedicated to civilian purposes'.[103] Non-exhaustive examples include: civilian Internet services, civilian social networks, civilian residences, commercial businesses, factories, libraries, and educational facilities.[104] The term 'normally

---

[99]   Additional Protocol I, Art. 52(2).
[100] ICRC CUSTOMARY IHL STUDY, commentary accompanying Rule 10.
[101] United States Department of Defense, CONDUCT OF THE PERSIAN GULF WAR: FINAL REPORT TO CONGRESS 616 (April 1992).
[102] ICRC ADDITIONAL PROTOCOLS COMMENTARY, para. 2195.
[103] Additional Protocol I, Art. 52(3). See also AMW MANUAL, commentary accompanying Rule 12(b).
[104] UK MANUAL, para. 5.4.2.

dedicated' denotes that the object has not been used for military purposes in any regular or substantial way. Infrequent or insignificant use by the military does not permanently deprive an object of civilian status.

7.   In cases where a particular nominated target is normally employed for civilian purposes but an attacker suspects that it may have been converted, at least in part, to military use, the target may only be attacked following a careful assessment of the situation. The assessment must be sufficient to establish that there are reasonable grounds to conclude that the conversion has occurred. In arriving at this conclusion, an attacker must take into account all the information available at the time. One important criterion in establishing the reasonableness of the conclusion is the apparent reliability of the information, including the credibility of the source or sensor, the timeliness of the information, the likelihood of deception, and the possibility of misinterpretation of data.

8.   Absolute certainty that an object has been so converted is not necessary. Doubt is often present in armed conflict and any such require-ment would clearly run contrary to State practice. What is required is sufficiently reliable information that would lead a reasonable commander to conclude the enemy is using the potential target for military purposes, that is, to make an effective contribution to military action. In other words, a reasonable attacker would not hesitate before conducting the strike despite the doubt.[105]

9.   Issues of doubt must be assessed in light of the information reasonably available to the attacker at the time of attack and not that revealed after the fact; the analysis is *ex ante*.[106] An attacker who has taken all feasible steps to discern the use of an object and reasonably concludes the enemy is using the target for military purposes has

---

[105] AMW MANUAL, commentary accompanying Rule 12(b).

[106] The UK Additional Protocols Ratification Statement para. (c) states, 'Military com-manders and others responsible for planning, deciding upon, or executing attacks necessarily have to reach decisions on the basis of their assessment of the information from all sources which is reasonably available to them at the relevant time.' Similarly, Canada made the following Statement of Understanding on ratification of Additional Protocol I: 'It is the understanding of the Government of Canada that, in relation to Articles 48, 51 to 60 inclusive, 62 and 67, military commanders and others responsible for planning, deciding upon or executing attacks have to reach decisions on the basis of their assessment of the information reasonably available to them at the relevant time and that such decisions cannot be judged on the basis of information which has subsequently come to light.' Canada Additional Protocol Ratification Statement, *reprinted in* DOCU-MENTS ON THE LAWS OF WAR 502 (Adam Roberts and Richard Guelff eds., 3rd ed. 2000).

complied with the requirements under this Rule. The reasonableness of the conclusion must be assessed based on the information gathering capabilities available to the attacker and not on information and intelligence capabilities that may be possessed by other armed forces or nations. Of course, in some circumstances, an attacker may lack the means to gather information reasonably to conclude the object is being so used; the absence of such means cannot be used to justify an attack.

10.   It must be recalled that formerly civilian objects that have become military objectives through use will revert to being civilian as soon as the military use ceases. For instance, where the military temporarily (perhaps even momentarily) uses an information system normally dedicated to civilian use, such as the temporary use of social networking media for military purposes, particular attention must be paid to the possibility of any reconversion to civilian use. As another example, consider a case in which a human intelligence source reports that a university computer system in enemy territory is being used for military purposes. A cyber operational planning team is charged with assessing the accuracy of this report, but is unable to confirm that the system is presently being put to military use. In this circumstance, it may not be attacked; only measures short of attack would be permissible. One must be cautious in this regard. If the cyber infrastructure might have been converted back to purely civilian use but will be used for military purposes in the future, it qualifies as a military objective by virtue of the purpose criterion (Rule 38).

11.   Defenders must facilitate an attacker's efforts to resolve the status of 'objects dedicated to religion, art, science or charitable purposes, historic monuments, hospitals, and places where the sick and wounded are collected' by means of distinctive markings or by notifying the attacker beforehand.[107]

SECTION 5:   MEANS AND METHODS OF WARFARE

1.   Cyber operations are not explicitly referred to in existing law of armed conflict treaties. However, in the *Nuclear Weapons* Advisory Opinion, the International Court of Justice affirmed that 'the established principles and rules of humanitarian law... appl[y] to all forms of warfare, and to all kinds of weapons, those of the past, those of the

---

[107]   Hague Regulations, Art. 27.

present and those of the future'.[108] The International Group of Experts adopted the same approach by concluding that the general rules that determine the legality of weapons will also determine the lawfulness of cyber methods and means of warfare.

2.   The Rules set out in this section apply in relation to methods and means of warfare that a State develops or procures for use by its own armed forces. Moreover, they apply to any means of warfare over which a State acquires control. A State that acquires control by cyber means over enemy weapons is subject to the law of armed conflict applicable to those weapons. Consider the case of an Unmanned Combat Aerial System (UCAS) armed with cluster munitions. If the State that acquires control over this system is a Party to the Cluster Munitions Convention,[109] it would be prohibited from using the UCAS to deliver such weapons. The notion of acquiring control implies that the Party using cyber means exercises sufficient control over the system to employ it as if it were its own. This situation must be distinguished from one in which cyber means are used to attack, neutralize, or otherwise interfere with enemy systems, as in the case of taking control of an enemy UCAS in order to cause it to crash.

Rule 41 – Definitions of means and methods of warfare

For the purposes of this Manual:

(a) 'means of cyber warfare' are cyber weapons and their associated cyber systems; and

(b) 'methods of cyber warfare' are the cyber tactics, techniques, and procedures by which hostilities are conducted.

1.   The terms 'means' and 'methods' of warfare are legal terms of art used in the law of armed conflict. They should not be confused with the broader, non-legal term 'cyber operation' used throughout this Manual. Cyber operation simply denotes a particular cyber activity. The definitions set forth in this Rule are applicable in both international and non-international armed conflict.

2.   For the purposes of this Manual, cyber weapons are cyber means of warfare that are by design, use, or intended use capable of causing either (i) injury to, or death of, persons; or (ii) damage to, or destruction

---

[108] *Nuclear Weapons* Advisory Opinion, para. 86.
[109] Convention on Cluster Munitions, 3 December 2008, 48 INTERNATIONAL LEGAL MATER-IALS 357 (2009).

of, objects, that is, causing the consequences required for qualification of a cyber operation as an attack (Rule 30).[110] The term means of cyber warfare encompasses both cyber weapons and cyber weapon systems. A weapon is generally understood as that aspect of the system used to cause damage or destruction to objects or injury or death to persons. Cyber means of warfare therefore include any cyber device, materiel, instrument, mechanism, equipment, or software used, designed, or intended to be used to conduct a cyber attack (Rule 30).

3.   A distinction must be drawn between the computer system, which qualifies as a means of warfare, and the cyber infrastructure (e.g., the Internet) that connects the computer system to the target that the system is used to attack. The cyber infrastructure is not a means of warfare because an object must be in the control of an attacking party to comprise a means of warfare.

4.   The term 'methods of warfare' refers to how cyber operations are mounted, as distinct from the instruments used to conduct them.[111] For instance, consider an operation using a botnet to conduct a distributed denial of service attack. In this example, the botnet is the means of cyber warfare while the distributed denial of service attack is the method of cyber warfare. Active cyber defences are encompassed in the notion of methods of cyber warfare, whereas passive cyber defences are not.

5.   The phrase 'cyber tactics, techniques, and procedures whereby hostilities are conducted'[112] does not include cyber activities that, for instance, involve communications between friendly forces. On the other hand, it is intended to denote more than those operations that rise to the level of an 'attack' (Rule 30). For example, a particular type of cyber operation designed to interfere with the enemy's capability to communicate may not qualify as an attack (as that term is used in this Manual), but would constitute a method of warfare.

---

[110] See AMW MANUAL, commentary accompanying Rule 1(t). See also International Committee of the Red Cross, A Guide to the Legal Review of New Weapons, Means, and Methods of Warfare: Measures to Implement Article 36 of Additional Protocol I of 1977, 88 INTERNATIONAL REVIEW OF THE RED CROSS, 931, 937 n. 17 (2006) (referring to a proposed definition of weapons put forward by the US DoD Working Group as, 'All arms, munitions, materiel, instruments, mechanisms or devices that have an intended effect of injuring, damaging, destroying or disabling personnel or property').

[111] See AMW MANUAL, Rule 1(v) and accompanying commentary.

[112] As to the meaning of tactics, techniques, and procedures, see US DEPARTMENT OF THE ARMY, FIELD MANUAL 3.0 (change 1), OPERATIONS, paras. D-5 to D-6 (27 February 2008).

Rule 42 – Superfluous injury or unnecessary suffering

It is prohibited to employ means or methods of cyber warfare that are of a nature to cause superfluous injury or unnecessary suffering.

1. This Rule is based on Article 23(e) of the Hague Regulations and Article 35(2) of Additional Protocol I.[113] It reflects customary international law and is applicable in both international and non-international armed conflict.[114]

2. This Rule applies only to injury or suffering caused to combatants, members of organized armed groups, and civilians directly participating in hostilities. Other individuals are immune from attack in the first place. Any incidental harm to them caused during an attack would be governed by the rule of proportionality and the requirement to take precautions in attack (Rules 51 to 58). In other words, superfluous injury and unnecessary suffering are not to be equated with the notion of incidental injury to civilians.

3. The term 'superfluous injury or unnecessary suffering' refers to a situation in which a weapon or a particular use of a weapon aggravates suffering without providing any further military advantage to an attacker.[115] As noted by the International Court of Justice, weapons may not 'cause a harm greater than that unavoidable to achieve legitimate military objectives'.[116]

4. The use of the word 'nature' confirms that a cyber means or method of warfare violates this Rule if it will necessarily cause unnecessary suffering or superfluous injury, regardless of whether it was intended

---

[113] These notions find their origin in the Preamble to the 1868 St Petersburg Declaration. *See also* Rome Statute, Art. 8(2)(b)(xx); Conventional Weapons Convention, Preamble; Convention on the Prohibition on the Use, Stockpiling, Production and Transfer of Anti-Personnel Mines and on their Destruction, Preamble, 3 December 1997, 2056 U.N.T.S. 211.

[114] *See* US Commander's Handbook, para. 9.1.1; UK Manual, para. 6.1; Canadian Manual, paras. 502, 506, 508; German Manual, paras. 401, 402; AMW Manual, Rule 5(b); NIAC Manual, paras. 1.2.3, 2.2.1.3; ICRC Customary IHL Study, Rule 70.

[115] Although there is historical significance to the use of the two terms, 'unnecessary suffering' and 'superfluous injury', for the purposes of this Manual the International Group of Experts treated them as a unitary concept. Doing so is consistent with the original authentic French text '*maux superflus*' in the 1899 and 1907 Hague Regulations. *See* AMW Manual, commentary accompanying Rule 5(b); ICRC Additional Protocols Commentary, para. 1426. Use of both terms emphasizes that the concept extends to both physical and severe mental harm.

[116] *Nuclear Weapons* Advisory Opinion, para. 78.

to do so. Means or methods of cyber warfare also violate the prohibition if designed to needlessly aggravate injuries or suffering.[117]

5.   Only the normal use of a means or method of cyber warfare is considered when assessing compliance with the Rule. The purpose is to judge its lawfulness *per se*. The assessment is made by reference to the envisioned use of the means or method of cyber warfare under normal circumstances and when directed at its intended category of target. The prohibition extends to the use of otherwise lawful means of warfare that have been altered in order to exacerbate suffering or injury.

6.   Means and methods of cyber warfare will only in rare cases violate this Rule. It is, however, conceivable that means or methods of warfare that are lawful in the abstract could bring about suffering that is unnecessary in relation to the military advantage sought. For example, consider an enemy combatant who has an Internet-addressable pacemaker device with a built-in defibrillator. It would be lawful to take control of the pacemaker to kill that individual or render him *hors de combat,* for example by using the defibrillation function to stop the heart. However, it would be unlawful to conduct the operation in a manner that is intended to cause additional pain and suffering for their own sake, that is, unrelated or patently excessive to the lawful military purpose of the operation.[118] Examples of such unlawful actions would include stopping the target's heart and then reviving him multiple times before finally killing him. Doing so would occasion suffering that served no military purpose.

Rule 43 – Indiscriminate means or methods

It is prohibited to employ means or methods of cyber warfare that are indiscriminate by nature. Means or methods of cyber warfare are indiscriminate by nature when they cannot be:

---

[117] The International Group of Experts took the same position in this regard as their counterparts who drafted the AMW Manual. AMW MANUAL, commentary accompanying Rule 5(b).

[118] Such conduct would amount to cruel, inhuman or degrading treatment or, under certain circumstances, even torture. For the definition of torture, see Convention against Torture and Other Forms of Cruel, Inhuman or Degrading Treatment or Punishment, Art. 1, 10 December 1984, 1465 U.N.T.S. 85. Regarding cruel, inhuman, or degrading treatment, see *Delalić* judgment, para. 543.

(a) directed at a specific military objective, or

(b) limited in their effects as required by the law of armed conflict

and consequently are of a nature to strike military objectives and civilians or civilian objects without distinction.

1.   Rule 43 is based on Article 51(4)(b) and (c) of Additional Protocol I and represents customary international law in both international and non-international armed conflict.[119] It derives from the customary principle of distinction, which is codified in Article 48 of Additional Protocol I and set forth in Rule 31.

2.   This Rule deals only with the lawfulness of means or methods of cyber warfare *per se,* as distinct from the lawfulness of their use in particular circumstances (with regard to the indiscriminate use of weapons, see Rule 49). In other words, the issue with which this Rule is concerned is whether the contemplated cyber weapon is inherently indiscriminate.

3.   *Lit.* (a) prohibits the use of any means or method of warfare that cannot be directed against a specific lawful target. This Rule does not prohibit imprecise means or methods of warfare. Instead, the prohibition extends only to those means or methods that are essentially 'shots in the dark'.[120] In other words, an indiscriminate cyber means or method under *lit.* (a) is one where it is impossible to predict whether it will strike a specific military objective rather than a computer or computer system protected by the law of armed conflict.

4.   *Lit.* (b) addresses cyber means or methods that are capable of being directed against a specific target in compliance with *lit.* (a), but are of a nature to have effects that cannot be limited in any circumstances.[121] The crux of *lit.* (b) is a prohibition on weapons that by their nature generate effects that are incapable of being controlled and therefore can spread uncontrollably into civilian and other protected computers and computer networks and cause the requisite degree of harm. In particular, *lit.* (b) encompasses cyber weapons that create an uncontrollable chain of events.[122] To illustrate, assume that malware employed by a State is

---

[119] US Commander's Handbook, para. 9.1.2; UK Manual, para. 6.4; Canadian Manual, para. 509; German Manual, paras. 401, 454–6; AMW Manual, Rule 5(a); NIAC Manual, para. 2.2.1.1; ICRC Customary IHL Study, Rules 12, 71. *See also* Rome Statute, Art. 8(2)(b)(xx); Amended Mines Protocol, Art. 3(8)(b) (prohibiting booby traps that 'cannot be directed at a specific military objective').

[120] AMW Manual, commentary accompanying Rule 5(a).

[121] ICRC Additional Protocols Commentary, para. 1963.

[122] AMW Manual, commentary accompanying Rule 5(a).

capable of targeting specific military computer networks. However, once introduced into such a network, it will inevitably, and harmfully, spread into civilian networks in a way that cannot be controlled by the attacker. Such malware would violate *lit.* (b) of this Rule. To the extent the effects of the means or method of warfare can be limited in particular circumstances, it does not violate *lit.* (b).

5.   The harmful effects that are likely to be uncontrollably spread by virtue of the cyber means or method in question must rise to the level of harm that would amount to collateral damage (Rule 51). In particular, the uncontrollable spread of harmless effects or those that are merely inconvenient or annoying is irrelevant when assessing the legality of a means or method of cyber warfare under *lit.* (b). Consider the employment of Stuxnet-like malware that spreads widely into civilian systems, but only damages specific enemy technical equipment. The malware does not violate *lit.* (b).

6.   Use of means of warfare that have indiscriminate effects in a particular attack due to unforeseeable system malfunction or reconfiguration does not violate this Rule. Of course, the weapon must only be fielded after it has been assessed as lawful, pursuant to a proper and thorough legal review (Rule 48).

7.   The International Group of Experts struggled to identify means and methods of cyber warfare that might violate this Rule. For instance, even though a cyber means of warfare may be unable to distinguish one target from another, it could lawfully be introduced into a closed military network. In such a case, there would be little risk of it striking protected systems or having uncontrollable effects on such systems. Nevertheless, in light of the rapidly advancing state of technology in this field, the International Group of Experts agreed that the inclusion of the Rule was useful.

Rule 44 – Cyber booby traps

It is forbidden to employ cyber booby traps associated with certain objects specified in the law of armed conflict.

1.   This Rule is derived from the Mines Protocol and Amended Mines Protocol. It reflects customary international law in both international and non-international armed conflict.[123] Both Protocols define a booby trap as

---

[123] US COMMANDER'S HANDBOOK, para. 9.6; UK MANUAL, para. 6.7; CANADIAN MANUAL, para. 522; GERMAN MANUAL, para. 415; NIAC MANUAL, para. 2.2.3.1; ICRC CUSTOMARY IHL STUDY, Rule 80. Note that the scope of Amended Protocol II extends to

'any device or material which is designed, constructed or adapted to kill or injure, and which functions unexpectedly when a person disturbs or approaches an apparently harmless object or performs an apparently safe act'.[124] Definitional factors significantly limit the scope of the prohibition.

2. The International Group of Experts struggled with the question of whether a cyber booby trap qualified as a device. The Experts agreed that the appropriate way to interpret the term in the cyber context is to focus on the function of the entity in question. In other words, there is no reason as a matter of law to differentiate between a physical object that serves as a booby trap and cyber means of achieving an equivalent objective. The alternative view is that only tangible equipment may constitute a device for the purposes of this Rule.

3. A number of other definitional factors affect the application of this Rule. First, a cyber booby trap must be deliberately configured to operate unexpectedly. Codes that inadvertently or incidentally function in an unforeseen manner are not booby traps in the legal sense, because they are not designed to operate as such. Second, to qualify as cyber booby traps, codes or malware must be 'designed, constructed, or adapted to kill or injure'.[125] In the cyber context the operation of the cyber means of warfare must eventually and intentionally result in such consequences. Cyber weapons that only harm objects are outside the scope of the definition. Third, to qualify as a cyber booby trap, a cyber weapon must appear innocuous or harmless to a reasonable observer, or the observer must be performing an apparently safe act. In other words, the person setting the cyber booby trap must intend the act that will trigger it to appear harmless.[126] Finally, the cyber weapon must in some way be associated with certain specified objects.[127] Several are of particular relevance in the cyber context. These include objects associated

non-international armed conflict for Parties thereto. Amended Mines Protocol, Art. 1(2). Note also that the Convention on Conventional Weapons extends to non-international armed conflict for Parties thereto that have ratified the extension in scope. Conventional Weapons Convention, Art. 1(2), as amended 21 December 2001, 2260 U.N.T.S. 82.

[124] Amended Mines Protocol, Art. 2(4); Mines Protocol, Art. 2(2).

[125] Amended Mines Protocol, Art. 2(4); Mines Protocol, Art. 2(2).

[126] Consider the example of a device fitted to a door, referred to in the UK MANUAL, para. 6.7.1.

[127] Amended Mines Protocol, Art. 7; Mines Protocol, Art. 6(1). The prohibition extends to 'any booby-trap in the form of an apparently harmless portable object which is specifically designed and constructed to contain explosive material and to detonate when it is disturbed or approached' and to those attached to: (i) internationally recognized protective emblems, signs or signals; (ii) sick, wounded or dead persons;

with medical functions; the care or education of children; religious functions; and cultural, historic, or spiritual functions.

3.   As an illustration of this Rule, consider an email with an attachment containing malware, such as an embedded kill-switch, sent to an employee of a water treatment plant, purportedly from his physician. When opened, the malware is designed to cause the purification process at the plant, which serves both military and civilian users, to be suspended, thus allowing untreated water into the water supply on which the soldiers rely. Illness is the intended purpose. The malware is an unlawful cyber booby trap because the recipient reasonably believes that the act of opening an email from his physician is safe to himself and others, and because it appears to be related to medical activities. This is so regardless of whether the operation complies with the principle of proportionality (Rule 51).

4.   Treaty provisions confirm that this Rule operates without prejudice to other aspects of the law of armed conflict. Thus, a cyber booby trap that does not violate the letter of this Rule may nonetheless violate the rule against perfidy (Rule 60) or other rules of the law of armed conflict. Moreover, note that the Mines Protocol and Amended Mines Protocol impose specific requirements regarding use of booby traps, including provisions as to precautions and removal.[128]

Rule 45 – Starvation

Starvation of civilians as a method of cyber warfare is prohibited.

1.   This Rule is based on Article 54(1) of Additional Protocol I and Article 14 of Additional Protocol II. It reflects customary international law in both international and non-international armed conflicts.[129]

2.   For the purposes of this Manual, the term 'starvation' means deliberately depriving a civilian population of nourishment (including water)

(iii) burial or cremation sites or graves; (iv) medical facilities, medical equipment, medical supplies or medical transportation; (v) children's toys or other portable objects or products specially designed for the feeding, health, hygiene, clothing or education of children; (vi) food or drink; (vii) kitchen utensils or appliances except in military establishments, military locations or military supply depots; (viii) objects clearly of a religious nature; (ix) historic monuments, works of art or places of worship which constitute the cultural or spiritual heritage of peoples; (x) animals or their carcasses. Mines Protocol, Art. 6(1).

[128] Amended Mines Protocol, Arts. 9, 10; Mines Protocol, Art. 7.

[129] UK MANUAL, paras. 5.27, 15.19; CANADIAN MANUAL, paras. 618, 708, 1721; AMW MANUAL, Rule 97(a); NIAC MANUAL, para. 2.3.10; ICRC CUSTOMARY IHL STUDY, Rule 53. See also Rome Statute, Art. 8 (2)(b)(xxv).

with a view to weakening or killing it.[130] The civilian population need not comprise the enemy's entire population.

3. Reference to 'as a method of cyber warfare' excludes from the Rule the incidental starvation of the civilian population as a result of the armed conflict. For the Rule to be breached, starvation must be a tactic deliberately employed by one of the parties to the conflict against the civilian population.

4. Only in exceptional cases will cyber operations violate this Rule. Such a violation could, however, arise during an armed conflict in which a party seeks to annihilate the enemy civilian population through starvation. As part of its campaign of starvation, it launches cyber operations for the exclusive purpose of disrupting transportation of food to civilian population centres and targets food processing and storage facilities in order to cause food stocks used by civilians to spoil. It is the hunger of civilians that these operations are designed to cause that qualifies the actions as prohibited starvation of the population (see also Rule 81 regarding protection of objects indispensable to the civilian population). Denying foodstuffs to enemy armed forces or organized armed enemy groups does not violate this Rule, even if the incidental effect affects civilians.[131] Such incidental starvation effect would instead be assessed pursuant to the rules of proportionality and precautions (Rules 51 to 58).

Rule 46 – Belligerent reprisals

Belligerent reprisals by way of cyber operations against:

(a) **prisoners of war;**
(b) **interned civilians, civilians in occupied territory or otherwise in the hands of an adverse party to the conflict, and their property;**
(c) **those *hors de combat*; and**
(d) **medical personnel, facilities, vehicles, and equipment are prohibited.**

---

[130] ICRC Additional Protocols Commentary, para. 2089. The AMW Manual, in the commentary accompanying Rule 97(a), refers to 'annihilating or weakening the civilian population by deliberately depriving it of its sources of food, drinking water or of other essential supplies, thereby causing it to suffer hunger or otherwise affecting its subsistence'.

[131] UK Manual, para. 5.27.1; AMW Manual, commentary accompanying Rule 97(a).

Where not prohibited by international law, belligerent reprisals are subject to stringent conditions.

1.   This Rule is based on the various prohibitions on belligerent reprisal set forth in the Geneva Conventions, the relevant provisions of which are discussed below. The concept of belligerent reprisal is limited to international armed conflict.[132]

2.   Belligerent reprisals are acts that would be in violation of the law of armed conflict were they not being undertaken in response to violations by the enemy.[133] Reprisals may only be undertaken in order to induce or compel compliance with the law by the enemy.[134] Their sole motivating purpose of securing future compliance by the adverse party is what distinguishes them from revenge, punishment, and retaliation.

3.   As dealt with in this Manual, belligerent reprisals are distinct from countermeasures (Rule 9). Unlike countermeasures, belligerent reprisals occur only during an armed conflict, are undertaken only in response to violations of the law of armed conflict, and may permit the use of armed force.

4.   International consensus as to the legality of some forms of belligerent reprisal is lacking. Nevertheless, the International Group of Experts agreed that it is incontrovertible that reprisals using cyber means are prohibited if undertaken against the wounded, sick, shipwrecked, medical personnel, medical units, medical establishments, or medical transports, chaplains;[135] prisoners of war;[136] and interned civilians and civilians in the hands of an adverse party to the conflict who are protected by Geneva Convention IV, or their property.[137] The near-universal ratification of the Geneva Conventions and consistent subsequent State practice confirm

---

[132] *See* ICRC CUSTOMARY IHL STUDY, Rule 148.

[133] *Naulilaa* arbitration, at 1025; US COMMANDER'S HANDBOOK, para. 6.2.4.

[134] US COMMANDER'S HANDBOOK, para. 6.2.4; Frits Kalshoven, BELLIGERENT REPRISALS 33 (2nd ed. 2005).

[135] Geneva Convention I, Art. 46; Geneva Convention II, Art. 47. *See also* US COMMANDER'S HANDBOOK, para. 6.2.4.2; UK MANUAL, para. 16.18.a; GERMAN MANUAL, paras. 476–9.

[136] Geneva Convention III, Art. 13. *See also* US COMMANDER'S HANDBOOK, para. 6.2.4.2; UK MANUAL, para. 16.18.b; CANADIAN MANUAL, para. 1019; GERMAN MANUAL, para. 479.

[137] Mines Protocol, Art. 3 (prohibiting the use of booby traps as a means of reprisal against the civilian population); Geneva Convention IV, Art. 33. *See also* US COMMANDER'S HANDBOOK, para. 6.2.4.2; UK MANUAL, para. 16.18.c; CANADIAN MANUAL, para. 1121; GERMAN MANUAL, para. 479; ICRC CUSTOMARY IHL STUDY, Rule 146.

that these prohibitions are now accepted as customary international law that binds all States.

5. With regard to belligerent reprisals other than against the persons and objects enumerated in this Rule, the ICRC Customary IHL Study concludes that to be lawful, reprisals: (1) may only be taken in reaction to a prior serious violation of the law of armed conflict and only for the purpose of inducing the adversary to comply with the law; (2) may only be carried out as a measure of last resort when no other lawful measures to induce the adversary to respect the law exist; (3) must be proportionate to the original violation; (4) must be approved by the highest level of government; and (5) must cease as soon as the adversary complies with the law.[138] States generally accept these conditions.[139]

6. There is no requirement that reprisals be in kind. Cyber operations may be used to conduct belligerent reprisals in response to kinetic violations of the law of armed conflict, and vice versa.

7. Consider a situation in which the armed forces of State A are bombing military medical facilities in State B, which is not a Party to Additional Protocol I.[140] In response and after repeated demands to desist, State B's Prime Minister approves a cyber attack against a power generation facility used exclusively to provide power to the civilian population. The cyber attack is intended solely to compel State A to refrain from continuing to attack medical facilities, and the Prime Minister has issued strict orders to cease reprisal operations as soon as State A does so. State B's belligerent reprisals would comply with this Rule (although the same result will not hold for a Party to Additional Protocol I for which Article 52(1) prohibits reprisals against civilian objects).

---

[138] ICRC CUSTOMARY IHL STUDY, Rule 145 and accompanying commentary. It must be noted that the Study suggests that it is difficult to 'assert that a right to resort to such reprisals continues to exist on the strength of the practice of only a limited number of States, some of which is ambiguous. Hence, there appears, at a minimum, to exist a trend in favour of prohibiting such reprisals.' *Ibid.*, commentary accompanying Rule 146. Anticipatory reprisals are not permitted, nor can they be in response to a violation of another type of law. The duty to make a prior demand for cessation of unlawful conduct before undertaking a belligerent reprisal and the obligation to make the purpose of a reprisal public are generally included as sub-conditions of the requirement that the taking of reprisals is a measure of last resort, or as separate conditions.

[139] *See generally* US COMMANDER'S HANDBOOK, para. 6.2.4.1; UK MANUAL, paras. 16.19.1, 16.19.2; CANADIAN MANUAL, para. 1507; GERMAN MANUAL, para. 478.

[140] That is, which is not subject to Additional Protocol I, Art. 52(1) (prohibiting reprisals against civilian property).

By contrast, a decision to conduct cyber attacks against State A's military medical facilities would be unlawful as a prohibited reprisal since, as noted, they are protected from attack in reprisal.

8.   A number of the members of the International Group of Experts were of the opinion that reprisals against cultural property are prohibited as a matter of customary international law.[141] Other members of the Group were not convinced that such a prohibition had matured to a rule of customary international law, but acknowledged that States Party to the 1954 Hague Cultural Property Convention would be prohibited by Article 4(4) from conducting such operations.

Rule 47 – Reprisals under Additional Protocol I

Additional Protocol I prohibits States Parties from making the civilian population, individual civilians, civilian objects, cultural objects and places of worship, objects indispensable to the survival of the civilian population, the natural environment, and dams, dykes, and nuclear electrical generating stations the object of a cyber attack by way of reprisal.

1.   Articles 20, 51(6), 52(1), 53(c), 54(4), 55(2), and 56(4) of Additional Protocol I provide the basis for this Rule, which applies in international armed conflicts.[142] Upon ratification of Additional Protocol I, certain States adopted understandings with regard to reprisals against civilians that have the effect of making the prohibition conditional. Noteworthy in this regard are the United Kingdom[143] and France.[144] Therefore, in application of this Rule, States must determine

---

[141] ICRC CUSTOMARY LAW STUDY, Rule 147.

[142] *See also* Amended Mines Protocol, Art. 3(7); Mines Protocol, Art. 3(2).

[143] The United Kingdom noted that: 'The obligations of Articles 51 and 55 are accepted on the basis that any adverse party against which the UK might be engaged will itself scrupulously observe those obligations. If an adverse party makes serious and deliberate attacks, in violation of Article 51 or Article 52 against the civilian population or civilians or against civilian objects, or, in violation of Articles 53, 54 and 55, on objects or items protected by those Articles, the UK will regard itself as entitled to take measures otherwise prohibited by the Articles in question to the extent that it considers such measures necessary for the sole purpose of compelling the adverse party to cease committing violations under those Articles, but only after formal warning to the adverse party requiring cessation of the violations has been disregarded and then only after a decision taken at the highest level of government.' UK Additional Protocol Ratification Statement, para. (m).

[144] In ratifying Additional Protocol I, France did not reserve in relation to Art. 51(6). It did, however, make a statement in relation to Art. 51(8) that appears to be intended

their position *vis-à-vis* Article 51(6) of Additional Protocol I and whether that instrument is applicable in the conflict in question.[145]

2. The International Criminal Tribunal for the Former Yugoslavia has held that reprisals against civilians violate customary international law.[146] However, commentators and States contest the Tribunal's assertion with respect to customary status.[147] Additionally, in its Customary IHL Study, the International Committee of the Red Cross concludes that, because of contrary practice, a customary rule prohibiting reprisal attacks on civilians has yet to crystallize.[148] Application of this Rule is accordingly limited to those States that are Party to Additional Protocol I and have not reserved on the issue.

3. The concept of belligerent reprisal does not exist in non-international armed conflict. Therefore, a rule setting forth a prohibition on conducting attacks against already protected persons and objects would be superfluous.

Rule 48 – Weapons review

(a) **All States are required to ensure that the cyber means of warfare that they acquire or use comply with the rules of the law of armed conflict that bind the State.**

(b) **States that are Party to Additional Protocol I are required in the study, development, acquisition, or adoption of a new means or method of cyber warfare to determine whether its employment would, in some or all circumstances, be prohibited by that Protocol or by any other rule of international law applicable to that State.**

1. The terms 'means' and 'method' of cyber warfare are defined in Rule 41.

2. *Lit.* (a) of this Rule derives from the general duty of compliance with the law of armed conflict as reflected in Article 1 of the 1907 Hague Convention IV and Common Article 1 of the Geneva Conventions. The International Group of Experts agreed that in the case of means of

---

to retain the possibility of reprisals against civilians. French Additional Protocol Ratification Statement, para. 11, *available at* www.icrc.org/ihl.nsf/NORM/D8041036B40EBC44C1256A34004897B2?OpenDocument.

[145] The UK position is set out in UK Manual, paras. 16.19.1, 16.19.2.

[146] *Prosecutor* v. *Kupreškić*, Case No. IT-95-16-T, Trial Chamber judgment, paras. 527–33 (Int'l Crim. Trib. for the Former Yugoslavia 14 January 2000).

[147] *See* US Commander's Handbook, para. 6.2.4; Yoram Dinstein, The Conduct of Hostilities under the Law of International Armed Conflict 260 (2nd ed. 2010).

[148] ICRC Customary IHL Study, commentary accompanying Rule 146.

warfare, this limited obligation has matured through State practice into customary international law.[149] *Lit.* (b) is based on Article 36 of Additional Protocol I. The International Group of Experts was divided as to whether it represented customary international law and therefore it is represented in this Manual as an obligation applicable only to States Party to that treaty, which applies only to international armed conflict.

3.   As regards *lit.* (a), the International Group of Experts was divided over whether there is an affirmative duty to conduct a formal legal review of means of warfare prior to their use. The majority took the position that this obligation is satisfied so long as a State has taken steps to ensure that their means of warfare are in accordance with the law of armed conflict. For instance, the advice of a legal advisor at the relevant level of command was deemed by these Experts to suffice in lieu of a formal legal review.

4.   *Lit.* (a) only requires States to take those steps necessary to ensure means of cyber warfare they acquire or use comply with the law of armed conflict. The International Group of Experts was divided over whether the obligation extends to methods of warfare. Some argued that it does, whereas others suggested that, although methods of warfare must comply with the law of armed conflict generally, there is no affirmative duty to take the specific step of conducting a formal legal review to ensure such compliance.

5.   The obligations set forth in *lit.* (b) are broader, encompassing the study, development, acquisition, and adoption of new means and methods of cyber warfare. Further, the paragraph requires the review to address whether employment of the means or method will comply with international law generally, not only the law of armed conflict. For instance, the review would necessarily include assessment of any applicable arms control regime.

6.   Article 36 prescribes no particular methodology for conducting the reviews required by *lit.* (b), nor is there any obligation for a State to disclose the review.[150]

7.   With regard to both *lit.* (a) and *lit.* (b), the fact that a supplying State has already reviewed a method or means of cyber warfare does not relieve an acquiring State of its obligation to consider the means by reference to its own international law obligations. In complying with this obligation, the acquiring State may be assisted by a legal assessment conducted by the supplying

---

[149]   US COMMANDER'S HANDBOOK, para. 5.3.4; UK MANUAL, paras. 6.20–6.20.1; CANADIAN MANUAL, para. 530; GERMAN MANUAL, para. 405; AMW MANUAL, Rule 9. *See also* US AIR FORCE, LEGAL REVIEW OF WEAPONS AND CYBER CAPABILITIES, AIR FORCE INSTRUCTION 51–402 (27 July 2011).

[150]   *See* ICRC ADDITIONAL PROTOCOLS COMMENTARY, para. 1470 (discussing disclosure).

State, but retains the obligation to satisfy itself as to compliance with the legal rules by which it is bound. A determination by any State that the employment of a weapon is prohibited or permitted does not bind other States.[151]

8. The determination of the legality of a means or method of cyber warfare must be made by reference to its normal expected use at the time the evaluation is conducted.[152] If a means or method of cyber warfare is being developed for immediate operational use, the lawyer who advises the commander planning to use it will be responsible for advising whether the cyber weapon and the intended method of using it accord with the State's international law obligations. Any significant changes to means or methods necessitate a new legal review. A State is not required to foresee or analyse possible misuses of a weapon, for almost any weapon can be misused in ways that would be prohibited.

9. For example, consider a cyber capability to degrade an adversary's land-based radar system. The software that causes the degradation of the radar signal is the weapon and requires a legal review, as does the rootkit required to enable the weapon to operate. Likewise, any significant changes to them require a new legal review. Minor changes that do not affect their operational effects, such as testing or debugging to eliminate unwanted functionality, would not trigger the requirement for a subsequent review.

10. Legal reviews of a means or method of cyber warfare should consider such matters as whether: (i) it is, in its normal or intended circumstances of use, of a nature to cause superfluous injury or unnecessary suffering (Rule 42); (ii) it is by nature indiscriminate (Rule 43); (iii) its use is intended or may be expected to breach law of armed conflict rules pertaining to the environment to which the State is Party;[153] and (iv) there is any ad hoc provision of treaty or customary international law that directly addresses it.

11. Information that might support a legal review includes a technical description of the cyber means or method, the nature of the generic targets it

---

[151] ICRC ADDITIONAL PROTOCOLS COMMENTARY, para. 1469.

[152] ICRC ADDITIONAL PROTOCOLS COMMENTARY, para. 1466.

[153] If the State is Party to the Environmental Modification Convention 1976, and the cyber means or method of warfare is intended to make use of environmental modification techniques, that would breach its obligations under that convention. Convention on the Prohibition of Military or Any Hostile Use of Environmental Modification Techniques, 18 May 1977, 1108 U.N.T.S. 151. For a State Party to Additional Protocol I or a State that otherwise accepts those rules, a cyber means or method of warfare that is intended, or may be expected, to cause widespread, long-term, and severe damage to the natural environment would breach Arts. 35(3) and 55 of Additional Protocol I and customary international law respectively.

is to engage, its intended effect on the target, how it will achieve this effect, its precision and ability to distinguish the target system from any civilian systems with which it is networked, and the scope of intended effects. Such information can come from sources like test results, reports as to past operational use, computer modelling, operational analysis, concepts of use documents, and general information regarding its employment.

SECTION 6: CONDUCT OF ATTACKS

Rule 49 – Indiscriminate attacks

Cyber attacks that are not directed at a lawful target, and consequently are of a nature to strike lawful targets and civilians or civilian objects without distinction, are prohibited.

1.   This Rule is based on Article 51(4)(a) of Additional Protocol I and is considered customary international law.[154] It applies in both international and non-international armed conflict.[155]

2.   Note that Article 51(4)(b) and (c) of Additional Protocol I also provides that attacks employing means or methods of warfare that cannot be directed, and those having uncontrollable effects, are indiscriminate and therefore prohibited. These issues are dealt with in Rule 43 and its accompanying Commentary.

3.   Rule 49 prohibits cyber attacks (Rule 30) that are not directed at a member of the armed forces, a member of an organized armed group, a civilian directly participating in hostilities, or a military objective, that is, a 'lawful target'. The cyber weapon in question is capable of being directed at a lawful target (and is therefore not prohibited by Rule 43), but the attacker fails so to direct it. For example, consider a cyber attack in which a malicious script is embedded in a file containing a digital image posted on a public website. When a vulnerable computer's browser downloads that file, the script runs and the computer is damaged. The attacker knows that both military and civilian users access the web server. The placement of the malware is indiscriminate because opening the image will infect the computer of anyone accessing the website who

---

[154] US COMMANDER'S HANDBOOK para. 5.3.2; UK MANUAL, paras. 5.23–5.23.2; CANADIAN MANUAL, paras. 416, 613; GERMAN MANUAL, para. 404; AMW MANUAL, Rule 13; ICRC CUSTOMARY IHL STUDY, Rules 11–12; SAN REMO MANUAL, Rule 42(b).

[155] Amended Mines Protocol, Art. 3(8); ICRC CUSTOMARY IHL STUDY, commentary accompanying Rule 11; NIAC MANUAL, para. 2.1.1.3.

has a computing device that is vulnerable to that attack vector. A discriminate means of warfare has been employed indiscriminately.

4.   Although not expressly stated in this Rule, the International Group of Experts unanimously agreed that cyber attacks employing means or methods of warfare that in the circumstances cannot be directed at a specific military objective, or which in the circumstances produce effects that cannot be limited as required by the law of armed conflict, are prohibited. This conclusion is based on Article 51(4)(b) and (c), which the Experts agreed accurately reflects customary international law. They noted that weapons that are otherwise discriminate might be incapable of being employed discriminately in certain circumstances. For example, consider malware designed to disable a certain type of SCADA system (and thereby damage systems which rely upon it) upon installation by using a flash drive. Use on a military base where its effects will be limited to the targeted system is discriminate. However, if the malware is delivered via flash drives left at various cyber conferences in the hope the drives will eventually be used at a military base (but it will also more than likely disable civilian systems), its use would violate this Rule.

5.   Indiscriminate attacks under this Rule must be distinguished from attacks intentionally directed against civilians and civilian objects (Rules 32 and 37). Whether an attack is indiscriminate should be assessed on a case-by-case basis. Factors to consider include: the nature of the system into which the malware is introduced or which is placed at risk; the nature of the method or means of cyber warfare employed; the extent and quality of planning; and any evidence of indifference on the part of the cyber operator planning, approving, or conducting the attack.[156]

6.   Indiscriminate attacks, like direct attacks against civilians and civilian objects, need not be successful to be unlawful. For instance, an indiscriminate cyber attack launched into a network serving both civilian and military users without regard for whom it will affect may be blocked by the network's firewall. The fact that the attack was launched suffices to violate this Rule.

7.   Rule 49 must be distinguished from Rule 50. Whereas the former prohibits attacks that are indiscriminate because they are not aimed, the latter prohibits another form of indiscriminate attacks, those that are

---

[156] *See, e.g., Martić* judgment, paras. 462–3 (reviewing the specific circumstance of an attack with cluster munitions into a densely populated area and finding that an indiscriminate attack occurred); UK Manual, para. 5.23.3; AMW Manual, commentary accompanying Rule 13(b).

aimed at cyber infrastructure that contains both military objectives and civilian cyber assets in situations in which the military objectives alone could have been targeted.

Rule 50 – Clearly separated and distinct military objectives

A cyber attack that treats as a single target a number of clearly discrete cyber military objectives in cyber infrastructure primarily used for civilian purposes is prohibited if to do so would harm protected persons or objects.

1.   This Rule is based on Article 51(5)(a) of Additional Protocol I. It reflects customary international law in both international and non-international armed conflict.[157]

2.   The attacks proscribed by the Rule violate the law of armed conflict because they are indiscriminate. In traditional armed conflict, this principle precludes targeting an area in which civilian objects and military objectives are comingled when it is feasible to individually attack the military targets therein. With regard to cyber operations, the prohibition should not be conceived of in the physical sense, and thus territorially. As an example, military computers may be connected to a network that predominantly hosts civilian computers. Assume that the military computers can be attacked individually (for instance, if their IP addresses are known). However, the attacker chooses a method of cyber attack that will neutralize the military computers, but also damage the civilian ones. This method of cyber attack would violate Rule 50 because the attacker treats the military computers as a single target and by doing so harms the civilian computers when it was not necessary to do so. Similarly, consider two military servers located in a server farm that is part of a large data centre primarily hosting servers for civilian use. An attack that shuts down the entire server farm's cooling system in order to overheat and damage the servers it contains would violate this Rule if it is technically feasible to use cyber means to just shut down the cooling subsystems of the server clusters containing the two military servers.

---

[157] Amended Mines Protocol, Art. 3(9); US COMMANDER'S HANDBOOK, para. 5.3.2; UK MANUAL, para. 5.23.2; CANADIAN MANUAL, para. 416; GERMAN MANUAL, para. 456; AMW MANUAL, commentary accompanying Rule 13(c); NIAC MANUAL, commentary accompanying 2.1.1.3; ICRC CUSTOMARY IHL STUDY, Rule 13.

3. The International Group of Experts took the position that this Rule applies even when the attack is proportionate (Rule 51). In other words, a cyber attack against a dual-use system will be unlawful whenever the individual military components thereof could have been attacked separately. In much the same way that area bombing is impermissible in an air attack when attacking individual targets located in a concentration of civilians, cyber attacks must be directed, if feasible, against individual military components of a cyber infrastructure consisting of military and civilian components.

Rule 51 – Proportionality

A cyber attack that may be expected to cause incidental loss of civilian life, injury to civilians, damage to civilian objects, or a combination thereof, which would be excessive in relation to the concrete and direct military advantage anticipated is prohibited.

1. This Rule is based on Articles 51(5)(b) and 57(2)(iii) of Additional Protocol I.[158] It is often referred to as the rule of proportionality, although as a technical legal matter the issue is one of excessiveness, not proportionality. This principle is generally accepted as customary international law applicable in international and non-international armed conflicts.[159]

2. As stated in Rules 32 and 37, it is unlawful to make civilians or civilian objects the object of cyber attack. By contrast, this Rule deals with situations in which civilians or civilian objects are incidentally harmed, that is, they are not the intended objects of attack. Incidental death or injury to civilians, or damage or destruction of civilian objects, is often termed 'collateral damage'. As this Rule makes clear, the fact that civilians or civilian objects suffer harm during a cyber attack on a lawful military objective does not necessarily render said attack unlawful *per se*. Rather, the lawfulness of an attack in which collateral damage results depends on the relationship between the harm an attacker reasonably expects to incidentally cause to civilians and civilian objects and the military advantage that he or she anticipates as a result of the attack.

---

[158] *See also* Second Cultural Property Protocol, Art. 7; Amended Mines Protocol, Art. 3(8); Mines Protocol, Art. 3(3).

[159] US COMMANDER'S HANDBOOK, para. 5.3.3; UK MANUAL, paras. 5.23.2, 15.15.1; CANADIAN MANUAL at GL-5; AMW MANUAL, Rule 14 and accompanying commentary; NIAC MANUAL, para. 2.1.1.4; ICRC CUSTOMARY IHL STUDY, Rule 14; ICRC ADDITIONAL PROTOCOLS COMMENTARY, para. 4772.

3.   This Rule envisages a situation where a cyber attack on a military objective will result in harm to civilian objects, including computers, networks, or infrastructure, or to civilians, that could not be avoided pursuant to Rules 52 to 58. It should be noted in this regard that cyber attacks on military objectives are sometimes launched via civilian communications cables, satellites, or other civilian infrastructure. When this is the case, they might harm that infrastructure. In other words, a cyber attack can cause collateral damage during transit and because of the cyber attack itself. Both forms of collateral damage are to be considered in application of this Rule.

4.   As an example of the operation of this Rule, consider the case of a cyber attack on the Global Positioning System. The system is dual-use and thus a lawful target. However, depriving the civilian users of key information such as navigational data is likely to cause damage to, for instance, merchant vessels and civil aircraft relying on Global Positioning System guidance. If this expected harm is excessive in relation to the anticipated military advantage of the operation, the operation would be forbidden.[160]

5.   Cyber operations may cause inconvenience, irritation, stress, or fear. Such consequences do not qualify as collateral damage because they do not amount to 'incidental loss of civilian life, injury to civilians, damage to civilian objects'.[161] Such effects are not to be considered when applying this Rule. The International Group of Experts agreed that the notion of 'damage to civilian objects' might, in certain circumstances, include deprivation of functionality (Rule 30). When this is the case, it is to be considered in a proportionality evaluation.

6.   Collateral damage can consist of both direct and indirect effects. Direct effects are 'the immediate, first order consequences [of a cyber attack], unaltered by intervening events or mechanisms'. By contrast, indirect effects of a cyber attack comprise 'the delayed and/or displaced second-, third-, and higher-order consequences of action, created through intermediate events or mechanisms'.[162] The collateral damage factored into the proportionality calculation includes any indirect effects that should be expected by those individuals planning, approving, or executing a cyber attack. For example, if Global Positioning Satellite data is blocked or otherwise disrupted, accidents involving transportation

---

[160]   Rome Statute, Art. 8(2)(b)(iv).
[161]   AMW MANUAL, commentary accompanying Rule 14.
[162]   JOINT CHIEFS OF STAFF, JOINT PUBLICATION 3–60: JOINT TARGETING I-10 (2007).

systems relying on the data can be expected in the short term, at least until adoption of other navigational aids and techniques. Similarly, an attacker may decide to insert malware into a specific military computer system that will not only disable that system, but also likely spread to a limited number of civilian computer systems, thereby causing the type of damage qualifying as collateral damage for the purposes of this Rule. These effects, if they are or should have been expected, must be considered in the proportionality analysis.[163] By contrast, if the malware is unexpectedly or unforeseeably transferred via, for instance, a portable storage device into civilian systems, the ensuing consequences will not be considered when assessing compliance with this Rule.

7. Only collateral damage that is excessive to the anticipated concrete and direct military advantage is prohibited. The term 'excessive' is not defined in international law. However, as stated in the AMW Manual, excessiveness 'is not a matter of counting civilian casualties and comparing them to the number of enemy combatants that have been put out of action'.[164] The amount of harm done to civilians and their property in the abstract is not the primary issue. Instead, the question is whether the harm that may be expected is excessive relative to the anticipated military advantage given the circumstances prevailing at the time. Despite an assertion to the contrary in the ICRC Additional Protocols Commentary,[165] the majority of the International Group of Experts took the position that extensive collateral damage may be legal if the anticipated concrete and direct military advantage is sufficiently great. Conversely, even slight damage may be unlawful if the military advantage expected is negligible.

8. The term 'concrete and direct' removes mere speculation from the equation of military advantage. While the advantage from a military action is seldom precisely predictable, requiring the anticipated advantage to be concrete and direct obliges decision-makers to anticipate a real and quantifiable benefit.[166] The commentary to Article 51 of Additional Protocol I states that 'the expression "concrete and direct" was intended

[163] This understanding of the Rule is supported by the US Commander's Handbook, which states that indirect effects of an attack may be one of the factors included when weighing anticipated incidental injury or death to protected persons. US COMMANDER'S HANDBOOK, para. 8.11.4.

[164] AMW MANUAL, commentary accompanying Rule 14.

[165] ICRC ADDITIONAL PROTOCOLS COMMENTARY, para. 1980.

[166] UK MANUAL, para. 5.33.3 (as amended); CANADIAN MANUAL, para. 415. The AMW Manual observes that the 'term "concrete and direct" refers to military advantage that is

to show that the advantage concerned should be substantial and relatively close, and that advantages which are hardly perceptible and those which would only appear in the long term should be disregarded'.[167]

9.   When determining the concrete and direct military advantage anticipated, it is generally accepted as customary international law that the 'military advantage anticipated from an attack is intended to refer to the advantage anticipated from the attack considered as a whole and not only from isolated or particular parts of the attack'.[168] For instance, a cyber operation could occur in conjunction with another form of military action, such as a cyber attack on an installation's air defence radar during conventional strikes on that installation. In this case, the concrete and direct military advantage to be considered with regard to the cyber attack would be that anticipated from the entire attack, not just the effect on the air defences. Similarly, a single cyber attack might be planned to convince the enemy that a particular target set is going to be the focus of forthcoming attacks, thereby causing the enemy to misdirect its defensive measures. The actual focus of the main attack lies elsewhere. Any expected collateral damage from the first cyber attack must be assessed in light of the anticipated military advantage deriving from the main attack.

10.   It is important to note that the standard for this Rule is prospective. The use of the words 'expected' and 'anticipated' indicates that its application requires an assessment of the reasonableness of the determination at the time the attack in question was planned, approved, or executed.[169] In making such determinations, all apparently reliable

---

clearly identifiable and, in many cases, quantifiable'. AMW Manual, commentary accompanying Rule 14.

[167] ICRC Additional Protocols Commentary, para. 2209.

[168] The text is drawn from the UK Additional Protocols Ratification Statement, para. (i). Australia, Germany, Italy, and the Netherlands have stated similar Understandings, *available at* www.icrc.org/ihl.nsf/WebSign?ReadForm&id=740&ps=P. *See also* UK Manual, para. 5.33.5; Canadian Manual, para. 415; German Manual, para. 444; ICRC Customary IHL Study, commentary accompanying Rule 14; NIAC Manual, commentary accompanying para. 2.1.1.4. For the purposes of international criminal law, the Rome Statute employs the term 'overall' in referring to military advantage. Rome Statute, Art. 8 (2)(b)(iv). Footnote 36 of Art. 8(2)(b)(iv) of the Rome Statute Elements of the Crimes states, 'The expression "concrete and direct overall military advantage" refers to a military advantage that is foreseeable by the perpetrator at the relevant time.'

[169] *See Galić* Trial Chamber judgment, paras. 58–60; *Trial of Wilhelm List and Others (The Hostages Trial)*, Case No. 47, VIII Law Reports of Trials of War Criminals 34, 69 (UN War Crimes Commission 1948) (setting forth 'Rendulic Rule'); AMW Manual, commentary accompanying Rule 14.

information that is reasonably available must be considered.[170] The Rule is not to be applied with the benefit of hindsight.

11. Expectation and anticipation do not require absolute certainty of occurrence. By the same token, the mere possibility of occurrence does not suffice to attribute expectation or anticipation to those planning, approving, or executing a cyber attack. The terms 'expected' and 'anticipated' allow for a 'fairly broad margin of judgment'.[171]

12. There was a discussion among the International Group of Experts over whether and to what extent uncertainty as to collateral damage affects application of the Rule. The issue is of particular relevance in the context of cyber attacks in that it is sometimes very difficult to reliably determine likely collateral damage in advance. A minority of the Experts took the position that the lower the probability of collateral damage, the less the military advantage needed to justify the operation through application of the rule of proportionality. The majority of Experts rejected this approach on the basis that once collateral damage is expected, it must be calculated into the proportionality analysis as such; it is not appropriate to consider the degree of certainty as to possible collateral damage. The attacker either reasonably expects it or the possibility of collateral damage is merely speculative, in which case it would not be considered in assessing proportionality.

13. The International Criminal Tribunal for the Former Yugoslavia addressed the question of the reasonableness of the ultimate proportionality decision in the *Galić* judgment. The Trial Chamber held 'In determining whether an attack was proportionate, it is necessary to examine whether a reasonably well-informed person in the circumstances of the actual perpetrator, making reasonable use of the information available to him or her, could have expected excessive civilian casualties to result from the attack.'[172]

---

[170] UK Manual, para. 5.20.4 (as amended); Canadian Manual, para. 418; NIAC Manual, commentary accompanying para. 2.1.1.4. *See also* UK Additional Protocols Ratification Statement, para. (c): 'Military commanders and others responsible for planning, deciding upon, or executing attacks necessarily have to reach decisions on the basis of their assessment of the information from all sources which is reasonably available to them at the relevant time.' Austria, Belgium, Canada, Italy, the Netherlands, New Zealand, and Spain made similar statements, *available at* www.icrc.org/ihl.nsf/WebSign?ReadForm&id=740&ps=P.

[171] ICRC Additional Protocols Commentary, para. 2210.

[172] *Galić* Trial Chamber judgment, para. 58.

14. Sparing one's own forces or capabilities was considered by a minority of the International Group of Experts to be a factor when performing a proportionality calculation. Consider a situation in which an attacker decides not to map the 'cyber battle space' for fear that doing so might reveal information that could enhance an enemy counterattack. The majority of the International Group of Experts rejected the premise that the maintenance of one's own forces and capabilities in this situation is appropriate for inclusion in the calculation of military advantage. Instead, they took the position that such considerations are only appropriate when evaluating feasibility in the precautions in attack context (Rules 52 to 58).

15. This Rule must be clearly distinguished from the requirement to take precautions in attack (Rules 52 to 58), which requires an attacker to take steps to minimize civilian harm regardless of whether expected collateral damage is excessive in relation to the military advantage anticipated.

SECTION 7: PRECAUTIONS

1. As noted in Article 49(3) of Additional Protocol I, the provisions on precautions 'apply to any land, air or sea warfare which may affect the civilian population, individual civilians or civilian objects on land. They further apply to all attacks from the sea or from the air against objectives on land but do not otherwise affect the rules of international law applicable in armed conflict at sea or in the air.' Therefore, the Rules of this section apply to any operation having effects on land.

2. The generally required standard under this section is 'feasibility'. There is a different standard for cyber operations at sea or in the air that are not directed against land-based targets, but which may have effects on the civilian population.[173] Article 57(4) of Additional Protocol I, which expressly relates to military operations at sea or in the air, states that 'all reasonable' rather than 'all feasible' precautions must be taken. This is reflected in the US Commander's Handbook, which uses the term 'all reasonable precautions'.[174] The ICRC commentary to the provision states

---

[173] ICRC ADDITIONAL PROTOCOLS COMMENTARY, para. 2230.
[174] US COMMANDER'S HANDBOOK, para. 8.3.1.

that the term 'reasonable' is to be interpreted as 'a little less far-reaching' than 'all feasible precautions'.[175]

3.   Consider the case of a cyber attack against a warship. According to the majority of the International Group of Experts, the necessary precautions would not encompass a mapping of the entire cyber infrastructure of which the warship is a part. Even though such mapping might be technically possible and militarily feasible, these Experts concluded that it would not be reasonable to undertake the mapping because the primary focus of the operation is a target beyond land territory. The minority of the International Group of Experts concluded that the distinction is so highly nuanced as to be of little practical relevance; the applicable legal regime is operationally the same.[176] This is the current International Committee of the Red Cross position. In the example above, these Experts maintained that the attacker must perform those precautionary measures that are both technically possible and militarily feasible.

4.   The duty of the attacker to take precautions is set forth in Rules 52 to 58. The obligations of the party to the conflict defending against attacks are set forth in Rule 59.

Rule 52 – Constant care

During hostilities involving cyber operations, constant care shall be taken to spare the civilian population, individual civilians, and civilian objects.

1.   The Rule is based on Article 57(1) of Additional Protocol I and is considered customary in both international armed conflict and non-international armed conflict.[177]

2.   The notion of hostilities is defined in the Commentary accompanying Rule 22. It is not limited to cyber attacks.[178]

---

[175] ICRC ADDITIONAL PROTOCOLS COMMENTARY, para. 2230.

[176] AMW MANUAL at commentary accompanying Rule 30.

[177] Second Cultural Property Protocol, Art. 7(b); Amended Mines Protocol, Art. 3(10); Mines Protocol, Art. 3(4); US COMMANDER'S HANDBOOK, para. 8.1; UK MANUAL, paras. 5.32 (as amended), 15.15, 15.15.1; GERMAN MANUAL, para. 447; AMW MANUAL, Rules 30, 34, chapeau to sec. G; NIAC MANUAL, para. 2.1.2; ICRC CUSTOMARY IHL STUDY, Rule 15.

[178] UK MANUAL, para. 5.32; ICRC ADDITIONAL PROTOCOLS COMMENTARY, para. 2191. See also ICRC ADDITIONAL PROTOCOLS COMMENTARY, para. 1875 (offering an explanation of the term 'operations').

3.   As used in this Rule, the term 'spare' refers to the broad general duty to 'respect' the civilian population, that is, to consider deleterious effects of military operations on civilians.[179] It supplements the obligation to distinguish between combatants and civilians and between military objectives and civilian objects (Rule 31), the rule of proportionality (Rule 51), and the requirement to take precautions in attack (Rules 52 to 58).

4.   The law of armed conflict does not define the term 'constant care'. The International Group of Experts agreed that in cyber operations, the duty of care requires commanders and all others involved in the operations to be continuously sensitive to the effects of their activities on the civilian population and civilian objects, and to seek to avoid any unnecessary effects thereon.[180]

5.   Use of the word 'constant' denotes that the duty to take care to protect civilians and civilian objects is of a continuing nature throughout all cyber operations; all those involved in the operation must discharge the duty. The law admits of no situation in which, or time when, individuals involved in the planning and execution process may ignore the effects of their operations on civilians or civilian objects.[181] In the cyber context, this requires situational awareness at all times, not merely during the preparatory stage of an operation.

6.   Given the complexity of cyber operations, the high probability of affecting civilian systems, and the sometimes limited understanding of their nature and effects on the part of those charged with approving cyber operations, mission planners should, where feasible, have technical experts available to assist them in determining whether appropriate precautionary measures have been taken.

7.   In light of the duty to respect the civilian population, it is self-evidently unlawful to use the presence of civilians to shield a lawful target from cyber attack or to otherwise shield, favour, or impede military operations. For instance, placing civilians at an electrical generating facility qualifying as a military objective in order to shield it from cyber attack would violate this Rule. This prohibition, set forth in Article 51(7) of the Additional Protocol, reflects customary law.[182] Although the

---

[179] ICRC ADDITIONAL PROTOCOLS COMMENTARY, para. 2191.

[180] UK MANUAL, para. 5.32.1.

[181] AMW MANUAL, commentary accompanying Rule 30.

[182] US COMMANDER'S HANDBOOK, para. 8.3.2; AMW MANUAL, Rule 45; ICRC CUSTOMARY IHL STUDY, Rule 97. *See also* Rome Statute, Art. 8(2)(b)(xxiii). Specific prohibitions on using prisoners of war and civilians protected under Geneva Convention IV exist. Geneva Convention III, Art. 23; Geneva Convention IV, Art. 28

prohibition does not extend to civilian objects in general (as distinct from civilians), it is expressly prohibited to use medical facilities for the purposes of shielding.[183] Extension of the prohibition to the use of medical cyber infrastructure as a shield is reasonable.

Rule 53 – Verification of targets

Those who plan or decide upon a cyber attack shall do everything feasible to verify that the objectives to be attacked are neither civilians nor civilian objects and are not subject to special protection.

1. This Rule is based on Article 57(2)(a)(i) of Additional Protocol I and is accepted as customary international law in both international and non-international armed conflicts.[184]

2. This Rule applies to cyber operations that qualify as an 'attack'. The term 'attack' is defined in Rule 30.

3. An important feature of Rule 53 is its focus on planners and decision-makers. Those who execute cyber attacks may sometimes also be the ones who approve them. In the case of certain attacks, the individual actually executing the attack has the capability to determine the nature of the target and to cancel the operation. This individual is thus in a position to decide whether the attack is to be undertaken and therefore is obligated to exercise his or her capability to verify that the person or object to be attacked is a lawful target. On other occasions, the person executing the attack may not be privy to information as to its character or even the identity of the target. He or she may simply be carrying out instructions to deliver the cyber weapon against a predetermined part of the cyber infrastructure. Under these circumstances, the duty of the individual carrying out the cyber attack would be limited to those measures that are feasible in the circumstances.[185]

4. The limitation to those who plan or decide upon cyber attacks should not be interpreted as relieving others of the obligation to take appropriate steps should information come to their attention that suggests an intended target of a cyber attack is a protected person or object, or that the attack would otherwise be prohibited. For example, assume

---

[183] Additional Protocol I, Art. 12(4).

[184] *Galić* Trial Chamber judgment, para. 58; US COMMANDER'S HANDBOOK, para. 8.1; UK MANUAL, para. 5.32.2 (as amended); CANADIAN MANUAL, para. 417; GERMAN MANUAL, para. 457; AMW MANUAL, Rule 32(a) and chapeau to sec. G; NIAC MANUAL, commentary accompanying para. 2.1.2; ICRC CUSTOMARY IHL STUDY, Rule 16.

[185] AMW MANUAL, commentary accompanying Rule 35.

that a cyber attack is planned and all preparations are completed, including mapping the network and determining the nature of the target system. The attackers are awaiting authorization by the approving authority. Assume further that an operator is continuously monitoring the network. Any material changes in the cyber environment of the proposed target must be relayed to the commander and other relevant personnel as soon as possible.

5.   The obligation to do 'everything feasible' is to be interpreted identically to the obligation to take 'all feasible precautions' in Rule 54. 'Feasible' has been widely interpreted as that which is 'practicable or practically possible, taking into account all circumstances ruling at the time, including humanitarian and military considerations'.[186] In the context of cyber attacks, feasible precautions might include gathering intelligence on the network through mapping or other processes in order to allow those responsible reasonably to determine the attack's likely effects, particularly on the civilian population or civilian objects. There is no obligation to take measures that are not feasible. It may, for example, not be feasible to map the target because doing so will disclose, and thus enable defences against, the intended operation.

6.   When gathering sufficient information to verify the target is not practicable or practically possible, the decision-maker may have to refrain from conducting an attack, or otherwise modify the concept of operations. For instance, if an attacker is unable to gather reliable information as to the nature of a proposed cyber target system, the decision-maker would be obligated to limit the scope of the attack to only those components or capabilities of the system with regard to which there is sufficient information to verify their status as lawful targets.

Rule 54 – Choice of means or methods

Those who plan or decide upon a cyber attack shall take all feasible precautions in the choice of means or methods of warfare employed in such an attack, with a view to avoiding, and in any event to minimizing, incidental injury to civilians, loss of civilian life, and damage to or destruction of civilian objects.

---

[186] Amended Mines Protocol, Art. 3(10); UK Additional Protocols Ratification Statement, para. (b). *See also* US COMMANDER'S HANDBOOK, para. 8.3.1; UK MANUAL, para. 5.32 (as amended); CANADIAN MANUAL at A-4; AMW MANUAL, Rule 1(q); ICRC CUSTOMARY IHL STUDY, commentary accompanying Rule 15.

1.   This Rule is based upon Article 57(2)(a)(ii) of Additional Protocol I. It reflects customary international law and is applicable in international and non-international armed conflicts.[187]

2.   Even if the harm to civilians and civilian objects expected to result during an attack is not excessive relative to the anticipated military advantage, and is therefore in compliance with Rule 51, feasible precautions must be taken to minimize collateral damage. Rule 54 specifically addresses the obligation to consider alternative weapons or tactics to minimize collateral damage to civilians or civilian property. It should be noted that the Rule requires consideration of both cyber and kinetic options for achieving the desired military effect while minimizing collateral damage.

3.   The term 'all feasible precautions' in this Rule has the same meaning as 'everything feasible' in Rule 53 and the Commentary to that Rule applies equally here. In particular, an attacker need not select alternative weapons or tactics that will yield less military advantage to the attacker.

4.   'Means' and 'methods' are defined in Rule 41.[188] With regard to the application of this Rule to those who execute attacks, see the Commentary to Rule 53.

5.   The issue of indirect effects is central to cyber operations because of the interconnectivity of computers, particularly between military and civilian systems. The US Commander's Handbook acknowledges the appropriateness of considering indirect effects as collateral damage.[189] The International Group of Experts agreed with this view. Therefore, a person who is planning or using a cyber means or method must take all feasible precautions to avoid, or at least minimize, indirect as well as direct collateral damage. This obligation affects not only the choice of the cyber means used, but also how it is employed.

6.   To illustrate operation of this Rule, consider the case of an attacker who seeks to insert malware into a closed military network. One method of doing so would involve placing the malware on a thumb drive used by someone working on that closed network. The attacker would have to assess the possibility that the thumb drive might also be used on computers connected to civilian networks and thereby cause collateral

---

[187]   UK MANUAL, paras. 5.32, 5.32.4 (both as amended); CANADIAN MANUAL, para. 417; GERMAN MANUAL, paras. 457, 510; AMW MANUAL, Rule 32(b), chapeau to sec. G; NIAC MANUAL, para. 2.1.2.b; ICRC CUSTOMARY IHL STUDY, Rule 17.

[188]   *See, e.g.*, UK MANUAL, para. 5.32.4. Further, para. 5.32.5 provides a list of factors to be considered when considering the appropriate means or method of attack.

[189]   US COMMANDER'S HANDBOOK, para. 8.11.4.

damage. In such a case, it might be possible to design different malware (means) that will minimize the likelihood of collateral damage. The Stuxnet attack appears to have been planned with this Rule in mind, in that the cyber weapon employed was designed to seek out a specific type of industrial process-control system, operating with a particular combination of hardware and software.

Rule 55 – Precautions as to proportionality

Those who plan or decide upon attacks shall refrain from deciding to launch any cyber attack that may be expected to cause incidental loss of civilian life, injury to civilians, damage to civilian objects or a combination thereof, which would be excessive in relation to the concrete and direct military advantage anticipated.

1. Rule 55 is based on Article 57(2)(a)(iii) of Additional Protocol I. It reflects customary international law and is applicable in international and non-international armed conflicts.[190]

2. This Rule is to be distinguished from Rule 51. Rule 51 sets forth the general rule on proportionality and is rooted in Article 51(5)(b) of Additional Protocol I. Rule 55 merely emphasizes that individuals who plan or decide upon cyber attacks have a continuing personal obligation to assess proportionality. As noted in the Commentary to Rule 53, in many situations an individual executing a cyber attack will be in a position to 'decide upon' it. This is particularly important in the context of Rule 55. For instance, if a cyber operator becomes aware that an attack being executed will unexpectedly result in excessive collateral damage, he or she must terminate the attack. Rule 57 addresses the duty to cancel or suspend attacks when new information becomes available that indicates the attack will violate the rule of proportionality.

3. Rule 55 applies in the same fashion as Rule 51. The Commentary to that Rule applies equally here.

Rule 56 – Choice of targets

For States Party to Additional Protocol I, when a choice is possible between several military objectives for obtaining a similar military advantage, the objective to be selected for cyber attack shall be that the

---

[190] CANADIAN MANUAL, para. 417; GERMAN MANUAL, para. 457; AMW MANUAL, Rule 32(c) and chapeau to sec. G; ICRC CUSTOMARY IHL STUDY, Rule 18.

attack on which may be expected to cause the least danger to civilian lives and to civilian objects.

1.   This Rule is based on Article 57(3) of Additional Protocol I. A substantial majority of the International Group of Experts agreed that this Rule reflects customary international law and is applicable in international and non-international armed conflicts.[191] However, a minority of the Experts took the position that Article 57(3) had not matured into customary international law and therefore this Rule is not binding on States that are not Party to that instrument.

2.   Rule 56 applies to cyber operations that qualify as an 'attack'. The term attack is defined in Rule 30.

3.   In contrast to the other sub-paragraphs of Article 57, Article 57(3) does not specify to whom it is directed. Therefore, Rule 56 has been drafted to apply to all persons who are involved in target selection, approval, and execution of the attack.

4.   Based upon the text of Article 57(3), the International Group of Experts understood the consequences of the danger referred to in this Rule as limited to injury, death, damage, or destruction by the direct or indirect effects of a cyber attack. Damage would, for the majority of the International Group of Experts, include, in certain circumstances, deprivation of functionality (Rule 30).

5.   Whether a choice is possible is a question of fact to be determined in the circumstances ruling at the time. For the Rule to apply the options must be more than mere possibilities; they must be reasonable with regard to such factors as practicality, military viability, and technological prospect of success.

6.   It must be borne in mind that the Rule only applies in the case of targets the attack upon which will yield similar military advantage. The military advantage does not have to be identical qualitatively or quantitatively. Instead, the issue is whether an attack on the alternative target would achieve comparable military effects.[192]

7.   The military advantage is to be determined in light of the operation as a whole and not based solely on that accruing from an individual attack. Thus, even if the alternative attack is likely to occasion less

---

[191] UK Manual, para. 5.32 (as amended); Canadian Manual, para. 716; German Manual, para. 457; AMW Manual, Rule 33, chapeau to sec. G; NIAC Manual, para. 2.1.2d; ICRC Customary IHL Study, Rule 21.
[192] AMW Manual, commentary accompanying Rule 33.

collateral damage, there will be no obligation to undertake it if it would not achieve the military purpose for which the original attack is designed.

8.   For instance, consider a situation in which an attacker seeks to disrupt enemy command and control. One option is to conduct cyber attacks against elements of the dual-use electrical grid on which the enemy's communication system relies. However, such attacks are likely to result in significant, albeit proportional, collateral damage. A second militarily feasible option is to conduct cyber attacks directly against the enemy's command and control network. If the latter would be expected to achieve the desired effect on enemy command and control (the same military advantage), while resulting in less collateral damage, this option must be selected.

Rule 57 – Cancellation or suspension of attack

Those who plan, approve, or execute a cyber attack shall cancel or suspend the attack if it becomes apparent that:

(a) **the objective is not a military one or is subject to special protection; or**

(b) **the attack may be expected to cause, directly or indirectly, incidental loss of civilian life, injury to civilians, damage to civilian objects, or a combination thereof that would be excessive in relation to the concrete and direct military advantage anticipated.**

1.   Rule 57 reflects Article 57(2)(b) of Additional Protocol I. It is customary in character and applies in both international armed conflict and non-international armed conflict.[193]

2.   This Rule applies to cyber operations that qualify as an 'attack'. The term attack is defined in Rule 30.

3.   *Lit.* (a) reflects the fact that the requirement to ensure that protected persons and objects are not attacked applies beyond the planning phase into its execution. It is a corollary to Rule 53, which sets forth a requirement to take feasible measures to verify the status of the target.

4.   *Lit.* (b) is a corollary to Rule 51, which sets forth the general rule of proportionality, and Rule 55, which applies to those who plan or approve attacks. It applies to situations in which, although all necessary precautions have been taken, new information makes it clear that an attack that has been previously decided upon will cause excessive collateral damage.

---

[193]   NIAC MANUAL, para. 2.1.2(c); ICRC CUSTOMARY IHL STUDY, Rule 19.

The interpretation of the terms used in this Rule is identical to that set forth in the Commentary to Rule 51.

5. The practicality of suspending or cancelling an attack is case-specific. For instance, in some cases, such as the placement of a logic bomb as part of a rootkit, there may be many opportunities to cancel or suspend an attack. Duration of the cyber attack itself, which can range from seconds to months, can also determine the attacker's ability to suspend or cancel.

6. The requirement of 'constant care' in Rule 52 implies a duty to take 'all feasible measures' to determine whether an attack should be cancelled or suspended. An example is monitoring the operation.

7. The notion of facts 'becoming apparent' is not entirely passive. Rather, an attacker who initiates a cyber attack has a duty to monitor the attack as long as it is feasible to do so. Some cyber attacks may be difficult to continuously monitor, thus making it practically difficult to know whether to cancel or suspend them. This would heighten the degree of scrutiny that is merited during the planning and decision phases of the attack.

8. Consider a case in which, before the initiation of hostilities, State A distributes rootkits in a segment of the military communication network of State B. After hostilities have commenced, a cyber operation to activate the logic bombs on board these rootkits is approved. In the course of this operation, the rootkits' sniffer component detects that State B has recently connected its emergency services communication system to its military communication network, thereby raising the issue of proportionality. State A must suspend its cyber attack until it can satisfy itself that the attack would be proportionate, for example by conducting further reconnaissance in order to ascertain the likely harm to the civilian population that will be caused by the disabling of the emergency services communication system.

Rule 58 – Warnings

Effective advance warning shall be given of cyber attacks that may affect the civilian population unless circumstances do not permit.

1. This Rule derives from Article 57(2)(c) of Additional Protocol I and Article 26 of the Hague Regulations. The International Group of Experts agreed that it is reflective of customary international law applicable in international armed conflicts.[194]

---

[194] UK MANUAL, para. 5.32.8; CANADIAN MANUAL, para. 420; GERMAN MANUAL, paras. 447, 453, 457; AMW MANUAL, Rule 37 and accompanying commentary; ICRC CUSTOMARY IHL STUDY, Rule 20.

2.   The International Group of Experts agreed that this Rule extends to non-international armed conflicts as a matter of customary international law, although they acknowledged the existence of arguments that its application was limited during such conflicts to certain treaty obligations.[195]

3.   Rule 58 applies only to cyber attacks as defined in Rule 30; it does not apply to cyber operations falling short of that level. Additionally, it does not apply to situations in which civilian objects will be damaged or destroyed without the civilian population being placed at risk. This point is especially important in the cyber context since cyber attacks will often damage civilian cyber infrastructure without risking harm to persons.

4.   The law of armed conflict does not define the term 'affect' as used in Article 57(2)(c) of Additional Protocol I. In light of the limitation of the Article's application to attacks and the reference to 'loss of civilian life [and] injury to civilians' in other aspects of the requirement to take precautions in attack (Rules 54 to 57), the majority of the International Group of Experts concluded that the Rule applies only in cases where civilians are at risk of injury or death. The minority took a broader approach by noting the requirement to take precautions to 'spare' the civilian population in Rule 52. All the Experts agreed that effects that consisted of mere inconvenience, irritation, stress, or fear to civilians would not meet the threshold of this Rule.[196]

5.   For the purposes of the Rule, 'effective' means that the intended recipient is likely to receive the warning and understand it in sufficient time to be able to act.[197] Cyber means may be an effective way of delivering a warning of both cyber and kinetic attacks. Other warning techniques may also be effective in giving warning of a cyber attack. The determination of whether a warning is likely to be effective depends on the attendant circumstances.

6.   Warnings may be conveyed through the enemy if it is reasonable to conclude in the circumstances that the enemy will warn its population. For instance, if dual-use cyber infrastructure is to be attacked, the attacking force may elect to warn the enemy of the impending attack

---

[195] For States Parties, Art. 3(11) of the Amended Mine Protocol sets forth a warning requirement in non-international armed conflict with respect to, inter alia, booby traps (Rule 44). Similarly, warning requirements exist with regard to cultural property (Rule 82) for States Party to the Second Cultural Property Protocol, Arts. 6(d), 13(2)(c)(ii). *See also* AMW MANUAL, Rule 96.
[196] AMW MANUAL, commentary accompanying Rule 37.
[197] *See* UK MANUAL, para. 5.32.8.

on the assumption that the enemy will warn the civilian population to take steps to minimize any expected collateral damage. However, if it is unreasonable to conclude the enemy will do so (perhaps because the enemy wants to use affected civilians and civilian objects as shields), such a warning will not suffice. Instead, the attacker would need to directly warn the civilian population itself, subject to the conditions set forth in this Commentary.

7. The means of warning need only be effective; there is no requirement that the means chosen be the most effective available. For instance, a party to the conflict may intend to attack a service provider that serves both military and civilian users. The attacker may elect to provide notice of the impending attack via national news media rather than by sending text messages to each civilian user. Even though the technique might be a more effective means of warning, notification through the media would be sufficiently effective to meet the requirements of this Rule.

8. The phrase 'unless circumstances do not permit' reflects the fact that warnings can prejudice an attack.[198] When cyber attacks require surprise, warnings do not have to be given. For example, surprise may be necessary to ensure that the enemy does not mount effective cyber defences against an attack. Similarly, surprise may be necessary to ensure the enemy does not pre-empt an attack by striking first at the attacker's cyber assets. Consider, for example, a cyber operation involving placement of a kill-switch into the target computer's control system, to be activated on the occurrence of some future event or after the passage of a specified period. A warning that would give the enemy an opportunity to locate and neutralize the device need not be given (or may be general). Surprise might also be necessary for force protection. As an example, a warning could allow the enemy to monitor the cyber attack such that it will be able to strike back. Equally, the cyber attack may form part of a broader military operation and advance warning may expose troops involved to greater risk. Given the current state of technology, the likelihood of warnings being feasible in the cyber context is low.

9. Warnings of cyber attacks, or cyber warnings of kinetic attacks, may have a general character. An example would be a warning that cyber attacks are to be conducted against dual-use electrical generation facilities throughout enemy territory without specifying precise targets.

---

[198] UK MANUAL para. 5.32.8; CANADIAN MANUAL, para. 420; AMW MANUAL, commentary accompanying Rule 37; ICRC ADDITIONAL PROTOCOLS COMMENTARY, para. 2223.

10.   A party to the conflict may issue a warning as a ruse, that is, in order to mislead the enemy (Rule 61). For instance, a false announcement of an attack affecting dual-use systems might prove militarily useful in causing the enemy to take its military assets off-line. However, even though ruses of war are not prohibited in this regard, they are unlawful if they have the effect of influencing the population to disregard future valid warnings of attack.

Rule 59 – Precautions against the effects of cyber attacks

The parties to an armed conflict shall, to the maximum extent feasible, take necessary precautions to protect the civilian population, individual civilians, and civilian objects under their control against the dangers resulting from cyber attacks.

1.   This Rule is based on Article 58(c) of Additional Protocol I. It reflects customary international law applicable in international armed conflicts.[199]

2.   The majority of the International Group of Experts took the position that the Rule's application was limited to international armed conflict. These Experts doubted that international law would impose a general obligation on a State to take actions to protect its own population from attacks during a non-international armed conflict; any decision to do so would be a matter within its discretion. A minority of the Experts would extend application of the Rule to non-international armed conflicts.[200]

3.   The obligation to take precautions under this Rule differs from that under Rules 52 to 58 insofar as this Rule relates to precautions against the effects of cyber attacks, that is, to 'passive precautions' that must be taken by the parties to the conflict in anticipation of the possibility of cyber attacks. In other words, whereas Rules 52 to 58 set forth an attacker's obligations as to precautions, Rule 59 addresses those of a defender. Examples of passive precautions include segregating military from civilian cyber infrastructure; segregating computer systems on which critical civilian infrastructure depends from the Internet; backing up important civilian data; making advance arrangements to ensure the timely repair

---

[199] US COMMANDER'S HANDBOOK, para. 8.3; UK MANUAL, paras. 5.36–5.36.2; CANADIAN MANUAL, para. 421; GERMAN MANUAL, para. 513; AMW MANUAL, Rules 42–5; ICRC CUSTOMARY IHL STUDY, Rule 22.

[200] ICRC CUSTOMARY IHL STUDY, Rule 22. *See also* the obligation to take passive precautions with respect to cultural property. Second Cultural Property Protocol, Art. 8; AMW MANUAL, chapeau to sec. H; NIAC MANUAL, para. 2.3.7 (placement of military objectives).

of important computer systems; digitally recording important cultural or spiritual objects to facilitate reconstruction in the event of their destruction; and using anti-virus measures to protect civilian systems that might suffer damage or destruction during an attack on military cyber infrastructure.

4. Not all sub-paragraphs of Article 58 of Additional Protocol I have been incorporated into this Rule since Article 58(c), which this Rule reflects, captures the totality of the requirement to take passive precautions; it is a 'catch-all' provision that encompasses the requirements set forth in the other sub-paragraphs. The omission of the remaining sub-paragraphs of Article 58 should therefore not be interpreted as implying that the obligation to take passive precautions is in any way diminished in the case of cyber attacks.

5. Note that Article 58(c) refers to protection against the 'dangers resulting from military operations', while Rule 59 limits applicability to 'attacks'. All members of the International Group of Experts agreed that precautions against cyber attacks were encompassed in the Rule. The majority, however, were unwilling to extend its application to all cyber operations on two grounds. First, these Experts maintained that Article 58 applies only to attacks, as indicated by the title of the Article in Additional Protocol I. Second, even if Article 58 is meant to apply to all operations, they took the position that no equivalent customary law exists. The minority took the contrary position on the basis that Article 58(c) refers to 'operations' and that therefore the norm should be understood in its broader sense.

6. Passive precautionary obligations are subject to the caveat 'to the maximum extent feasible'. The term 'maximum extent' emphasizes the importance of taking the requisite measures. It does not imply, however, the existence of an obligation to do everything that, though theoretically possible, is not practically possible.[201] Indeed, the ICRC commentary to Article 58 notes 'it is clear that precautions should not go beyond the point where the life of the population would become difficult or even impossible'.[202] As to the meaning of the word 'feasible' for the purposes of this Manual, see the Commentary accompanying Rule 53.

7. It may not always be feasible for parties to the conflict to segregate potential military objectives from civilian objects. For example, a power generation plant or an air traffic control centre may serve both military

---

[201] See Commentary accompanying Rule 53.
[202] ICRC ADDITIONAL PROTOCOLS COMMENTARY, para. 2245.

and civilian purposes. Civilians and civilian objects might be present at these lawful targets and it may not be feasible to segregate them in accordance with this Rule. Similarly, it might be impossible to segregate the civilian and military functions of the infrastructure. When segregation cannot be accomplished, a party to the conflict remains obliged, to the maximum extent feasible, to take other measures to protect civilians and civilian objects under its control from the dangers attendant to cyber attacks.

8.   The concept of 'control' was thought of in territorial terms during the negotiations of Additional Protocol I.[203] The International Group of Experts was divided over the meaning to be attributed to the term in the cyber context. A majority of the Experts concluded that all civilian cyber infrastructure and activities located in territory under the control of a party to the conflict are subject to this Rule. This would include the party's unoccupied territory and occupied enemy territory. A minority took a more nuanced approach, asserting that the prohibition should not necessarily be conceived of territorially. For them, not every computer system within territory controlled by a party is within its control for the purpose of the Rule. As an example, military communications may travel through civilian computer systems, servers, and routers over which a party has no de facto control. For these Experts, the obligation in this Rule would not apply in such cases. In view of the 'maximum extent feasible' caveat, this division of opinion results in only minor differences in application of the Rule. All the Experts agreed that if the party can dictate the operations of a civilian computer system, it is under the control of that party.

9.   On the one hand, the International Group of Experts agreed that the term 'dangers' does not refer to the risk of inconvenience or irritation. For example, the Rule does not require a party to the conflict to protect civilians from cyber operations that cause temporary inability to access a website. Similarly, the party is not obliged to protect against the mere defacement of websites. On the other hand, the Experts also agreed that the dangers the Rule is designed to protect against include death or injury to civilians or damage to civilian property, that is, collateral damage. A minority of the International Group of Experts would include negative effects falling short of this threshold, such as major disruption of day-to-day life (as distinct from mere inconvenience or irritation).

---

[203] ICRC Additional Protocols Commentary, para. 2239.

10. Although paragraphs (a) and (b) of Article 58 of Additional Protocol I are not restated in this Rule, they provide useful guidance. Article 58(a) imposes a requirement to remove civilians and civilian objects from the vicinity of military objectives.[204] Two scenarios in the cyber context illustrate the danger contemplated. First, a military objective may be attacked by cyber means in a way that harms nearby civilians or civilian objects. In such a case, the physical removal of the civilians and civilian objects would be required to the extent feasible. Second, cyber attacks may have indirect effects on civilian computers, computer networks, or cyber infrastructure. Appropriate precautions in such situations may include separating, compartmentalizing, or otherwise shielding civilian cyber systems.

11. The obligation in Article 58(b) of Additional Protocol I to 'avoid locating military objectives within or near densely populated areas', which is implicit in this Rule, addresses the situation in which civilian objects are not (yet) located in the vicinity of military objectives; it is preventive in character.[205] In the cyber context, there is no direct equivalent to 'densely populated areas'. For instance, although civilians primarily use social networking media, these cannot be equated with densely populated areas, because the notion involves physical presence. However, the requirement does apply with respect to physically locating cyber infrastructure liable to attack in densely populated areas.

12. The commentary to Article 58 offers several further examples of passive precautions. These include well-trained civil defence forces, systems for warnings of impending attacks, and responsive fire and emergency services.[206] Cyber equivalents might include distributing protective software products, monitoring networks and systems, maintaining a strategic cyber reserve of bandwidth and cyber capability, and developing response capabilities that prevent bleed over into the civilian system.

13. Rule 59 does not bear on the 'dual-use' issue (Rule 39). State practice clearly establishes the legality of using cyber infrastructure for both military and civilian purposes. Instead, this Rule addresses the issue of proximity (whether real or virtual) of civilians and civilian objects to cyber infrastructure that qualifies as a military objective, including dual-use targets.

---

[204] AMW Manual, Rule 43; ICRC Customary IHL Study, Rule 24.
[205] AMW Manual, Rule 42; ICRC Customary IHL Study, Rule 23.
[206] ICRC Additional Protocols Commentary, paras. 2257–8. See also ICRC Customary IHL Study, commentary accompanying Rule 22.

14.   State practice also demonstrates that the failure of a defender to take passive precautions does not, in itself, preclude the other side from conducting a cyber attack.[207] Nevertheless, the International Group of Experts agreed that even when the enemy does not take passive precautions, an attacker remains bound by the Rules governing attacks, especially distinction, proportionality, and the requirement to take active precautions (Rules 31 and 51 to 58).[208] Some of the Experts took the position that the failure of a party to take passive precautions is an appropriate consideration when determining whether an attacker has complied with its obligations to take active precautions.

SECTION 8:   PERFIDY, IMPROPER USE, AND ESPIONAGE

Rule 60 – Perfidy

In the conduct of hostilities involving cyber operations, it is prohibited to kill or injure an adversary by resort to perfidy. Acts that invite the confidence of an adversary to lead him to believe he or she is entitled to receive, or is obliged to accord, protection under the law of armed conflict with intent to betray that confidence constitute perfidy.

1.   Perfidy, also referred to as 'treachery', is defined in Article 37(1) of Additional Protocol I as '[a]cts inviting the confidence of an adversary to lead him to believe that he is entitled to, or is obliged to accord, protection under the rules of international law applicable in armed conflict, with the intent to betray that confidence'. The prohibition against killing or wounding by perfidy also appears in Article 23(b) of the Hague Regulations. This Rule applies in both international and non-international armed conflict and is considered customary international law.[209]

2.   Whereas Article 37(1) of Additional Protocol I includes acts that result in the capture of an adversary, the majority of the International

---

[207] ICRC CUSTOMARY IHL STUDY, commentary accompanying Rule 22.
[208] See Additional Protocol I, Art. 51(8); AMW MANUAL, Rule 46; ICRC CUSTOMARY IHL STUDY, commentary accompanying Rule 22.
[209] Hague Regulations, Art. 23(f); US COMMANDER'S HANDBOOK, para. 12.1.2; UK MANUAL, paras. 5.9, 15.12; CANADIAN MANUAL, paras. 603, 706, 857; GERMAN MANUAL, para. 472; AMW MANUAL, commentary accompanying Rule 111(a); NIAC Manual, para. 2.3.6; ICRC CUSTOMARY IHL STUDY, Rule 65. See also Rome Statute, Arts. 8(2)(b)(xi), 8(2)(e)(ix).

Group of Experts concluded that customary international law prohibits only those perfidious acts intended to result in death or injury.[210] This position is based in part on the fact that capture is not referred to in the Hague Regulations or the Rome Statute.[211] A minority of the Experts took the position that as a matter of customary international law, the prohibition also extends to capture.[212] Of course, the prohibition of perfidious acts leading to capture extends as a matter of treaty law to States Party to Additional Protocol I during conflicts in which that instrument applies.

3. The prohibition has four elements: (1) an act inviting particular confidence of the adversary; (2) an intent to betray that confidence; (3) a specific protection provided for in international law; and (4) death or injury of the adversary.[213]

4. The notion of 'adversary' is sufficiently broad to encompass the situation in which the deceived person is not necessarily the person whose death or injury results from the deception, provided the individual killed or injured was an intended target of the attack.

5. In order to breach the prohibition against perfidy, the perfidious act must be the proximate cause of the death or injury.[214] Consider the case of a perfidious email inviting the enemy to a meeting with a representative of the International Committee of the Red Cross, but which is actually intended to lead enemy forces into an ambush. The enemy is deceived, and, while travelling to the purported meeting, their vehicle strikes a landmine (which was not foreseen by the senders of the email). Any resulting deaths were not proximately caused by the perfidious email because they were not foreseeable; therefore, the prohibition set forth in this Rule has not been breached.

6. Proximate cause should not be confused with temporal proximity. In the cyber context, it is possible that a perfidious act inviting the adversary's confidence will occur at a point in time that is remote from the act that causes the death or injury. An example is an email sent by a military unit to the adversary indicating an intention to surrender some days later at a specific location. At the appointed time and location, the adversary is ambushed and some of its troops are killed. Rule 60 has

---

[210] See AMW MANUAL, commentary accompanying Rule 111(a) (discussing whether the prohibition against perfidy extends to acts resulting in capture).

[211] Hague Regulations, Art. 23(b). See also Rome Statute, Art. 8(2)(b)(xi).

[212] ICRC CUSTOMARY IHL STUDY, Rule 65.

[213] ICRC ADDITIONAL PROTOCOLS COMMENTARY, para. 1500; Rome Statute Elements of the Crimes, Arts. 8(2)(b)(xi), 8(2)(e)(ix).

[214] Bothe et al., NEW RULES FOR VICTIMS OF ARMED CONFLICTS 204 (1982).

been violated, even though substantial time has passed since the initiating perfidious act.

7.   The International Group of Experts was split as to whether the perfidious act must actually result in the injury or death of the adversary. The ICRC commentary to Article 37 indicates that the issue was problematic, but that 'it seems evident that the attempted or unsuccessful act also falls under the scope of this prohibition'.[215] On this basis, some Experts took the position that the perfidious act need not be successful. Others were of the view that this position does not accurately reflect customary law, as evidenced in part by the plain text of Article 23(b) of the Hague Regulations and Article 37 of Additional Protocol I.

8.   The confidence that is invited must be that the person or object involved is either protected by the law of armed conflict or is obliged to accord such protection to the party that is the subject of the deception. Examples include feigning the status of civilians (Rule 29), civilian objects (Rule 38), medical personnel or entities (Rules 70 and 71), United Nations personnel or objects (Rule 74), or persons who are *hors de combat* (Rule 34).

9.   The International Group of Experts was divided as to whether the confidence referred to in this Rule encompasses that of a cyber system. Some Experts were of the view that it does. An example would be a situation in which the enemy commander is known to have a pacemaker. Malware that will disrupt the rhythm of the pacemaker and induce a heart attack is programmed to falsely authenticate itself as being generated by a legitimate medical source. The false authentication is accepted by the enemy's computer network and the malware attacks the pacemaker of the adversary commander, causing a heart attack. In this example, the confidence of the adverse party's computer system has been betrayed and, according to the majority of the Experts, the Rule has been violated. Other Experts took the position that the notion of confidence presupposes human involvement, such that influencing a machine's processes without consequently affecting human perception falls outside the Rule.

10.   The perfidy Rule does not extend to perfidious acts that result in damage or destruction of property.[216] Such perfidious conduct might, however, be prohibited by another rule of the law of international armed conflict. For example, the feigning of United Nations observer status to gain access to an adversary's military headquarters to enable a close access

---

[215] ICRC ADDITIONAL PROTOCOLS COMMENTARY, para. 1493.
[216] AMW MANUAL, commentary accompanying Rule 111(a).

operation against its secure computer network would not breach the perfidy rule, but would nonetheless be prohibited (Rule 63).

11.   Perfidy must be distinguished from espionage (Rule 66). However, a cyber operation with the primary purpose of espionage that fulfils the perfidy criteria and results in the death or injury of an adversary violates this Rule.

12.   In an armed conflict, simply failing to identify oneself as a combatant is not perfidy, although it may result in a loss of entitlement to claim combatant immunity or prisoner of war status (Rule 26).[217] Similarly, in the cyber context there is no obligation specifically to mark websites, IP addresses, or other information technology facilities that are used for military purposes in order to distinguish them from civilian objects. However, it may be perfidious to make such websites (or other cyber entities) appear to have civilian status with a view to deceiving the enemy in order to kill or injure.

13.   There is a distinction between feigning protected status and masking the originator of the attack. A cyber attack in which the originator is concealed does not equate to feigning protected status. It is therefore not perfidious to conduct cyber operations that do not disclose the originator of the operation.[218] The situation is analogous to a sniper attack in which the location of the attacker or identity of the sniper may never be known. However, an operation that is masked in a manner that invites an adversary to conclude that the originator is a civilian or other protected person is prohibited if the result of the operation is death or injury of the enemy.

14.   The integrated nature of cyber infrastructure makes it likely that civilian cyber infrastructure will be involved in cyber attacks. The fact that cyber attacks causing death or injury are conducted over civilian cyber infrastructure does not in itself make them perfidious. In this respect, cyber infrastructure is no different from civilian infrastructure used to launch a kinetic attack. Examples include roads used by military convoys or civilian airports used by military aircraft. The exception to this general rule is infrastructure that enjoys specially protected status, such as a medical computer network. This issue is further discussed below at Rule 71.

---

[217] See Rules 25 and 31 for further discussion on the requirement for combatants to distinguish themselves from the civilian population.

[218] Recalling, however, that if captured, that combatant may subsequently be denied combatant or prisoner of war status.

15.   Perfidy must be distinguished from ruses, which are permissible. Ruses are acts designed to mislead, confuse, or induce an adversary to act recklessly, but that do not violate the law of armed conflict (Rule 61).

Rule 61 – Ruses

Cyber operations that qualify as ruses of war are permitted.

1.   This Rule is drawn from Article 37(2) of Additional Protocol I. Ruses are permitted in both international and non-international armed conflict.[219]

2.   Ruses of war are acts intended to mislead the enemy or to induce enemy forces to act recklessly, but that do not violate the law of armed conflict. They are not perfidious because they do not invite the confidence of the enemy with respect to protected status. The following are examples of permissible ruses:[220]

(a) creation of a 'dummy' computer system simulating non-existent forces;
(b) transmission of false information causing an opponent erroneously to believe operations are about to occur or are underway;
(c) use of false computer identifiers, computer networks (e.g., honeynets or honeypots), or computer transmissions;
(d) feigned cyber attacks that do not violate Rule 36;
(e) bogus orders purported to have been issued by the enemy commander;
(f) psychological warfare activities;
(g) transmitting false intelligence information intended for interception; and
(h) use of enemy codes, signals, and passwords.

3.   A common element of ruses of war is the presentation to the enemy of a 'false appearance of what is actually going on, thereby lawfully gaining a military advantage'.[221] Consider, for example, the use of a software decoy to deceive the enemy. In response to a rogue software agent that is tasked with modifying XML tags, the software decoy deflects

---

[219] US Commander's Handbook, para. 12.1.1; UK Manual, paras. 5.17, 15.12; German Manual, para. 471; AMW Manual, commentary accompanying Rule 113; NIAC Manual, commentary accompanying para. 2.3.6; ICRC Customary IHL Study, Rule 57.

[220] For examples of ruses in the conventional context, see Department of the Army, Field Manual 27–10, The Law of Land Warfare para. 51 (1956). See also US Commander's Handbook, para. 12.1.1; UK Manual, para. 5.17.2; Canadian Manual, para. 856; AMW Manual, Rule 116.

[221] AMW Manual, commentary accompanying Rule 116(a).

the enemy's cyber operators by redirecting their attention to a honeypot that contains false XML tags that appear to have greater military value than those under attack. The action is a lawful ruse.

4.   It is permissible to camouflage persons and objects to blend in with (i.e., to be visually indistinct from) surroundings, including civilian surroundings, so long as doing so does not amount to perfidy (Rule 60).[222] The International Group of Experts was split, however, as to whether it would be lawful to camouflage a computer or computer network to blend in with a civilian system in a manner that did not constitute perfidy. For instance, a military computer system might use a .com domain in order to appear to be commercial in nature to make it harder to detect. The majority of the Experts took the position that doing so would be unlawful if the operation undermined the principle of distinction (Rule 31) by placing civilians and civilian objects at increased risk.[223] The minority suggested that only the rule of perfidy applies to such cases.

Rule 62 – Improper use of the protective indicators

It is prohibited to make improper use of the protective emblems, signs, or signals that are set forth in the law of armed conflict.

1.   This Rule of customary and treaty law applies during both international and non-international armed conflict.[224]

2.   The Red Cross and the Red Crescent (as well as the Red Lion and Sun, now in disuse[225]) have long been recognized as distinctive protective emblems.[226] Additional Protocol III to the 1949 Geneva Conventions establishes the Red Crystal as an additional distinctive emblem with equal

---

[222]   AMW MANUAL, Rule 116(e) and accompanying commentary.

[223]   AMW MANUAL, commentary accompanying Rule 116(e).

[224]   Hague Regulations, Art. 23(f); Additional Protocol I, Art. 38(1); Additional Protocol II, Art. 12; Additional Protocol III, Art. 6(1); US COMMANDER'S HANDBOOK, para. 8.5.1.6; UK MANUAL, para. 5.10 (as amended); CANADIAN MANUAL, paras. 604–5; GERMAN MANUAL, paras. 641, 932; AMW MANUAL, Rule 112(a) and (b). NIAC MANUAL, para. 2.3.4; ICRC CUSTOMARY IHL STUDY, Rules 58, 59, 61. *See also* Rome Statute, Art. 8(2)(b)(vii). It is important to note that the latter provision is of more limited scope, applying only when 'resulting in death or serious personal injury'. Moreover, the Rome Statute contains no equivalent rule in relation to non-international armed conflict.

[225]   The Red Lion and Sun has not been used since 1980. In that year, the government of the Islamic Republic of Iran declared that it would use the Red Crescent. *See* AMW MANUAL, n. 404.

[226]   Geneva Convention I, Arts. 38–44; Geneva Convention II, Arts. 41–5; US COMMANDER'S HANDBOOK, para. 8.5.1.1.

status.[227] This Rule also encompasses improper use of the distinctive sign for civil defence,[228] the distinctive emblem for cultural property,[229] the flag of truce,[230] and electronic protective markings such as those set forth in Annex I of Additional Protocol I.[231] Improper use of these distinctive indicators jeopardizes identification of the protected persons and objects entitled to display them, undermines the future credibility of the indicators, and places persons and objects entitled to their protection at greater risk.

3.   Unlike the previous Rule relating to perfidy, this Rule's prohibitions are absolute.[232] They are not limited to actions resulting (or intending to result) in the death, injury, or, in the case of a State Party to Additional Protocol I, capture of an adversary.

4.   The term 'improper use' generally refers to 'any use other than that for which the emblems were intended', namely identification of the objects, locations, and personnel performing or serving a protected function.[233] The mere display of a protective emblem, even when a reasonable person would realize its false nature, violates the Rule. Improper use does not encompass feigning protected status when protective indicators are not being displayed or used. As an example, consider an email from a Hotmail account to enemy forces that includes a bare assertion that the sender is a delegate of the International Committee of the Red Cross. The action does not breach the Rule because it does not misuse the organization's emblem.

5.   The International Group of Experts struggled with the issue of whether the prohibitions set forth in this Rule applied beyond the recognized and specified indicators. For instance, they discussed whether the use of an email employing the International Committee of the Red Cross domain name for purposes related to the conflict violate this Rule. The Experts took two different approaches.

---

[227]   Additional Protocol III, Art. 2(1).
[228]   Additional Protocol I, Art. 66; US COMMANDER's HANDBOOK, para. 8.5.1.2; UK MANUAL, para. 5.10, n. 41.
[229]   Cultural Property Convention, Arts. 16, 17; US COMMANDER's HANDBOOK, para. 8.5.1.4; AMW MANUAL, commentary accompanying Rule 112(a).
[230]   Hague Regulations, Art. 23(f); Additional Protocol I, Art. 38(1); US COMMANDER's HANDBOOK, para. 8.5.1.5; AMW MANUAL, commentary accompanying Rule 112; ICRC CUSTOMARY IHL STUDY, Rule 58.
[231]   Additional Protocol I, Annex I, Art. 9, as amended 30 November 1993. See also US COMMANDER's HANDBOOK, paras. 8.5.2.1, 8.5.2.3.
[232]   ICRC ADDITIONAL PROTOCOLS COMMENTARY, para. 1532.
[233]   ICRC CUSTOMARY IHL STUDY, commentary accompanying Rule 61.

6. By the first approach, based upon strict textual interpretation of the underlying treaty law, this Rule bears only on protective indicators, as distinct from the protected persons or objects they identify. For proponents of this approach, only cyber operations that employ electronic reproductions of the relevant graphic emblems, or which display the other protective indicators set forth in the law of armed conflict, are prohibited. Consider, for example, the use of an email message with the 'icrc.org' address extension in order to bypass the enemy's network data filters and deliver a piece of malware to the military network. As this operation does not specifically misuse the Red Cross symbol, the Experts taking this position concluded that the action would not violate this Rule.

7. By the second approach, based upon a teleological interpretation of the underlying treaty law, the key factor in analysing such situations is use of an indicator upon which others would reasonably rely in extending protection provided for under the law of armed conflict. For these Experts, the previous example would violate this Rule because the domain name 'icrc.org' invites confidence as to the affiliation of the originator.[234]

8. This Rule is without prejudice to the adoption of an agreement between parties to the conflict as to cyber or other indicators of specially protected status.[235]

Rule 63 – Improper use of United Nations emblem

It is prohibited to make use of the distinctive emblem of the United Nations in cyber operations, except as authorized by that organization.

1. Both treaty and customary international law recognize that unauthorized use of the distinctive emblem of the United Nations is prohibited in international and non-international armed conflict.[236]

---

[234] An argument in favour of this view would be to treat Art. 44 of Geneva Convention I as extending not only to the words 'Red Cross' or 'Geneva Cross' but also to 'ICRC'.

[235] Geneva Conventions I–III, Art. 6; Geneva Convention IV, Art. 7; ICRC ADDITIONAL PROTOCOLS COMMENTARY, para. 1557.

[236] Additional Protocol I, Art. 38(2); US COMMANDER'S HANDBOOK, para. 12.4; UK MANUAL, para. 5.10.c; CANADIAN MANUAL, para. 605(c); AMW MANUAL, Rule 112(e); NIAC MANUAL, commentary accompanying para. 2.3.4; ICRC CUSTOMARY IHL STUDY, Rule 60. *See also* Rome Statute, Art. 8(2)(b)(vii).

2. Any use of its emblem not authorized by the organization constitutes a violation of this Rule, subject to the exception set forth in the following paragraph. For instance, sending an email masquerading as a United Nations communication and containing the United Nations emblem is prohibited. The prohibition applies irrespective of whether United Nations personnel are deployed to the area of armed conflict.

3. In circumstances where the United Nations becomes a party to an armed conflict or militarily intervenes in an on-going one, the emblem loses its protective function since United Nations military personnel and equipment are lawful targets. Of course, United Nations personnel performing non-military functions, and their material and equipment, remain protected under the law of armed conflict as civilians and civilian objects respectively.

4. As in the case of the protective indicators addressed in Rule 62, the International Group of Experts was split on the issue of whether the emblem has to be used in order to violate this Rule. Whereas some took the position that it does, others maintained that any unauthorized use of an apparently authoritative indication of United Nations status suffices. For a discussion of this matter, see the Commentary accompanying Rule 62.

Rule 64 – Improper use of enemy indicators

It is prohibited to make use of the flags, military emblems, insignia, or uniforms of the enemy while visible to the enemy during an attack, including a cyber attack.

1. This Rule is based on Article 23(f) of the Hague Regulations and Article 39(2) of Additional Protocol I. It applies in both international and non-international armed conflict and reflects customary international law.[237]

2. There was consensus among the International Group of Experts that the use of enemy uniforms, insignia, and emblems is prohibited when engaging in an attack during both international and non-international armed conflict.[238] Article 39(2) of Additional Protocol I extends the prohibition beyond use during attacks to actions intended to shield,

---

[237] US COMMANDER's HANDBOOK, para. 12.5.3; UK MANUAL, para. 5.11; CANADIAN MANUAL, para. 607; GERMAN MANUAL, para. 473; AMW MANUAL, Rule 112(c); NIAC MANUAL, para. 2.3.5; ICRC CUSTOMARY IHL STUDY, Rule 62. See also Rome Statute, Art. 8(2)(b)(vii).

[238] Combatants captured while wearing enemy uniforms do not enjoy belligerent immunity and are not entitled to prisoner of war status. See commentary accompanying Rules 25 and 26.

favour, protect, or impede military operations.[239] The extension is not generally considered to form part of customary international law.[240]

3.   This Rule originates from a historical requirement for visual distinction between opposing forces and their equipment on the battlefield. As such, the terms "'emblem, insignia, or uniforms" refer only to concrete visual objects, including national symbols marked on military vehicles and aircraft'.[241] It is unlikely that improper use of enemy uniforms and other indicators will occur during a remote access cyber attack, as the cyber operators would not be in visual contact with the adversary. However, the use of them during a close access cyber attack is prohibited.

4.   The reference to 'while visible to the enemy' has been included in this Rule because the International Group of Experts split over the issue of whether customary law prohibits use during any attack, irrespective of the attendant circumstances. The majority of the International Group of Experts took the position that such a broad interpretation would serve no purpose since it is only when the attacker's use is apparent to the enemy that the act benefits the attacker or places its opponent at a disadvantage. In their estimation, the prohibition therefore only applies when the individual conducting the cyber attack is physically visible to his or her adversary. The other Experts were of the view that no such limitation should be placed on the prohibition since it appears in neither Article 39(2) of Additional Protocol I, nor in the ICRC Customary IHL Study's discussion of that Article. However, all the Experts agreed that the conduct cited in this Rule violated customary international law.

5.   Unlike misuse of protective indicators (Rule 62), the Rule does not extend to use of the enemy's emblem or other indicators of enemy status in the cyber communications themselves. In other words, it is permissible to feign enemy authorship of a cyber communication. This distinction is supported by State practice regarding lawful ruses. For instance, the UK Manual cites the following examples of ruses, each of which is adaptable to cyber operations: 'transmitting bogus signal messages and sending bogus despatches and newspapers with a view to their being intercepted by the enemy; making use of the enemy's signals, passwords, radio code

---

[239] Canada has made a reservation to its application of Art. 39(2) to the effect that it would apply the prohibition only while engaging in attacks and not in order to shield, favour, protect, or impede military operations. CANADIAN MANUAL, para. 607.

[240] There are divergent views as to what constitutes improper use. *See* AMW MANUAL, commentary accompanying Rule 112(c); NIAC MANUAL, commentary accompanying para. 2.3.5; ICRC CUSTOMARY IHL STUDY, commentary accompanying Rule 62.

[241] Bothe et al. at 214.

signs, and words of command; conducting a false military exercise on the radio while substantial troop movements are taking place on the ground; pretending to communicate with troops or reinforcements which do not exist ... and giving false ground signals to enable airborne personnel or supplies to be dropped in a hostile area, or to induce aircraft to land in a hostile area'.[242]

6.   The application of this Rule is somewhat problematic in the cyber context because of the possibility of remotely acquiring control of enemy systems without having physical possession of them. Military computer hardware is regularly marked. However, such markings are seldom used to distinguish it from enemy computer hardware. For this reason, the International Group of Experts agreed that the Rule has no application with regard to enemy marked computer hardware over which control has been remotely acquired and that is used for conducting attacks against the enemy.

7.   Situations involving cyber operation employed to gain control of other enemy military equipment are more complicated. For instance, it might be possible to acquire control of an enemy surface-to-air missile site that has been marked with the enemy emblem. In such a case, it would be impossible to remove the enemy's emblem before using the site to attack enemy aircraft. The ICRC commentary to Article 39(2) addresses the analogous situation of capturing an enemy tank on the battlefield and using it against the enemy. The commentary asserts that enemy markings would first have to be removed. As justification for applying such a strict rule, the commentary cites the persistent abuse of enemy uniforms and emblems following the Second World War.[243] The majority of the International Group of Experts took the position that military equipment, the control of which is taken by cyber means, may not be used for an attack while bearing enemy markings. A minority of the Experts noted that the commentary both labelled the issue 'a delicate question' and observed that the equipment could be withdrawn to the rear in order to be re-marked.[244] These Experts took the position that the tank scenario should have been resolved by assessing the feasibility of removing or obscuring the enemy markings. In the surface-to-air missile

---

[242] UK MANUAL, para. 5.17.2. *See also* US COMMANDER'S HANDBOOK, para. 12.1.1; CAN-ADIAN MANUAL, para. 856; GERMAN MANUAL, para. 471; AMW MANUAL, commentary accompanying Rule 116(c).

[243] ICRC ADDITIONAL PROTOCOLS COMMENTARY, para. 1576.

[244] ICRC ADDITIONAL PROTOCOLS COMMENTARY, para. 1576.

site scenario, they concluded that the site might be used to conduct attacks since it is not feasible to remove or obscure the enemy markings prior to doing so. They argued that the Rule is not absolute; it is context-dependent, particularly with regard to feasibility.

8. An exception to Article 39(2) of Additional Protocol I exists for the conduct of armed conflict at sea. The exception allows a warship to fly enemy (or neutral) flags as long as it displays its true colours immediately before an armed engagement.[245] Therefore, warships flying the enemy or neutral flag may conduct cyber operations until an engagement commences. The International Group of Experts agreed that the law is unsettled as to whether a cyber attack (as distinct from a cyber operation) would be prohibited as an engagement from a warship displaying enemy or neutral flags.

9. The International Group of Experts noted the existence of separate requirements beyond the scope of this Rule to mark warships and military aircraft. For instance, in air warfare only properly marked military aircraft may exercise belligerent rights.[246] Such issues arise in the case of acquiring control of enemy warships or military aircraft to conduct belligerent activities other than attack. Consider a cyber operation to assume control of an enemy's unmanned aerial vehicle (UAV) while in flight. The question is whether it must be marked with the capturing party's military marks before undertaking, for example, reconnaissance missions. Some Experts took the view that most States would not interpret this requirement as absolute in character. In their view, the captured UAV would not have to first land immediately and be marked with the acquiring State's markings. Cyber operations, in their estimation, undercut the basis for asserting the absolute character of the Rule. Other Experts, however, considered that there is an absolute prohibition on employing the captured vehicle for military purposes until the relevant military and national markings have been applied.

Rule 65 – Improper use of neutral indicators

In cyber operations, it is prohibited to make use of flags, military emblems, insignia, or uniforms of neutral or other States not party to the conflict.

---

[245] US COMMANDER'S HANDBOOK, para. 12.5.1; SAN REMO MANUAL, Rule 110.

[246] US COMMANDER'S HANDBOOK, Chapter 12; AMW MANUAL, Rules 1(x), 17; Hague Air Warfare Rules, Arts. 3, 13.

1.   This Rule is based on Article 39(1) of Additional Protocol I. It applies to international armed conflict and is considered part of customary international law.[247] An exception to the Rule exists in relation to naval warfare.[248]

2.   It is unsettled whether this Rule applies to non-international armed conflict. The ICRC Customary IHL Study argues that there is a 'legitimate expectation that the parties to a non-international armed conflict abide by this rule'.[249] A contrary view is that the Rule does not apply in non-international armed conflict because the concept of neutrality is limited to international armed conflicts.[250]

3.   The phrase 'other States not party to the conflict' is drawn from the text of Article 39(1). It was included in order to cover States that have adopted a narrow interpretation of neutrality.

4.   The International Group of Experts agreed that wearing the uniform of a neutral State's armed forces to conduct a close access cyber attack would be prohibited under this Rule. However, as in the case of protective indicators (Rule 62) and United Nations emblems (Rule 63), the Group was divided over whether employment of other indicators of neutral status is prohibited. For example, there was a lack of consensus as to use of a neutral State's government domain name. For a discussion of the two positions, see the Commentary accompanying Rule 62.

5.   See Rules 91 to 95 and accompanying Commentary for further discussion on neutrality.

Rule 66 – Cyber espionage

(a) **Cyber espionage and other forms of information gathering directed at an adversary during an armed conflict do not violate the law of armed conflict.**

---

[247] US COMMANDER'S HANDBOOK, para. 12.3.3; UK MANUAL, para. 5.11; CANADIAN MANUAL, para. 606; GERMAN MANUAL, para. 473; AMW MANUAL, Rule 112(d); ICRC CUSTOMARY IHL STUDY, Rule 63.

[248] Additional Protocol I, Art. 39(3) (stating that it does not affect 'the existing generally recognized rules of international law applicable to espionage or to the use of flags in the conduct of armed conflict at sea'); US COMMANDER'S HANDBOOK, para. 12.3.1; SAN REMO MANUAL, Rule 110.

[249] ICRC CUSTOMARY IHL STUDY, commentary accompanying Rule 63. *See also* NIAC MANUAL, para. 2.3.4.

[250] AMW MANUAL, commentary accompanying Rule 112(d). The AMW Manual notes that the conduct would nevertheless 'be regarded as improper'.

(b) **A member of the armed forces who has engaged in cyber espionage in enemy-controlled territory loses the right to be a prisoner of war and may be treated as a spy if captured before re-joining the armed forces to which he or she belongs.**

1.   The formulation of this Rule is based on customary international law, Articles 29 and 31 of the Hague Regulations, and Article 46 of Additional Protocol I.[251] *Lit.* (b) applies only in international armed conflict because the concept of espionage is limited to inter-State relations[252] and because the notions of prisoner of war status and combatant immunity have no application in non-international armed conflicts.

2.   For the purposes of this Manual, 'cyber espionage' is defined narrowly as any act undertaken clandestinely or under false pretences that uses cyber capabilities to gather (or attempt to gather) information with the intention of communicating it to the opposing party. The act must occur in territory controlled by a party to the conflict.[253] 'Clandestinely' refers to activities undertaken secretly or secretively,[254] as with a cyber espionage operation designed to conceal the identity of the persons involved or the fact that it has occurred. An act of cyber information collection is 'under false pretences' when so conducted as to create the impression that the individual concerned is entitled to access the information in question.[255] In the cyber domain, it often consists of an individual masquerading as a legitimate user by employing that user's permissions to access targeted systems and data.

3.   Cyber espionage must be distinguished from computer network exploitation (CNE), which is a doctrinal, as distinct from an international law, concept. CNE often occurs from beyond enemy territory, using remote access operations. Cyber operators sometimes also use the term 'cyber reconnaissance'. The term refers to the use of cyberspace capabilities to obtain information about enemy activities, information resources, or system capabilities. CNE and cyber reconnaissance are not cyber espionage when conducted from outside enemy-controlled territory.

---

[251]   US COMMANDER'S HANDBOOK, paras. 12.8, 12.9; ICRC CUSTOMARY IHL STUDY, Rule 107.
[252]   AMW MANUAL, chapeau to sec. R.
[253]   Note the definition of 'spy' at Hague Regulations, Art. 29; US COMMANDER'S HANDBOOK, para. 12.8; AMW MANUAL, Rule 118.
[254]   AMW MANUAL, commentary accompanying Rule 118.
[255]   ICRC ADDITIONAL PROTOCOLS COMMENTARY, para. 1779.

4.   Although there is no express prohibition on cyber espionage in the law of armed conflict (or international law more generally), it is subject to all prohibitions set forth in that body of law. For instance, cyber espionage can in some circumstances violate the prohibition on perfidy (Rule 60). Such conduct may also amount to 'direct participation in hostilities' by any civilians involved, thereby rendering them subject to attack (Rule 35). Although cyber espionage, whether by civilians or members of the armed forces, does not violate international law, it may violate the domestic law of States that enjoy jurisdiction over the individual or the offence.[256]

5.   Article 29 of the Hague Regulations employs the term 'zone of operations of a belligerent'. Article 46(2) of Additional Protocol I expands the geographical scope of the concept to any territory controlled by enemy forces. State practice supports this extension as a matter of customary international law.[257] Given the geographic limitation to territory controlled by the enemy, cyber espionage will most likely occur as a close access cyber operation, such as when a flash drive is used to gain access to a computer system.

6.   Cyber information gathering that is performed from outside terri-tory controlled by the adverse party to the conflict is not cyber espionage but, in certain circumstances, may be punishable under the domestic criminal law of the State affected or of the neutral State from which the activity is undertaken. However, since no cyber espionage is involved, belligerent immunity would attach when appropriate (Rule 26).

7.   The International Group of Experts agreed that the information in question must be gathered on behalf of a party to the conflict. For example, it is not cyber espionage for the purposes of this Rule for a corporation located in the territory of a party to the conflict to use cyber means to surreptitiously gather information about the commercial activities of a corporation in the territory of another party to the conflict.

8.   The majority of the International Group of Experts took the position that the nature of the information gathered has no bearing on the characterization of the activity as cyber espionage. By contrast, the minority agreed with the AMW Manual position that the information involved must be of some military value.[258]

---

[256] AMW MANUAL, Rule 119 and accompanying commentary.
[257] UK MANUAL, para. 4.9.1; CANADIAN MANUAL, para. 611; AMW MANUAL, commentary accompanying Rule 118.
[258] AMW MANUAL, Rule 118 and accompanying commentary.

9. Certain acts of cyber espionage involve more than mere information-gathering activities and can cause damage to computer systems. Therefore, acts whose primary purpose is cyber espionage may sometimes amount to a cyber attack, in which case the Rules as to cyber attack apply (Chapter 4).

10. With respect to *lit.* (b), it is well accepted that spies who are captured in enemy-controlled territory do not enjoy combatant immunity or prisoner of war status. However, 'a spy who, after re-joining the army to which he belongs, is subsequently captured by the enemy, is treated as a prisoner of war, and incurs no responsibility for his previous acts of spying'.[259] This provision applies to cyber espionage. Accordingly, if a member of the armed forces who has engaged in cyber espionage in enemy-controlled territory succeeds in re-joining his own forces, he or she is no longer liable to prosecution for those cyber espionage activities.[260]

SECTION 9: BLOCKADE AND ZONES

A. Blockades

1. The question of whether and to what extent the law of blockade applies in the cyber context proved to be a particularly challenging issue for the International Group of Experts. Blockade is a method of warfare consisting of belligerent operations to prevent all vessels and aircraft (enemy and neutral) from entering or exiting specified ports, airports, or coastal areas belonging to, occupied by, or under the control of an enemy belligerent State.[261] A blockade may be established as part of military operations directed against military forces or as an economic operation with the strategic goal of weakening an enemy's military power through the degradation of its economy.[262]

---

[259] Hague Regulations, Art. 31.

[260] Additional Protocol I, Art. 46(4); US COMMANDER'S HANDBOOK, para. 12.9; UK MANUAL, para. 4.9.4 (as amended); CANADIAN MANUAL, para. 320; AMW MANUAL, Rule 122.

[261] US COMMANDER'S HANDBOOK, para. 7.7.1. For a definition of aerial blockade, *see* AMW MANUAL, chapeau to sec. V.

[262] US COMMANDER'S HANDBOOK, para. 7.7.5. As part of economic warfare, a blockade has a direct impact on the commercial relations between neutral States and the blockaded State. It is considered a method of warfare designed to weaken the economy of an enemy. However, since World War II, States have established blockades most often as an integral part of military operations directed against military forces (e.g., to deny supplies, armaments, and reinforcements). *See* GERMAN MANUAL, paras. 1014, 1051–53.

2.   While the law of blockade originally evolved in the context of maritime operations, the advent of aviation made blockade law relevant to aircraft as well. Not only are aircraft used to enforce a naval blockade, but it has also been recognized that a blockade to prevent aircraft from entering or exiting specified airfields or coastal areas belonging to, occupied by, or under the control of the enemy, constitutes a lawful method of aerial warfare.[263]

3.   The common elements of a blockade are: it must be declared and notified; the commencement, duration, location, and extent of the blockade must be specified in the declaration; the blockade must be effective; the forces maintaining the blockade may be stationed at a distance from the coast determined by military requirements; a combination of lawful methods and means of warfare may enforce the blockade; access to neutral ports, coasts, and airfields may not be blocked; cessation, lifting, extension, re-establishment, or other alteration of a blockade must be declared and notified; and the blockading party must apply the blockade impartially to the aircraft and vessels of every State.[264]

4.   Given the increasing use of computers and computer systems in the operation of vessels and aircraft, cyber means can be used to facilitate the establishment and enforcement of a naval or aerial blockade. Rule 67 reflects this practice. A more difficult question is whether the use of cyber means to block neutral and enemy cyber communications to or from enemy territory or areas under enemy control – a so-called 'cyber blockade' – is subject to the law of blockade.[265]

5.   The issue of whether these operations amount to a blockade as a matter of law prompted significant debate within the International Group of Experts. That debate centred on the applicability of the criteria for blockade in the cyber context, the technical feasibility of a cyber

---

[263] AMW Manual, chapeau to sec. V.

[264] US Commander's Handbook, paras. 7.7.2–7.7.2.5; UK Manual, paras. 13.65–13.73; Canadian Manual, para. 848; German Manual, para. 1052; AMW Manual, sec. V; San Remo Manual, Rules 93–5, 97, 99–101.

[265] This question was prompted by the statement made by the Estonian Minister of Defence, who declared that the 2007 distributed denial of service attacks against his nation 'can effectively be compared to when your ports are shut to the sea'. While the Defence Minister did not explicitly use the term 'blockade', it is obvious that he drew a parallel between the closure of ports and distributed denial of service attacks that blocked Estonia's important websites. Johnny Ryan, 'iWar': A New Threat, its Convenience – and our Increasing Vulnerability, NATO Review (Winter 2007), available at www.nato.int/docu/review/2007/issue4/english/analysis2.html.

blockade and, thus, characterization of the rules governing cyber blockade as *lex lata* or *lex ferenda*.

6.   A minority of the Experts considered such cyber operations to be mere electronic jamming, that is, akin to electronic warfare. The majority took notice of the fact that naval or aerial blockades were often designed to create a particular effect that could be achieved by cyber means. For example, a legitimate goal of blockade has always been to affect negatively the enemy's economy. Since much of present day economic activity is conducted through communications via the Internet, the majority of the International Group of Experts concluded that it is reasonable to apply the law of blockade to operations designed to block cyber communications into and out of territory under enemy control. For them, these operations are qualitatively distinct from jamming communications.

7.   The establishment of a blockade traditionally required the specification of a particular geographical line that aircraft or vessels might not cross. This raises the question of whether a line of blockade can be articulated in a declaration of cyber blockade and whether it is feasible to block all cyber communications crossing it. The Technical Experts advised that it is possible to do both.

8.   A further conceptual difficulty is that blockade law, as presently understood, is geographically restricted. Naval and air blockades involve preventing access to or from 'specified ports, airfields, or coastal areas'.[266] In light of the relative freedom of navigation of neutral vessels and aircraft in international waters and airspace, the concept only has relevance when blockade operations are mounted in these areas, thereby interfering with neutral rights. The minority of the International Group of Experts strictly applied this paradigm in the cyber context, with the result that it would be conceptually impossible to establish a cyber blockade of landlocked territory. The majority concluded that a cyber blockade is a meaningful notion in these circumstances because it may be effectively enforced solely from belligerent territory without breaching the neutrality of adjacent States.

9.   The International Group of Experts struggled with the meaning of the effectiveness criterion in its application to cyber blockades. A minority of the Experts took the position that sufficient effectiveness was unattainable because the communications in question could be achieved by other

---

[266] US COMMANDER'S HANDBOOK, para. 7.7.1; AMW MANUAL, chapeau to sec. V.

means, such as radio and telephone. The majority drew support for their position by reference to air and sea movements. They pointed to the fact that the carriage of materials by air, which could not be shipped by sea due to a naval blockade, did not make a naval blockade ineffective, and vice versa.

10.   A cyber blockade may be rendered effective by other than cyber means. For example, a party to the conflict could enforce a cyber blockade with a combination of cyber (e.g., denying access to Internet route servers by modifying the routing tables), electronic warfare (e.g., employing directed energy weapons to interfere with radio frequency communication), and kinetic means (e.g., severing Internet trunk lines and destroying network centres in enemy territory by airstrikes).

11.   Cyber blockades may not bar, or otherwise seriously affect, the use of neutral cyber infrastructure for communications between the neutral State and other neutral States.[267]

12.   The law of blockade applies in international armed conflicts. In a non-international armed conflict, a State that is a party to the conflict may impose restrictions on the entry into and exit from areas that were formerly under its control and that are subject to its territorial sovereignty. So long as the State limits its operations to its own territory, waters, and airspace, they do not amount to a blockade in a legal sense. It is a matter of dispute whether a State involved in a non-international armed conflict may establish and enforce a blockade in international waters or airspace. Non-State actors are not entitled to establish and enforce a naval, aerial, or, a fortiori, cyber blockade.[268]

13.   To summarize, some members of the International Group of Experts completely rejected the notion of a cyber blockade as a matter of existing law. Others accepted it conceptually, but pointed to practical difficulties in meeting the legal criteria (or took divergent approaches to their application in the cyber context). Still others asserted that cyber blockades are lawful, capable of meeting traditional criteria, and practically and technically feasible. Since the International Group of Experts could not achieve consensus on Rules regarding the existence, establishment, and enforcement of a cyber blockade, the following Rules only address how cyber means may be used as a component of a traditional naval or air blockade.

---

[267] US COMMANDER'S HANDBOOK, para. 7.7.2.5; UK MANUAL, para. 13.71; CANADIAN MANUAL, para. 848; AMW MANUAL, Rule 150; SAN REMO MANUAL, Rule 99.
[268] AMW MANUAL, chapeau to sec. V.

B. Zones

1.   The concept of zones is grounded in operational doctrine and not international law. Operational zones include, inter alia, exclusion zones, no-fly zones, warning zones, and the immediate vicinity of naval or aerial operations.[269] They are not 'free fire zones' or 'areas of unrestricted warfare'. During an armed conflict, belligerents remain fully subject to the law of armed conflict within zones.[270] Neutral, civilian, and other protected objects or persons retain their protection under that law when they enter such zones, even if they have ignored the instructions issued by the party that established them.

2.   Penetration of a zone may be considered when assessing whether the object or person concerned qualifies as a lawful target.[271] Consider the penetration of a closed and sensitive military network (i.e., the equivalent of a zone) during an armed conflict. The system provides a clear warning that intrusion will subject the intruder to automatic 'hack-back' or other measures. Despite having been placed on sufficient notice and afforded the opportunity to withdraw or desist, the intruder persists. In this case, it would generally be reasonable to conclude that the intrusion is hostile. As such, those individuals authorizing or executing the intrusion and the hardware and software they employ may reasonably be considered lawful targets (Rules 34, 35, 37, and 38).

3.   Cyber exclusion zone issues arise in two contexts – use of cyber means or methods in the enforcement of naval and aerial zones and the creation of unique cyber exclusion zones. The former is dealt with in the Rules that follow. With respect to the latter, the Technical Experts emphasized the difficulty of defining zones in cyberspace. Moreover, compliance with the terms of a defined zone might be technically

---

[269] *See generally* US COMMANDER'S HANDBOOK, para. 7.9; UK MANUAL, paras. 12.58–58.2, 13.77–13.80; CANADIAN MANUAL, para. 852; GERMAN MANUAL, paras. 448, 1048–50; AMW MANUAL, sec. P; SAN REMO MANUAL, paras. 105–8.

[270] US COMMANDER'S HANDBOOK, para. 7.9; UK MANUAL, paras. 13.77, 13.78; CANADIAN MANUAL, para. 852; GERMAN MANUAL, para. 1050; AMW MANUAL, chapeau to sec. P, Rules 105(a), 107(a). During peacetime, international law regarding self-defence (Rules 13 to 17) and force protection applies fully within such zones.

[271] The *jus ad bellum* significance of penetrating a zone is that the act may be a relevant consideration when assessing whether an armed attack has occurred or is imminent. AMW MANUAL, commentary accompanying Rule 105(a). In certain narrowly defined circumstances, the mere fact that a zone has been penetrated can be sufficiently determinative that an armed attack (Rule 13) is underway.

challenging since in many cases the communications concerned may rely upon cyber infrastructure over which the sender has no control.

4.   In light of the facts that zones are operational concepts, that those who establish them are not relieved of their legal obligations, and that maintenance is technically difficult, the International Group of Experts agreed that the articulation of Rules governing cyber zones was inappropriate. Consequently, the sole zones issue addressed in this Manual is the use of cyber operations in support of aerial and naval zones (Rule 69).

Rule 67 – Maintenance and enforcement of blockade

Cyber methods and means of warfare may be used to maintain and enforce a naval or aerial blockade provided that they do not, alone or in combination with other methods, result in acts inconsistent with the law of international armed conflict.

1.   Conducted appropriately, cyber operations can prove valuable to a military commander in maintaining and enforcing a naval or aerial blockade. Remote access cyber operations against propulsion and navigation systems are examples of the sort of cyber operations that can support blockades. Any use of cyber operations to enforce or maintain a blockade is subject to the same restrictions as kinetic means and methods of warfare. In particular, a blockade is unlawful when the damage to the civilian population is, or may be expected to be, excessive in relation to the concrete and direct military advantage anticipated from the blockade.[272]

Rule 68 – Effect of blockade on neutral activities

The use of cyber operations to enforce a naval or aerial blockade must not have the effect of barring, or otherwise seriously affecting, access to neutral territory.

1.   According to well-established principles of the international law applicable to armed conflict, belligerent measures must be applied with due regard to, and must not violate, the rights of neutral States. For instance, Article 1 of Hague Convention V provides that 'the territory of

---

[272] CANADIAN MANUAL, para. 850; AMW MANUAL, Rule 157(b); SAN REMO MANUAL, para. 102(b).

neutral Powers is inviolable'.[273] In the context of aerial and naval blockades, both the AMW Manual and the San Remo Manual provide that a blockade may not bar access to the airspace, ports, and coasts of neutral States.[274] The same position has been adopted for the purposes of the present Manual.

2. The term 'access' in this Rule denotes physical access by aircraft or vessels. Cyber operations can have the effect of barring access in many situations. For instance, a cyber operation that interferes with the propulsion or navigation systems of neutral aircraft or vessels can effectively prevent them from operating in neutral airspace or sea areas. Similarly, a cyber operation that interferes with port or airfield operations can effectively keep vessels or aircraft from using those facilities and, thus, from accessing neutral territory. To the extent they physically bar access, cyber operations in support of a blockade are prohibited. A majority of the Experts agreed that the law of naval or aerial blockade does not prohibit cyber operations used to enforce a blockade that have the effect of interfering with access to neutral cyber infrastructure or with cyber communications between neutral States.

3. Those Experts who accepted the concept of cyber blockade (see chapeau to Section 9) agreed that such a blockade, as distinct from cyber measures taken to enforce a naval or aerial blockade, would be subject to a prohibition on cyber operations that impede access to neutral cyber infrastructure or interfere with cyber communications between neutral States. In particular, they noted that the cyber infrastructure physically situated in the territory of a neutral State is already protected by that State's territorial sovereignty (Rule 1) unless the protection is lost pursuant to international law (Rules 18 and 92). These Experts would limit operation of the prohibition to cyber communications between neutral States. Article 54 of the Hague Regulations provides that submarine cables connecting an occupied territory with neutral territory may be seized or destroyed 'in case of absolute necessity', subject to restoration and compensation after the end of war.

---

[273] *See also* Hague Convention XIII, Art. 1 (stating 'Belligerents are bound to respect the sovereign rights of neutral Powers and to abstain, in neutral territory or in neutral waters, from any act which would, if knowingly permitted by any Power, constitute a violation of neutrality').

[274] AMW MANUAL, Rule 150; SAN REMO MANUAL, Rule 99. *See also* US COMMANDER'S HANDBOOK, para. 7.7.2.5; UK MANUAL, para. 13.71; CANADIAN MANUAL, para. 848.

Rule 69 – Zones

To the extent that States establish zones, whether in peacetime or during armed conflict, lawful cyber operations may be used to exercise their rights in such zones.

1. As discussed in the chapeau to this section, various types of zones may be established during an armed conflict. The existence of such zones has no bearing on the legal rights and obligations of States, whether belligerent or neutral, within and beyond sovereign territory. For instance, States enjoy the rights of self-defence, of freedom of navigation, and to conduct hostilities in international sea areas and airspace (subject to the due regard principle). However, the existence of a zone may affect the exercise of such rights. As an example, a warship may take penetration of a warning zone into account when assessing whether an aircraft is about to attack it.

2. Cyber operations may be used to declare and notify the establishment of a zone, and subsequently to maintain it. For example, cyber means may serve to communicate restrictions regarding passage through a zone or to warn aircraft or vessels that are approaching it. Similarly, where activity within a zone leaves a vessel or aircraft open to attack as a military objective, cyber operations may be used to assist in, or carry out, the attack, as long as the cyber attack complies with the law of armed conflict.

5

Certain persons, objects, and activities

1. In addition to the general protection afforded to civilians and civilian objects, the law of armed conflict makes particular provision as to the protection of specific classes of persons, objects, and activities. The Rules set forth in this chapter apply these provisions in the cyber context.

2. These Rules are without prejudice to the right of the parties to a conflict to enter into special agreements. They may agree at any time to protect persons or objects not otherwise covered by the law of armed conflict, as well as to make additional provisions for protected persons or objects beyond those required by that law. As a rule, special agreements may only be concluded with a view to enhancing protection.[1] For example, the parties to a conflict may conclude a special agreement providing greater protection for computers and computer networks supporting the operation of works and installations containing dangerous forces than that set forth in Rule 80 by agreeing to an absolute prohibition on attacks against them, whether by cyber or kinetic means.[2] Similarly, a special agreement could be concluded to protect computers and computer networks supporting sensitive facilities not addressed by the Rule, such as oil production installations, oil drilling platforms, petroleum storage facilities, oil refineries, or chemical production facilities.[3] The unique nature of cyberspace and the activities that occur therein may render such agreements particularly relevant and useful. An impartial humanitarian organization, such as the International Committee of the Red Cross, may facilitate the conclusion and implementation of special agreements.[4]

---

[1] See Geneva Conventions I–IV, Art. 3; Geneva Conventions I–III, Art. 6; Geneva Convention IV, Art. 7. *See also* AMW MANUAL, Rule 99 and accompanying commentary.

[2] AMW MANUAL, commentary accompanying Rule 99.

[3] AMW MANUAL, commentary accompanying Rule 99.

[4] AMW MANUAL, commentary accompanying Rule 99.

3.   The fact that certain persons, objects, and activities that enjoy specific protection under the law of armed conflict are not addressed in this chapter's Rules must not be interpreted as implying that they lack such protection in the cyber context. Where the application of a particular law of armed conflict protective norm did not raise issues peculiar to cyber warfare, the International Group of Experts concluded that it was not necessary to reflect this in the present Manual. Therefore, it is essential to bear in mind that, to the extent persons, objects, and activities benefit from the protection of the law of armed conflict generally, they will equally enjoy such protection with regard to cyber operations and attacks.

SECTION 1:   MEDICAL AND RELIGIOUS PERSONNEL AND MEDICAL UNITS, TRANSPORTS, AND MATERIAL

Rule 70 – Medical and religious personnel, medical units and transports

Medical and religious personnel, medical units, and medical transports must be respected and protected and, in particular, may not be made the object of cyber attack.

1.   The general obligations to respect and protect medical units, medical means of transport, and medical personnel are set forth in Articles 19, 24, 25, 35, and 36 of Geneva Convention I; Articles 22, 24, 25, 27, 36 to 39 of Geneva Convention II; Articles 18 to 22 of Geneva Convention IV; Articles 12, 15, 21 to 24, and 26 of Additional Protocol I; and Article 9 of Additional Protocol II. Religious personnel are protected pursuant to Article 24 of Geneva Convention I; Chapter 4 of Geneva Convention II; Article 33 of Geneva Convention III; Article 15 of Additional Protocol I; and Article 9 of Additional Protocol II. The Rule applies in both international and non-international armed conflict as customary international law.[5] Medical and religious personnel, medical units, and medical transports may lose their protected status pursuant to Rule 73.

---

[5] US COMMANDER'S HANDBOOK, paras. 8.2.4.1, 8.2.4.2, 8.9.1.4; UK MANUAL, paras. 7.10–7.22, 7.30, 15.45–15.47 (as amended); CANADIAN MANUAL, Chapter 9, sec. 3; GERMAN MANUAL, paras. 610, 612, 624, 816; AMW MANUAL, secs. K, L; NIAC Manual, paras. 3.2, 4.2.1; ICRC Customary IHL Study, Rules 25, 27, 28, 29, 30. *See also* Rome Statute, Arts. 8(2)(b)(xxiv), 8(2)(e)(ii).

2. The term 'religious personnel' does not refer to every member of a religious society. Rather, it denotes those individuals defined in Article 8(d) of Additional Protocol I. In particular, it encompasses chaplains attached to the armed forces. The International Group of Experts agreed that this term applies in the same sense in non-international armed conflict.[6]

3. Although not addressed in this Rule, it must also be borne in mind that places of worship are specifically protected, albeit not absolutely, from attack or any other hostile act in accordance with Article 27 of the Hague Regulations and Article 53 of Additional Protocol I, which in the opinion of the International Group of Experts reflect customary international law.[7]

4. The requirement to 'respect and protect' involves separate obligations. The duty to respect is breached by actions that impede or prevent medical or religious personnel, medical units, or medical transports from performing their medical or religious functions, or that otherwise adversely affect the humanitarian functions of medical or religious personnel, units, or transports.[8] It includes, but is not limited to, the prohibition on attacks. For instance, this Rule prohibits altering data in the Global Positioning System of a medical helicopter in order to misdirect it, even though the operation does not qualify as an attack on a medical transport (Rule 30). Similarly, blocking the online broadcast of a religious service for combat troops is prohibited. It must be cautioned that the Rule does not extend to situations that occur only incidentally, as in the case of the overall blocking of enemy communications.

5. By contrast, the duty to protect implies the taking of positive measures to ensure respect by others (e.g., non-State actors) for medical and religious personnel, medical units, and medical transports.[9] For instance, the obligation would require a military force with the capability to do so to defend a hospital in an area under its control against cyber attacks by hacktivists, when and to the extent feasible.[10]

---

[6] ICRC CUSTOMARY IHL STUDY, commentary accompanying Rule 27.
[7] US COMMANDER'S HANDBOOK, para. 8.2; UK MANUAL, paras. 5.25, 15.18; CANADIAN MANUAL, paras. 443, 1723; AMW MANUAL, Rules 1(o), 95(a).
[8] AMW MANUAL, commentary accompanying Rule 71.
[9] AMW MANUAL, commentary accompanying Rule 71.
[10] See Hague Regulations, Art. 27 (concerning 'hospitals and places where the sick and wounded are collected').

Rule 71 – Medical computers, computer networks, and data

Computers, computer networks, and data that form an integral part of the operations or administration of medical units and transports must be respected and protected, and in particular may not be made the object of attack.

1. The protection set forth in this Rule derives from the broader protection to which medical personnel, units, and transports are entitled (Rule 70). It applies in both international and non-international armed conflict as customary international law.[11]

2. The concepts of 'respect' and 'protect' are explained in the Commentary to Rule 70. It would not violate this Rule to conduct non-damaging cyber reconnaissance to determine whether the medical facility or transports (or associated computers, computer networks, and data) in question are being misused for militarily harmful acts (Rule 73).

3. The 'data' referred to in this Rule are those that are essential for the operation of medical units and transports. Examples include data necessary for the proper use of medical equipment and data tracking the inventory of medical supplies. Personal medical data required for the treatment of individual patients is likewise protected from alteration, deletion, or any other act by cyber means that would negatively affect their care, regardless of whether such acts amount to a cyber attack.

4. If the objects referred to in this Rule are also being used to commit, outside their humanitarian functions, acts harmful to the enemy, they lose their protection against attack, subject to Rule 73. This situation is particularly relevant in the cyber context because medical data can be stored in the same data centre, server, or computer as military data.

Rule 72 – Identification

All feasible measures shall be taken to ensure that computers, computer networks, and data that form an integral part of the operations or administration of medical units and transports are clearly identified through appropriate means, including electronic markings. Failure to so identify them does not deprive them of their protected status.

---

[11] US COMMANDER'S HANDBOOK, para. 8.9.1.4; UK MANUAL, paras. 7.10–7.22 (as amended), 15.45–15.47; CANADIAN MANUAL, paras. 447, 448, 918; AMW MANUAL, commentary accompanying sec. K; NIAC MANUAL, para. 4.2.1; ICRC CUSTOMARY IHL STUDY, Rules 25, 28, 29, 30.

1. This Rule applies the law of armed conflict provisions as to the marking of medical units and medical transports with a distinctive emblem to computers, computer networks, and data that form an integral part of their operations. It applies in both international and non-international armed conflict as customary international law.[12]

2. For the meaning of the term 'data' in this context, see the Commentary accompanying Rule 71.

3. Electronic markings are provided for under Articles 8(m) and 18(5) of Additional Protocol I as additional means to facilitate the identification of medical units and transports. These markings may be used to supplement the distinctive emblems. Use of appropriate electronic markings by States not Party to Additional Protocol I is also encouraged.

4. It is the contribution to the medical function that computers, computer networks, and data that form an integral part of the operations or administration of medical units and transports make that determines their protected status.[13] Distinctive emblems and other means of identification only facilitate identification and do not, of themselves, confer protected status. This principle is codified in Article 1 of Annex I of Additional Protocol I (as amended in 1993) and in paragraph 4 of the Preamble to Additional Protocol III. Since protected status is not derived from the distinctive emblem or other means of identification *per se*, such computers, computer networks, and data are protected regardless of whether they bear the distinctive emblem or other means of identification.[14] The phrase 'all feasible measures' is included in this Rule to emphasize the fact that military, humanitarian, technical, or other considerations might make marking impractical in certain circumstances.

5. In the cyber context, marking could be achieved by adding identifiers to the data or by notifying, directly or indirectly, the other party to the conflict of unique identifiers related to the relevant computers,

---

[12] Additional Protocol I, Art. 18; Additional Protocol II, Art. 12; Geneva Convention I, Art. 42; Geneva Convention II, Arts. 43, 44; Geneva Convention IV, Arts. 18, 20–2; US COMMANDER'S HANDBOOK, para. 8.5.1.1; UK MANUAL paras. 7.23–7.23.3 (as amended), 15.48; CANADIAN MANUAL, paras. 915, 916, 917; GERMAN MANUAL paras. 635, 638; AMW MANUAL, Rule 72(a), chapeau to sec. K; NIAC MANUAL, commentary accompanying para. 3.2.

[13] *See* AMW MANUAL, commentary accompanying Rule 72(c).

[14] *See* US COMMANDER'S HANDBOOK, para. 8.2.4.1; GERMAN MANUAL, para. 612; AMW MANUAL, Rule 72(d) and accompanying commentary; ICRC CUSTOMARY IHL STUDY, commentary accompanying Rule 30.

computer networks, or data.[15] Consider the storage of military medical data in a cloud computing data centre. The party storing the data notifies the enemy that the files containing its military medical data have the unique name extension '.mil.med.B' and that this naming convention will not be used on any file that is not exclusively medical. The enemy verifies the nature of these files through intelligence analysis and incorporates special protections for this data into its cyber operational planning process. Both parties have complied with this Rule.

Rule 73 – Loss of protection and warnings

The protection to which medical units and transports, including computers, computer networks, and data that form an integral part of their operations or administration, are entitled by virtue of this section does not cease unless they are used to commit, outside their humanitarian function, acts harmful to the enemy. In such situations protection may cease only after a warning setting a reasonable time limit for compliance, when appropriate, remains unheeded.

1.   This Rule applies in international and in non-international armed conflicts and reflects customary international law.[16] With respect to international armed conflicts, the Rule is based on Article 27 of the Hague Regulations, Articles 21 and 22 of Geneva Convention I, Articles 34 and 35 of Geneva Convention II, Article 19 of Geneva Convention IV, and Article 13 of Additional Protocol I. In the case of non-international armed conflicts, it is based on Article 11(2) of Additional Protocol II.

2.   'Acts harmful' in this Rule has the same meaning as 'hostile acts' in Article 11(2) of Additional Protocol II.[17] The notion of 'acts harmful to the enemy' encompasses acts the purpose or effect of which is to harm the enemy by impeding their military operations, or enhancing

---

[15] Additional Protocol I, Annex I, Art. 1(4), as amended 30 November 1993 (providing, 'The High Contracting Parties and in particular the Parties to the conflict are invited at all times to agree upon additional or other signals, means or systems which enhance the possibility of identification and take full advantage of technological developments in this field').

[16] US COMMANDER'S HANDBOOK, para. 8.9.1.4; UK MANUAL, para. 7.13.1; CANADIAN MANUAL, paras. 447, 918; GERMAN MANUAL, paras. 613, 618–19; AMW MANUAL, Rule 74(a), (b); NIAC MANUAL, para. 4.2.1; CUSTOMARY IHL STUDY, Rules 25, 28–9.

[17] ICRC ADDITIONAL PROTOCOLS COMMENTARY, para. 4720.

one's own.[18] It not only includes acts inflicting harm on the enemy by direct attack, but also those adversely affecting enemy military operations, as with collecting intelligence and transmitting military communications.[19]

3.   Acts that are not considered harmful to the enemy include:

(a) that the personnel of a medical unit are equipped with light individual weapons for their own defence or for that of the wounded, sick, or shipwrecked in their charge;
(b) that a medical unit is guarded by sentries or an escort;
(c) that portable arms and ammunition taken from the wounded and sick, and not yet handed to the proper service, are found in the medical unit; or
(d) that members of the armed forces or other combatants are in the medical unit for medical or other authorized reasons, consistent with the mission of the medical unit.[20]

4.   The fact that a medical computer system is equipped with software that, although not intended to be used for acts harmful to the enemy, is capable of being so used, does not *per se* deprive it of protected status. Consider a software application or software agent resident on a medical computer system that is capable of being used to generate a DDoS script. The system as a whole retains its protection, although the agent or application becomes a lawful military objective if used or going to be used for military purposes (provided all other requirements for qualification as a military objective have been met). Similarly, the installation of intrusion detection software designed to prevent an attack on a medical computer system will not deprive it of its protected status.

5.   Even if there is a valid reason for discontinuing the specific protection of medical units or transports (including medical computers, computer networks, and data), due warning must be issued setting, where appropriate, a reasonable time limit for compliance before an attack may

---

[18] ICRC Additional Protocols Commentary, para. 550. *See also* AMW Manual, commentary accompanying Rule 74(a); ICRC Geneva Convention I Commentary at 200–1.
[19] AMW Manual, commentary accompanying Rule 74(a).
[20] Additional Protocol I, Art. 13; Geneva Convention I, Art. 22; Geneva Convention IV, Art. 19. *See also* AMW Manual, commentary accompanying Rule 74(c). Note that the reference to 'light individual weapons' appears in Art. 13(2)(a) of Additional Protocol I, which applies only to civilian medical facilities. No similar reference is contained in the Geneva Conventions with regard to military medical facilities.

be conducted.[21] The warning may take various forms, such as an email to the hospital, a radio message, or a press release. In many instances, it may simply consist of an order to cease the harmful act within a specified period.[22] The relevant legal question is whether the means selected are such that the warning is sufficiently likely to reach the enemy.

6. As noted in this Rule, the requirement to set a reasonable time limit for compliance only arises 'whenever appropriate', that is, when it is feasible to do so.[23] For instance, if the misuse of the medical computers in question is causing immediate serious harm, it will typically not be feasible to afford an opportunity for compliance before responding, or it may be necessary substantially to reduce the time limit for compliance.

SECTION 2:   UNITED NATIONS PERSONNEL, INSTALLATIONS, MATERIEL, UNITS, AND VEHICLES

Rule 74 – United Nations personnel, installations, materiel, units, and vehicles

(a) As long as they are entitled to the protection given to civilians and civilian objects under the law of armed conflict, United Nations personnel, installations, materiel, units, and vehicles, including computers and computer networks that support United Nations operations, must be respected and protected and are not subject to cyber attack.

(b) Other personnel, installations, materiel, units, or vehicles, including computers and computer networks, involved in a humanitarian assistance or peacekeeping mission in accordance with the United Nations Charter are protected against cyber attack under the same conditions.

---

[21] Additional Protocol I, Art. 13(1); Additional Protocol II, Art. 11(2); Geneva Convention I, Art. 21; Geneva Convention II, Art. 34; Geneva Convention IV, Art. 19. *See also* US COMMANDER'S HANDBOOK, para. 8.9.1.4; UK MANUAL, para. 7.13.1; CANADIAN MANUAL, para. 918; GERMAN MANUAL, para. 618; AMW MANUAL, commentary accompanying Rule 74(b).
[22] AMW MANUAL, commentary accompanying Rule 74(b).
[23] *See* Additional Protocol I, Art. 13(1); Additional Protocol II, Art. 11(2); Geneva Convention I, Art. 21; Geneva Convention II, Art. 34; Geneva Convention IV, Art. 19; AMW MANUAL, Rule 74(b).

1. This Rule is drawn from a number of sources. The obligation to respect and protect United Nations personnel, installations, materiel, units, or vehicles, and by extension their computers and computer networks, derives from the United Nations Safety Convention. Article 7(1) specifies that United Nations personnel, units, vehicles, equipment, and premises 'shall not be made the object of attack or of any action that prevents them from discharging their mandate' and that Contracting Parties have a duty to ensure the safety and security of United Nations personnel. The extension of protection from attack to those involved in a humanitarian or peacekeeping operation finds support in Articles 8(2)(b)(iii) and 8(2)(e)(iii) of the Rome Statute. Rule 74 is applicable in both international and non-international armed conflicts as customary law.[24]

2. The notion of 'respect' in *lit.* (a) of this Rule encompasses an obligation to refrain from interference with the fulfilment of the mandate. This obligation refers only to United Nations personnel as defined under international law[25] and to the installations, materiel, units, or vehicles, including computers and computer networks, which support United Nations operations. It does not apply to those persons and objects referred to in *lit.* (b).[26]

---

[24] *See also* UK Manual, paras. 14.9, 14.15; AMW Manual, commentary accompanying Rule 98(b), (c); NIAC Manual, para. 3.3; ICRC Customary IHL Study, Rule 33.

[25] United Nations Safety Convention, Art. 1(a). The Article defines 'United Nations personnel' as: '(i) Persons engaged or deployed by the Secretary-General of the United Nations as members of the military, police or civilian components of a United Nations operation; (ii) Other officials and experts on mission of the United Nations or its specialized agencies or the International Atomic Energy Agency who are present in an official capacity in the area where a United Nations operation is being conducted.'

[26] Art. 1(c) defines a 'United Nations operation' as: 'an operation established by the competent organ of the United Nations in accordance with the Charter of the United Nations and conducted under United Nations authority and control: (i) Where the operation is for the purpose of maintaining or restoring international peace and security; or (ii) Where the Security Council or the General Assembly has declared, for the purposes of this Convention, that there exists an exceptional risk to the safety of the personnel participating in the operation.'

In addition, Art. II of the Optional Protocol to the UN Safety Convention expands the term 'United Nations operation' to include: 'all other United Nations operations established by a competent organ of the United Nations in accordance with the Charter of the United Nations and conducted under United Nations authority and control for the purposes of: (a) Delivering humanitarian, political or development assistance in peace building, or (b) Delivering emergency humanitarian assistance.' Optional Protocol to the Convention on the Safety of United Nations and Associated Personnel, Art. II, 8 December 2005, UN Doc. A/RES/60/518.

3.   The obligation to respect and protect United Nations personnel means that it is prohibited to attack, threaten, or harm them in any way, including through cyber operations. Additionally, there may be no interference with the accomplishment of the mandate, for example, by directing cyber operations against the implementing force's networks.[27] The prohibition extends to persons or locations placed under United Nations protection within the context of the mandate. 'Protect' refers to the duty to take those feasible steps necessary to ensure that others do not attack, threaten, harm, or interfere with them.

4.   Attacks against United Nations personnel, whether kinetic or cyber, are prohibited as long as the United Nations is not a party to the armed conflict and so long as its forces or civilian personnel do not take a direct part in hostilities (Rule 35).[28] United Nations forces must refrain, in particular, from conducting cyber attacks; to do otherwise will result in the loss of their protected status. Of course, United Nations personnel have the right to act in self-defence and, when so authorized by a Security Council resolution, may forcibly resist armed attempts to interfere with the execution of the mandate.[29]

5.   If the threshold of armed conflict is crossed during hostilities between United Nations forces and those of a State or organized armed group (Rule 20), or if United Nations forces become a party to an on-going armed conflict, the law of armed conflict will apply to their operations.[30] In such cases, United Nations military personnel may be treated as combatants and their military equipment, including military computers and information systems, as military objectives subject to attack, including by cyber means. United Nations non-military

---

[27] AMW Manual, commentary accompanying Rule 98(a); ICRC Customary IHL Study, commentary accompanying Rule 33.

[28] UK Manual, para. 14.15; AMW Manual, Rule 98(b).

[29] UK Manual, para. 14.9. See also UN Secretariat, United Nations Peacekeeping Operations: Principles and Guidelines 34–5 (2008).

[30] UK Manual, para. 14.4; UN Secretary General, Secretary-General's Bulletin on the Observance by United Nations Forces of International Humanitarian Law, UN Doc. ST/SGB/1999/13 (6 August 1999). In accordance with Art. 2(2) of the United Nations Safety Convention, this Rule does not apply to 'a United Nations operation authorized by the Security Council as an enforcement action under Chapter 7 of the Charter of the United Nations, in which any of the personnel are engaged as combatants against organized armed forces and to which the law of international armed conflict applies'. For a discussion of combatants and organized armed groups (forces), see Commentary accompanying Rule 26.

personnel, like other civilians, must not be made the object of attack unless they directly participate in hostilities.[31]

6.   The dividing line between reacting to an attack in self-defence and becoming a party to an international or non-international armed conflict is, in principle, subject to the same criteria that apply to other actors (Rule 20). Consider the case of an international armed conflict to which United Nations-mandated national contingents have been deployed to enforce a peace settlement. The peace agreement breaks down and the armed forces of one of the parties to the conflict undertake cyber attacks against the military communications networks of the United Nations-mandated forces, which they suspect of supplying intelligence to their enemy. By limiting their cyber or other actions in response to those necessary to stop the attacks, the United Nations-mandated forces remain protected by the previous Rule.

7.   *Lit.* (b) applies to personnel who do not qualify as United Nations personnel. It also applies to operations that are not United Nations operations in the sense of Article 1(c) of the United Nations Safety Convention because they are not 'conducted under United Nations authority and control'.

8.   Although not conducted under United Nations authority and control, for *lit.* (b) to apply the mission in question must be 'in accordance with the United Nations Charter'.[32] This will usually mean that the Security Council has authorized it. Additionally, the purpose of such a mission must either be to deliver humanitarian assistance or conduct peacekeeping. Humanitarian assistance and peacekeeping operations presuppose consent by the host nation and any States that are parties to the conflict.

9.   As in the case of United Nations personnel, protection against attack ceases when a force of the sort referred to in *lit.* (b) becomes a party to the armed conflict. Protection of individual members of that force ceases when they directly participate in the conflict.

SECTION 3:   DETAINED PERSONS

1.   This section addresses certain cyber-relevant provisions of the law of armed conflict governing the treatment of prisoners of war, interned

---

[31] AMW Manual, commentary accompanying Rule 98(b).
[32] Rome Statute Arts. 8(2)(b)(iii), 8(2)(e)(iii).

protected persons, and others who are detained, including security detainees, detained civilians who have taken a direct part in hostilities, and those detained on criminal charges with a nexus to the armed conflict. It must be understood that there is an extensive body of law governing the treatment of detained persons. The following Rules deal only with those few aspects of that law that raise issues relating to cyber operations and activities.

2.   The legal regime governing detention of the various categories of detained persons differs based on the characterization of the conflict (Rules 22 and 23). In particular, and with the exception of Common Article 3, the protections set forth in Geneva Conventions III and IV apply only in international armed conflict, although certain analogous customary provisions may apply to non-international armed conflict.

Rule 75 – Protection of detained persons

Prisoners of war, interned protected persons, and other detained persons must be protected from the harmful effects of cyber operations.

1.   The categories of prisoner of war under Geneva Convention III and interned civilians under Geneva Convention IV relate only to international armed conflicts. Those instruments and Article 75 of Additional Protocol I, which the Experts considered to reflect customary international law, govern their treatment. The treatment of detained persons in the context of a non-international armed conflict is governed by Common Article 3 of the 1949 Geneva Conventions, customary international law, and, where applicable, the relevant provisions of Additional Protocol II.[33]

2.   Detaining parties[34] are responsible for the security and well-being of prisoners of war, interned protected persons, and other detainees.[35] Precautions must be taken to protect them from the harmful effects of

---

[33] Additional Protocol II, Arts. 4, 5 (as well as other applicable law, such as, in certain circumstances, human rights law).

[34] In an international armed conflict, the correct term is 'detaining power'. However, because this Rule encompasses norms applicable in international and non-international armed conflict, the generic term 'detaining party' has been adopted in this Manual.

[35] See generally Geneva Convention III, Art. 12; Geneva Convention IV, Art. 29; Hague Regulations, Arts. 4, 7; US COMMANDER'S HANDBOOK, paras. 11.1–11.8; UK MANUAL, paras. 8.26, 9.37–9.118; CANADIAN MANUAL, paras. 1014, 1129; GERMAN MANUAL, paras. 592–5, 702, 704, 714–26.

cyber operations.[36] All detained persons are also protected from cyber activities that contribute to or result in outrages on personal dignity, torture, or cruel, inhuman, humiliating or degrading treatment.[37]

3.   It is prohibited to employ cyber means to prevent or frustrate a detaining party's efforts to honour its obligations, such as recording personal details, with respect to prisoners of war, interned protected persons, and other detainees.[38]

4.   Feasible measures must be taken to protect personal data relating to prisoners of war and interned protected persons from the effects of cyber operations, for example by being stored separately from data or objects that constitute a military objective. Such data must be respected and may not be modified or publicly exposed.[39] This applies to data in the possession of the detaining party, any Protecting Power, and the International Committee of the Red Cross.

5.   Detaining parties must ensure their networks and computers are not employed to violate the honour or respect owed to prisoners of war and interned protected persons.[40] Protection extends beyond the physical person.[41] Prohibited cyber actions include posting defamatory information that reveals embarrassing or derogatory information or their emotional state.[42] This would embrace, for example, posting information or images on the Internet that could be demeaning or that could subject prisoners of war or interned protected persons to public ridicule or public curiosity.

6.   Treaties governing the treatment of prisoners of war and interned protected persons generally guarantee a detention regime of privacy and protection from public abuse and curiosity.[43] Detaining parties must

---

[36] Additional Protocol II, Art. 5(2)(c); Geneva Convention III, Art. 23; Geneva Convention IV, Art. 83; UK MANUAL, paras. 8.35, 8.39, 9.39; GERMAN MANUAL, paras. 543, 710, 714.

[37] Additional Protocol I, Art. 75(2)(b), 85(4)(c); Additional Protocol II, Art. 4(2)(e); Geneva Conventions I–IV Art. 3; Geneva Convention III, Art. 14; Geneva Convention IV, Art. 27; UK MANUAL, paras. 8.29(d), 9.21; GERMAN MANUAL, paras. 595, 704.

[38] Additional Protocol II, Art. 5(2)(b); Geneva Convention III, Arts. 70, 71 (stating provisions accounting for prisoners writing to family members); Geneva Convention IV, Arts. 106, 107.

[39] Geneva Convention III, Art. 13; Geneva Convention IV, Art. 27.

[40] Geneva Convention III, Arts. 13, 14; Geneva Convention IV, Art. 27.

[41] ICRC GENEVA CONVENTION III COMMENTARY at 144; ICRC GENEVA CONVENTION IV COMMENTARY at 201–2.

[42] ICRC GENEVA CONVENTION III COMMENTARY at 145 (discussing protection against 'libel, slander, insult and any violation of secrets of a personal nature'); ICRC GENEVA CONVENTION IV COMMENTARY at 202. See also CANADIAN MANUAL, para. 1016; GERMAN MANUAL, paras. 595, 704.

[43] Geneva Convention III, Art. 13; Geneva Convention IV, Art. 27. See also UK MANUAL, paras. 8.28, 8.29(d), 9.21.

guard against intrusion by public and private actors into the communications, financial assets, or electronic records of prisoners of war or
interned protected persons.[44]

Rule 76 – Correspondence of detained persons

**The right of prisoners of war, interned protected persons, and other
detained persons to certain correspondence must not be interfered
with by cyber operations.**

1.   In an international armed conflict, detaining parties must permit
prisoners of war and interned protected persons to maintain relations
with the exterior[45] and to notify families of their detention within one
week of arrival at a place of internment.[46] The obligations reflect customary international law.[47]

2.   Individuals detained for security reasons in non-international
armed conflict are entitled under customary international law to correspond with their families, subject to reasonable conditions. In particular,
persons who are detained in the context of a non-international armed
conflict to which Additional Protocol II applies are specifically permitted
to maintain correspondence with family members.[48]

3.   The correspondence addressed in this Rule denotes communication with family or other private persons of a strictly personal, non-
military, non-political nature. Traditionally, the term 'correspondence'
referred to letters or other handwritten communications. It is unclear
whether, as a matter of law, correspondence includes electronic communications, for example email. This is because the law is clear that a right
of correspondence exists, but is not prescriptive as to its form.

4.   The detaining party may take into consideration such factors as
the difficulty of achieving an acceptable level of assurance that electronic
communications are not being misused when determining which mode
of communication to allow. Although this Rule is meant to apply to the

---

[44]   UK MANUAL, para. 8.29(d); ICRC CUSTOMARY IHL STUDY, commentary accompanying
Rule 122.
[45]   Geneva Convention III, Arts. 69–77; Geneva Convention IV, Arts. 105–16; UK Manual,
paras. 8.62, 8.63, 9.61, 9.62; German Manual, paras. 595, 721.
[46]   Geneva Convention III, Art. 70; Geneva Convention IV, Art. 106; UK MANUAL, paras.
8.42, 9.45.
[47]   ICRC CUSTOMARY IHL STUDY, Rule 125.
[48]   Additional Protocol II, Art. 5(2)(b). See also UK MANUAL, para. 15.41.b; NIAC MANUAL,
para. 3.6 (regarding notification of status and location).

detaining party and not to interference by others, the detaining party will, if it permits electronic correspondence, be obliged to take basic reasonable and feasible security measures to ensure the message is delivered intact to the recipient.

5. The customary right of detained persons to correspond with their families is subject to reasonable conditions relating, inter alia, to frequency and to the need for censorship by the authorities.[49] If the detaining party decides to permit electronic communications, the setting of conditions will be particularly important because of factors like the difficulty of verifying the identity of the recipient of outgoing communications and the risk of malware being spread through incoming messages. Such conditions do not constitute interference with correspondence for the purpose of this Rule.[50]

6. The term 'interference' denotes activities by the detaining party that deny or impede the detainees' right to correspond or which take advantage of that right for its own purposes. For instance, manipulating such correspondence to include malicious computer codes in order to engage in espionage, conduct a cyber attack, or mount a psychological operation is prohibited by the terms of this Rule.

Rule 77 – Compelled participation in military activities

Prisoners of war and interned protected persons shall not be compelled to participate in or support cyber operations directed against their own country.

1. This Rule is based on Article 23(h) of the Hague Regulations; Articles 50 and 130 of Geneva Convention III; and Articles 40, 51, and 147 of Geneva Convention IV. It reflects customary international law in international armed conflict.[51] Indeed, the law of armed conflict extends the prohibition beyond those encompassed by this Rule. For example, nationals of a State who find themselves in enemy territory and protected

---

[49] Geneva Convention III, Art. 76; Geneva Convention IV, Art. 112; UK MANUAL, paras. 9.59, 9.66.

[50] So long as they do not violate Geneva Convention III, Art. 76, or Geneva Convention IV, Art. 112.

[51] See also Rome Statute, Art. 8(2)(a)(v); US COMMANDER'S HANDBOOK, para. 11.3.1.2; CANADIAN MANUAL, paras. 1030, 1124; UNITED STATES ARMY, ARMY REGULATION 190–8: ENEMY PRISONERS OF WAR, RETAINED PERSONNEL, CIVILIAN INTERNEES AND OTHER DETAINEES, paras. 4-4-4-5 (1997); GERMAN MANUAL, paras. 596, 720.

persons in occupied territory enjoy the same protection.[52] The Rule is not applicable in non-international armed conflict.

2. The general rule is particularly relevant in the cyber context. Prisoners of war, by virtue of their former duties with enemy armed forces, may possess knowledge as to enemy computer systems or networks. Such knowledge would be of great value to a detaining party planning a cyber attack. Certain civilian detainees might likewise possess expertise or knowledge of operationally or strategically important information systems. Notwithstanding the obvious advantage of compelling these individuals to engage in cyber operations harmful to their country, doing so is clearly prohibited.

SECTION 4:   CHILDREN

Rule 78 – Protection of children

It is prohibited to conscript or enlist children into the armed forces or to allow them to take part in cyber hostilities.

1. This Rule applies in international and non-international armed conflict and reflects customary international law.[53] More specific treaty law obligations are to be found in Article 38 of the Convention on the Rights of the Child; Articles 1, 2, and 4 of the Optional Protocol to the Convention on the Rights of the Child on the Involvement of Children in Armed Conflict; Article 77(2) of Additional Protocol I; and Article 4(3)(c) of Additional Protocol II. It should be noted that Article 4 of the Optional Protocol applies to organized armed groups, as distinct from the armed forces of a State. These rules are consistent with the general protection afforded to children under the law of armed conflict.[54]

---

[52] Geneva Convention IV, Arts. 40, 51; UK MANUAL, paras. 9.30, 9.77.

[53] *Lubanga* judgment, paras. 600–28; GERMAN MANUAL, paras. 306, 505; NIAC MANUAL, para. 3.5; ICRC CUSTOMARY IHL STUDY, Rules 136, 137. *See also* Rome Statute, Arts. 8(2)(b)(xxvi), 8(2)(e)(vii); Sierra Leone Statute, Art. 4(c).

[54] *See* CRC Optional Protocol, preamble (stating, 'Considering therefore that to strengthen further the implementation of rights recognized in the Convention on the Rights of the Child there is a need to increase the protection of children from involvement in armed conflict'). *See also* Convention concerning the Prohibition and Immediate Action for the Elimination of the Worst Forms of Child Labour, Art. 3(a), 17 June 1999, I.L.O. Convention No. 182. The International Criminal Court has observed, 'These provisions recognise the fact that "children are particularly vulnerable [and] require privileged treatment in comparison with the rest of the civilian population". The principal objective underlying these prohibitions historically is to protect children under the age of 15 from

2. For the purposes of this Rule, the term 'children' refers to persons under the age of fifteen years.[55] Provisions of the Optional Protocol apply the prohibition to persons under the age of eighteen years and bind States Party to that instrument.[56] The International Group of Experts did not achieve consensus on whether customary international law had evolved to this standard or remained at fifteen years. Accordingly, this Rule adopts the position that children under the age of fifteen may never be used in the conduct of cyber hostilities.[57]

3. Rule 78 prohibits the conscription or enlistment of children into the armed forces or any other organized armed group under any circumstances. The prohibition extends to the conscription and enlistment of children who are not subsequently used to participate in hostilities.

4. States must, therefore, take all feasible measures to ensure that children do not participate in hostilities (Rule 35).[58] The State's obligation in this regard applies regardless of whether the children are to be used by the armed forces or organized armed groups or operate on their own.[59] There is no reason to exclude engaging in cyber activities from the ambit of participation.

5. The term 'take part' was adopted from Rule 137 of the ICRC Customary IHL Study. Various instruments dealing with the use of children in armed conflicts employ different criteria regarding the activities in question. For instance, Additional Protocol I uses the phrase 'direct part in hostilities',[60] while Additional Protocol II refers to 'take part'.[61] The Rome Statute uses the phrase 'participate actively in hostilities'.[62] Interpretations of these criteria vary. Some commentators and tribunals treat 'active' and 'direct' participation as synonymous, while others take the position that they are distinct.[63] In light of the

---

the risks that are associated with armed conflict, and first and foremost they are directed at securing their physical and psychological well-being.' *Lubanga* judgment, para. 605.

[55] Rome Statute, Art. 8(2)(b)(xxvi); Convention on the Rights of the Child Art. 38(2)–(3); UK Manual, paras. 4.11, 15.7–15.7.1; Canadian Manual, para. 1714; German Manual, paras. 306, 505; ICRC Customary IHL Study, commentary accompanying Rule 136.

[56] CRC Optional Protocol Arts. 1, 2, 4(1).   [57] *Lubanga* judgment, paras. 620–8.

[58] CRC Optional Protocol, Arts. 1, 4(2); Rome Statute, Arts. 8(2)(b)(xxvi), 8(2)(e)(vii); Convention on the Rights of the Child, Art. 38(2).

[59] CRC Optional Protocol, Arts. 1, 4(2).   [60] Additional Protocol I, Art. 77(2).

[61] Additional Protocol II, Art. 4(3)(c).   [62] Rome Statute, Art. 8(2)(b)(xxvi), 8(2)(e)(vii).

[63] Compare *Akayesu* judgment, para. 629, and ICRC Interpretive Guidance, fn. 84, with *Lubanga* judgment, para. 627.

prohibition's object and purpose, the International Group of Experts agreed that the term 'take part' was appropriate.

SECTION 5:   JOURNALISTS

Rule 79 – Protection of journalists

Civilian journalists engaged in dangerous professional missions in areas of armed conflict are civilians and shall be respected as such, in particular with regard to cyber attacks, as long as they are not taking a direct part in hostilities.

1.   This Rule, based on Article 79 of Additional Protocol I, reflects customary international law applicable in international and non-international armed conflict.[64] It is especially relevant in the cyber context because of the heavy reliance of contemporary journalists on computers and communication systems and networks.

2.   Some Experts took the position that Rule 34 of the ICRC Customary IHL Study accurately reflects customary international law. According to that rule, 'civilian journalists engaged in professional missions in areas of armed conflict must be respected and protected, as long as they are not taking a direct part in hostilities'. The accompanying commentary asserts 'there is also practice which indicates that journalists exercising their professional activities in relation to an armed conflict must be protected'.

3.   The majority of the International Group of Experts took the view that the only customary obligation is to 'respect' journalists, rather than 'protect' them. Parties to the conflict must not harm journalists, but are not obliged to protect them from being harmed by others, for instance, by cyber means. A majority of the Experts also took the position that this Rule applies only to the obligation to respect the journalists themselves and not to their journalistic activities or products, such as content posted on a website. They were unwilling to go beyond the text

---

[64] UK MANUAL, para. 8.18; CANADIAN MANUAL, paras. 313, 441; GERMAN MANUAL, para. 515; NIAC MANUAL, para. 3.10; ICRC CUSTOMARY IHL STUDY, Rule 34; US Department of Defense, *Memorandum on 1977 Protocols Additional to the Geneva Conventions: Customary International Law Implications* (9 May 1986) *reprinted in* UNITED STATES ARMY JUDGE ADVOCATE GENERAL'S SCHOOL, LAW OF WAR DOCUMENTARY SUPPLEMENT 234 (2011) (citing with approval Additional Protocol I, Art. 79, 'as supportable for inclusion in customary law through state practice').

of Article 79 of Additional Protocol I. This is particularly relevant in the cyber context given the dependency of many journalistic activities on systems and equipment that are vulnerable to cyber operations. Of course, such systems and equipment are protected as civilian objects unless they become military objectives pursuant to Rule 38. In some circumstances, they may be requisitioned or confiscated in accordance with Rule 90.

4. For purposes of this Rule, 'journalists' includes reporters, cameramen, photographers, and sound technicians.[65] The ICRC commentary to Article 79 of Additional Protocol I limits the term to persons 'working for the press and other media'.[66] The International Group of Experts agreed that the term 'journalist' extends to those affiliated with established, exclusively online, media organizations. No consensus was reached as to whether it includes private individuals who produce web logs (blogs) unaffiliated with the established media.

5. The law of armed conflict distinguishes 'war correspondents' from 'journalists engaged in dangerous professional missions'.[67] War correspondents are formally accredited by the armed forces they accompany. They are civilians, although, unlike journalists, they have prisoner of war status if captured.[68] Members of the armed forces conducting journalism as part of their duties are not journalists, but rather combatants.[69]

6. The law of armed conflict does not prohibit the censorship of journalists and war correspondents by cyber or other means.[70] The lack of such a prohibition has practical significance in military operations. Consider the case of imminent or on-going offensive operations. A potential implication of the speed and pervasiveness of modern journalistic communications is that any report could

---

[65] This definition accords generally with the United Nations Convention on the Protection of Journalists Engaged in Dangerous Missions in Areas of Armed Conflict, Annex I, Art. 2(a), UN Doc. A/10147 (1 August 1975) (identifying as 'journalists' any 'correspondent, reporter, photographer, and their technical film, radio and television assistants who are ordinarily engaged in any of these activities as their principal occupation').

[66] ICRC ADDITIONAL PROTOCOLS COMMENTARY, para. 3260.

[67] *Compare* Geneva Convention III, Art. 4A(4), *with* Additional Protocol I, Art. 79(1)–(2). *See also* CANADIAN MANUAL, paras. 313–14; ICRC CUSTOMARY IHL STUDY, commentary accompanying Rule 34.

[68] Geneva Convention III, Art. 4A(4); US COMMANDER'S HANDBOOK, para. 11.5; UK MANUAL, para. 8.18; CANADIAN MANUAL, para. 314; GERMAN MANUAL, para. 515.

[69] ICRC ADDITIONAL PROTOCOLS COMMENTARY, para. 3262.

[70] To the extent censorship rules exist, they are in the domain of municipal or domestic law.

jeopardize the success of the operations or place those involved at increased risk. It would not be a violation of the law of armed conflict to prevent or restrict reports on them.

7. Journalistic equipment does not enjoy special status. Equipment belonging to or used by journalists in their professional activities is civilian objects protected as such, unless it qualifies as military objectives pursuant to Rule 38. Thus, computers, data, networks, communications, and connections used for journalism enjoy no protection beyond their status as civilian objects.

8. As civilians, journalists are subject to the Rule regarding direct participation in hostilities. Although journalistic activities such as investigating, conducting interviews, taking notes, and making recordings using cyber facilities and materials are not regarded as acts of direct participation *per se*, such actions, if undertaken in direct support of military operations, could rise to that level or constitute espionage (Rules 35 and 66).

9. The issue of whether the use of electronic or other media to spread propaganda qualifies as direct participation in hostilities (and the associated question of whether the objects used qualify as military objectives) is unsettled. The majority of the International Group of Experts took the position that broadcasts used to incite war crimes, genocide, or crimes against humanity render a journalist a direct participant and make the equipment used military objectives liable to attack, including by cyber means.[71] A minority disagreed. The majority of the International Group of Experts also took the position that spreading propaganda does not *per se* constitute direct participation in hostilities,[72] while the minority suggested that the use of networks or computers to spread propaganda might convert journalistic equipment into a military objective for purposes of cyber attacks.[73] In any case, these issues are highly fact contingent.

---

[71] The direct participation constituent elements of 'threshold of harm' and 'direct causation' can be met by harm to protected persons or objects. ICRC INTERPRETIVE GUIDANCE at 47–57. On incitement to genocide, see *Ferdinand Nahimana et al.* v. *Prosecutor*, paras. 677–715, Case No. ICTR 99-52-A, Appeals Chamber judgment (Int'l Crim. Trib. for Rwanda 28 November 2007).

[72] ICRC INTERPRETIVE GUIDANCE at 51.

[73] *But see* Final Report to the Prosecutor by the Committee Established to Review the NATO Bombing Campaign Against the Federal Republic of Yugoslavia, 39 INTERNATIONAL LEGAL MATERIALS 1257, para. 76 (13 June 2000).

SECTION 6: INSTALLATIONS CONTAINING DANGEROUS FORCES

Rule 80 – Duty of care during attacks on dams, dykes, and nuclear electrical generating stations

In order to avoid the release of dangerous forces and consequent severe losses among the civilian population, particular care must be taken during cyber attacks against works and installations containing dangerous forces, namely dams, dykes, and nuclear electrical generating stations, as well as installations located in their vicinity.

1. Article 56 of Additional Protocol I and Article 15 of Additional Protocol II provide that, subject to certain exceptions, the works and installations referred to in this Rule cannot be attacked, even when they are military objectives, if such attack may cause the release of dangerous forces and result in severe losses among the civilian population. There is general agreement that the two Articles do not constitute customary international law.[74] This Rule, which is drawn from Rule 42 of the ICRC Customary IHL Study, reflects a more limited prohibition than those in the Additional Protocols. The International Group of Experts agreed that it is customary in nature.[75] It follows that Parties to the two instruments are bound to a higher level of protection than that set forth in this Rule.[76]

2. Rule 80 is a special precautionary Rule regarding the degree of care to be taken when undertaking a cyber attack on an installation containing dangerous forces that qualifies as a military objective (Rule 38).[77] Even States not Party to Additional Protocols I or II acknowledge that the civilian population enjoys protection against excessive collateral damage that is to be expected from attacks on dams, dykes, and nuclear electrical generating stations pursuant to the rule of

---

[74] ICRC CUSTOMARY IHL STUDY, commentary accompanying Rule 42.

[75] *See also* AMW MANUAL, Rule 36; NIAC MANUAL, para. 4.2.3.

[76] UK MANUAL, paras. 5.30 (as amended) –5.30.10, 15.51–15.51.1; CANADIAN MANUAL, para. 444; GERMAN MANUAL, paras. 464–70; AMW MANUAL, commentary accompanying Rule 36. Some States Parties have qualified their obligations under Art. 56 of Additional Protocol I for purposes of reprisal. For instance, the United Kingdom made a statement on ratification reserving the right for high levels of command to authorize attack of installations that contribute to the enemy's war effort. UK Additional Protocols Ratification Statement, para. (n).

[77] ICRC ADDITIONAL PROTOCOLS COMMENTARY, para. 4817.

proportionality (Rule 51).[78] In that the risk of collateral damage is especially acute when attacking such objects, particular care must be taken to avoid the release of dangerous forces likely to cause severe losses among the civilian population.

3.   The majority of the International Group of Experts took the position that the term 'particular care' means that in determining which precautions are practically possible, account must be taken of the particular dangers posed by the forces referred to in the Rule. Consider malware intended to reduce enemy electrical supply by taking a nuclear power plant off-line. Paying insufficient attention when planning the attack to safeguarding the core from meltdown by ensuring the continued integrity of its cooling system would violate this Rule.

4.   A minority of the Experts were of the view that the word 'particular' should not appear in the Rule because the requirement to take precautions in attack (Rules 52 to 58) already requires doing everything feasible to avoid collateral damage. In their view, the notion of particular care adds nothing to the requirement to take all feasible precautions. For instance, in the example above, the precautions requirement would likewise have necessitated consideration of the possibility of reactor meltdown. However, as they considered that the words add nothing of substance to the Rule, they decided not to block consensus on the point.

5.   The term 'severe losses' is drawn from Article 56(1) of Additional Protocol I. The determination as to whether the release of dangerous forces will cause severe losses among the civilian population must be judged in good faith on the basis of objective elements, such as the existence of densely populated areas of civilians that could be affected by the release of dangerous forces.[79]

6.   This Rule is confined to dams, dykes, nuclear electrical generating stations, and military objectives located in their vicinity,[80] as well as to computers and computer networks that form an integral part of and support the operations of such works or installations. It does not apply to any other works or installations containing dangerous forces or

---

[78] US COMMANDER'S HANDBOOK, para. 8.9.1.7. The Handbook states: 'Dams, dikes, levees, and other installations, which if breached or destroyed would release flood waters or other forces dangerous to the civilian population, should not be bombarded if the anticipated harm to civilians would be excessive in relation to the anticipated military advantage to be gained by bombardment.'

[79] ICRC ADDITIONAL PROTOCOLS COMMENTARY, paras. 2154, 4821.

[80] ICRC ADDITIONAL PROTOCOLS COMMENTARY, paras. 2147–53.

substances, such as chemical plants and petroleum refineries.[81] Rules 37 to 39 and 51 to 58 govern attacks on these facilities.

7.   The requirement to take particular care when attacking the installations and supporting cyber infrastructure referred to in this Rule does not apply when they are used regularly in direct support of military operations and attack is the only feasible way to terminate the use.[82] Such support must be a departure from the installation's ordinary function. For example, occasional military use of electricity generated by a nuclear power station does not bar the application of the Rule. If the protection ceases and any of the computers and computer networks that support the dams, dykes, and nuclear electrical generating stations are the object of a cyber attack, all feasible precautions must be taken to avoid the release of the dangerous forces in accordance with the general requirement to take precautions in attack (Rules 52 to 58).[83] Of course, the principle of proportionality also applies (Rule 51).

8.   Article 56(6) of Additional Protocol I provides for the optional identification of works and installations containing dangerous forces. As a matter of good practice, and when feasible, works and installations containing dangerous forces should also be identified with agreed-upon electronic markings, which would be particularly useful with regard to cyber operations.[84] Such electronic markings can be used to supplement the special sign that indicates dams, dykes, and nuclear electrical generating stations. The absence of electronic or physical markings does not deprive them of their protected status.

SECTION 7: OBJECTS INDISPENSABLE TO THE SURVIVAL OF THE CIVILIAN POPULATION

Rule 81 – Protection of objects indispensable to survival

Attacking, destroying, removing, or rendering useless objects indispensable to the survival of the civilian population by means of cyber operations is prohibited.

---

[81] AMW MANUAL, commentary accompanying Rule 36.
[82] Additional Protocol I, Art. 56(2). *See also* UK MANUAL, paras. 5.30.5, fn. 124 (p. 406); CANADIAN MANUAL, para. 444; GERMAN MANUAL, para. 465.
[83] Additional Protocol I, Art. 56(3).
[84] Additional Protocol I, Art. 56(6). Art. 56(7) sets forth a physical means of marking installations containing dangerous forces. *See also* US COMMANDER'S HANDBOOK, figure 8-1j; UK MANUAL, para. 5.30.9.

1. This Rule is based on Article 54(2) of Additional Protocol I for international armed conflict and reflects customary international law. It supplements the protection of civilians against direct attack (Rule 32). While it is a distinct and independent rule, it should also be considered together with the Rule prohibiting starvation of civilians as a method of warfare (Rule 45).

2. The majority of the International Group of Experts took the position that the Rule applies in non-international armed conflict as a matter of customary international law.[85] A minority of the Experts noted that Article 14 of Additional Protocol II prohibits the stated activities only when undertaken for the purpose of starvation of civilians as a method of combat. Accordingly, they concluded that customary law applicable in non-international armed conflict is only violated when the stated activities are undertaken to starve the civilian population.

3. Application of the Rule, as with Article 54(2), is limited to situations in which the objects are attacked, destroyed, removed, or rendered useless for the 'specific purpose of denying them for their sustenance value to the civilian population or to the adverse Party'. The motive underlying this intent is irrelevant so long as the purpose is to deny the civilian population their sustenance value. Operations with other purposes having this effect are not prohibited by this Rule.[86] Thus, for example, objects incidentally destroyed during a cyber attack on a military objective (collateral damage) do not come within its scope of application.[87] Similarly, if any of these objects qualify in the circumstances ruling at the time as a military objective, an attack against them does not violate the Rule.

4. The cited provisions of Additional Protocols I and II offer the following examples of objects indispensable to the survival of the civilian population: foodstuffs, agricultural areas for the production of foodstuffs,

---

[85] See *Partial Award, Western Front, Aerial Bombardment and Related Claims 1, 3, 5, 9–13, 14, 21, 25 and 26 (Eri. v. Eth.)* 26 R.I.A.A. paras. 98–105 (Eritrea-Ethiopia Claims Commission 2005); US COMMANDER'S HANDBOOK, para. 8.3; UK MANUAL, para. 5.27; CANADIAN MANUAL, para. 445; GERMAN MANUAL, para. 463; AMW MANUAL, Rule 97(b); NIAC MANUAL, commentary accompanying para. 2.3.10; ICRC CUSTOMARY IHL STUDY, Rule 54. *See also* Rome Statute, Art. 8(2)(b)(xxv).

[86] Additional Protocol I, Art. 54(2). *See, e.g.,* UK Additional Protocols Ratification Statement, para. (l) (stating this provision 'has no application to attacks that are carried out for a specific purpose other than denying sustenance to the civilian population or the adverse Party'); AMW MANUAL, commentary accompanying Rule 97(b).

[87] UK MANUAL, para. 5.27.2.

crops, livestock, drinking water installations and supplies, and irrigation works. Food and medical supplies are also generally accepted as essential to the survival of the civilian population, and Additional Protocol I mentions clothing, bedding, and means of shelter.[88] Although these lists are not exhaustive, the objects to which the Rule applies must be 'indispensable to survival'.[89] This is a very narrow category; objects not required for survival (e.g., those that merely enhance civilian well-being or quality of life) fall outside the scope of application of this Rule, although they are protected by the general rules on the protection of civilian objects (Rules 37 to 39).

5. The Internet (or other communications networks) does not, in and of itself, qualify as an object indispensable to the survival of the civilian population. In the context of cyber operations, however, cyber infrastructure indispensable to the functioning of electrical generators, irrigation works and installations, drinking water installations, and food production facilities could, depending on the circumstances, qualify.

6. As is clear from its text, the Rule extends beyond a prohibition of cyber attack. It proscribes any act designed to deny sustenance to the civilian population or to the adverse party.

7. In international armed conflicts,[90] the prohibition does not apply if the objects in question are used by the enemy solely for the sustenance of their forces or in direct support of military action.[91] The majority of the International Group of Experts concluded that, despite these two exceptions, cyber operations may not be conducted against objects if those operations can be expected to so deprive the civilian population of food or water that it starves or is forced to move.[92] A minority suggested that insufficient State practice existed to support the proposition.

---

[88] Additional Protocol I, Art. 69(1) (governing occupied territory); Additional Protocol II, Art. 18(2); Geneva Convention IV, Art. 55 (limited to Art. 4 protected persons); US COMMANDER's HANDBOOK, para. 8.3; UK MANUAL, para. 5.27; CANADIAN MANUAL, para. 445; GERMAN MANUAL, para. 463; AMW MANUAL, Rule 97(b); NIAC MANUAL, commentary accompanying para. 2.3.10.

[89] ICRC ADDITIONAL PROTOCOLS COMMENTARY, para. 2103.

[90] ICRC CUSTOMARY IHL STUDY, commentary accompanying Rule 54 (asserting that this exception does not apply to non-international armed conflicts 'because Article 14 of Additional Protocol II does not provide for it and there is no practice supporting it').

[91] Additional Protocol I, Art. 54(3).

[92] See, e.g., UK MANUAL, para. 5.19; CANADIAN MANUAL, para. 445; ICRC CUSTOMARY IHL STUDY, commentary accompanying Rule 54.

SECTION 8:   CULTURAL PROPERTY

Rule 82 – Respect and protection of cultural property

The parties to an armed conflict must respect and protect cultural property that may be affected by cyber operations or that is located in cyberspace. In particular, they are prohibited from using digital cultural property for military purposes.

1.   This Rule reflects the general theme contained in the 1954 Hague Cultural Property Convention and its Protocols of 1954 and 1999, as well as Additional Protocols I and II. It applies in both international and non-international armed conflict and is customary international law.[93]

2.   Cultural property comprises 'moveable or immoveable property of great importance to the cultural heritage of every people'.[94] Under the 1999 Second Protocol to the 1954 Hague Cultural Property Convention, cultural property that is the 'cultural heritage of the greatest importance for humanity' enjoys enhanced protection.[95] This Manual adopts the former definition because it reflects customary international law;[96] the latter definition is relevant only for States Party to the Second Protocol.

3.   The reference to 'respect and protect' in this Rule is drawn from Articles 2 and 4 of the 1954 Hague Cultural Property Convention. In addition to a prohibition on attacking cultural property,[97] 'respect' refers, in particular, to the obligation to take all feasible measures to avoid harming cultural property during the conduct of military operations.[98]

---

[93]   Additional Protocol I, Art. 53; Additional Protocol II, Art. 16; Cultural Property Convention, Arts. 18–19. Apart from the 1954 Convention, other relevant international treaty law supports the proposition generally. Hague Regulations, Art. 27; Convention (IX) concerning Bombardment by Naval Forces in Time of War, Art. 5, 18 October 1907, 1 Bevans 681; Treaty on the Protection of Artistic and Scientific Institutions and Historic Monuments (Roerich Pact), 15 April 1935, 167 L.N.T.S. 279; US COMMANDER'S HANDBOOK, para. 8.9.1.6; UK MANUAL, paras. 5.25–5.26.8 (as amended), 15.18–15.18.3, 15.52; CANADIAN MANUAL, paras. 111, 443; NIAC MANUAL, para. 4.2.2; ICRC CUSTOMARY IHL STUDY, Rules 38, 39. *See also* Rome Statute, Arts. 8(2)(b)(ix), 8(2)(e)(iv).

[94]   Cultural Property Convention, Art. 1(a) (providing examples of the categories of property); AMW MANUAL, Rule 1(o).

[95]   Second Cultural Property Protocol, Art. 10(a) (requiring also that objects enjoy domestic legal protection and not be used for military purposes).

[96]   UK MANUAL, paras. 5.25, 5.25.2; AMW MANUAL, Rule 1(o).

[97]   UK MANUAL, para. 5.25.1; GERMAN MANUAL, para. 903; AMW MANUAL, Rules 95, 96.

[98]   UK MANUAL, para. 5.25.3; GERMAN MANUAL, para. 903; AMW MANUAL, Rule 95(c) and commentary accompanying Rule 96.

The International Group of Experts agreed that this obligation extends to cyber operations. 'Protect', by contrast, denotes the obligation to take feasible protective measures to safeguard cultural property against harm caused by others during military operations.[99] For States Party to the 1954 Hague Cultural Property Convention and its 1999 Second Protocol, additional protective measures are required.

4. The International Group of Experts considered whether intangible items could qualify as 'property' for law of armed conflict purposes. Recall that in the context of civilian objects, as that term is used in Article 52 of Additional Protocol I, the Group generally rejected characterization of intangible items such as data as an 'object' (Rule 38). Problematic in this regard is the fact that Article 53 of the same instrument refers to 'cultural objects'. For some members of the Group, this led to the conclusion that cultural property must be tangible in nature and that intangible items like data do not qualify.

5. Other Experts emphasized that the term 'property' is not always limited to tangible objects. An example of a notion of intangible property that is well accepted in international law and that appears in most domestic legal systems is intellectual property. For these Experts, the critical question is whether the intangible property is cultural in nature. Examples include objects that are created and stored on a computing device and therefore only exist in digital form, such as musical scores, digital films, documents pertaining to e-government, and scientific data. Certain copies of objects of which a physical manifestation exists (or has existed) that can be used to create replicas also qualify as cultural property.[100]

6. No member of the International Group of Experts taking this position asserted that all digital manifestations of cultural property are entitled to the protection of this Rule. Protection only applies to digital copies or versions where the original is either inaccessible or has been destroyed, and where the number of digital copies that can be made is limited. Consider the example of a single extremely high-resolution image of Leonardo da Vinci's *Mona Lisa* comprising a terabyte of information. Such a digital copy might, and in the event of the destruction of the original *Mona Lisa* would, qualify as cultural property. However, due to

---

[99] AMW MANUAL, Rule 94.
[100] An important historical example of objects used for the purpose of building replicas are the historical maps, photographs, building plans, etc., which facilitated the rebuilding of Warsaw's Old Town after World War II.

the high speed and low cost of digital reproduction, once such a digital image has been replicated and widely downloaded, no single digital copy of the artwork would be protected by this Rule. This is because protection of cultural property is afforded based on the value and irreplaceability of the original work of art, and on the difficulty, time, and expense involved in reproducing faithful copies of that original. The logic underlying this Rule does not apply in cases where large numbers of high-quality reproductions can be made.

7. In the digital cultural property context, the term 'respect and protect' prohibits any alteration, damage, deletion, or destruction of the data, as well as its exploitation for military purposes. For instance, the use of digitized historical archives regarding a population to determine the ethnic origin of individuals with a view to facilitating genocide is clearly unlawful. Merely temporarily denying or degrading access, for example by affecting the functioning of electronic devices used for such access, is beyond the ambit of the protection of cultural property.

8. Like its physical counterpart, digital cultural property may not be used for military purposes. As an example, steganographically modified pieces of digital art lose any protection as cultural property in light of their use for military ends.

9. Article 16 of the Cultural Property Convention establishes a distinctive emblem for marking cultural property. It is appropriate to use such markings on qualifying digital cultural property. Additionally, use of a digital marking equivalent that places attackers on notice that the digital items qualify as protected cultural property is appropriate. Whilst no such marking has been formally established, multiple technological solutions are possible, including file-naming conventions, the use of tagging-data with machine-interpretable encoding schemes, published lists of IP addresses of digital cultural property, or generic top-level domain names.

10. Although cultural property may be attacked if it qualifies as a military objective, a decision to conduct such an attack must be taken at an appropriately high level. Parties to the conflict must give due consideration to the fact that the target is cultural property. Moreover, an attacker is required to provide an effective advance warning when feasible and may only conduct an attack when the warning remains unheeded after a reasonable period for compliance.[101]

---

[101] Second Cultural Property Protocol, Arts. 6(d), 13(2)(c)(ii); AMW MANUAL, Rule 96.

SECTION 9:   THE NATURAL ENVIRONMENT

Rule 83 – Protection of the natural environment

(a) **The natural environment is a civilian object and as such enjoys general protection from cyber attacks and their effects.**

(b) **States Party to Additional Protocol I are prohibited from employing cyber methods or means of warfare which are intended, or may be expected, to cause widespread, long-term, and severe damage to the natural environment.**

1.   *Lit.* (a) is based on the principle of distinction as well as the prohibition on attacking civilian objects (Rules 31 and 37). The International Group of Experts agreed that it accurately reflects customary international law in international armed conflict.[102] The majority of the International Group of Experts took the position that *lit.* (a) also applies to non-international armed conflicts.[103]

2.   *Lit.* (b) is based on Articles 35(3) and 55 of Additional Protocol I. Since the International Group of Experts was divided over whether *lit.* (b) reflects customary international law,[104] it has been drafted to apply only to States that are Party to the Protocol. Although Additional Protocol I does not apply to non-international armed conflict, certain Experts took the position that its provisions on the environment apply as a matter of customary law in such conflicts.

3.   There is no generally accepted definition of the 'natural environment'.[105] For the purposes of this Manual, the International Group of Experts adopted, with the exception of outer space, the definition set forth in Article II of the 1977 Environmental Modification Convention: 'the dynamics, composition or structure of the Earth, including its biota, lithosphere, hydrosphere and atmosphere'.[106] The Experts were divided over whether the term should encompass outer space. Those

---

[102]   US COMMANDER'S HANDBOOK, para. 8.4; CANADIAN MANUAL, paras. 446, 620, 709; GERMAN MANUAL, para. 401; AMW MANUAL, chapeau to sec. M; ICRC CUSTOMARY IHL STUDY, Rule 43.

[103]   UK MANUAL, para. 15.20; AMW MANUAL, commentary accompanying Rules 88, 89; NIAC Manual, para. 4.2.4; ICRC CUSTOMARY IHL STUDY, commentary accompanying Rule 43.

[104]   ICRC CUSTOMARY IHL STUDY, Rule 45.   [105]   AMW MANUAL, chapeau to sec. M.

[106]   Environmental Modification Convention, Art. II.

Experts opposing inclusion based their view on the lack of conclusive State practice and *opinio juris*.

4.   All members of the International Group of Experts concluded that the environment is a civilian object that, as such, is protected from direct cyber attacks unless and until it becomes a military objective (Rules 37 to 39). Therefore, those who plan, approve, or conduct a cyber attack must apply the rule of proportionality and the requirement to take precautions in attack (Rules 51 to 58) with respect to expected collateral damage to the natural environment.[107] For example, when planning a cyber attack against a military petroleum storage facility, the expected damage to the natural environment through any spillage of petroleum must be considered.

5.   Furthermore, the destruction of the natural environment carried out wantonly is prohibited.[108] 'Wanton' means that the destruction is the consequence of a deliberate action taken maliciously, that is, the action cannot be justified by military necessity.[109] For instance, it would be unlawful to use cyber means to trigger a release of oil into a waterway simply to cause environmental damage.

6.   States Party to Additional Protocol I are prohibited from conducting cyber attacks that are intended or may be expected to cause 'widespread, long-term, and severe' damage to the natural environment.[110] As to the expression, the ICRC commentary to Additional Protocol I notes that during negotiations at the Diplomatic Conference,

> The time or duration required (i.e., long-term) was considered by some to be measured in decades. Some representatives referred to twenty or thirty years as being a minimum period. Others referred to battlefield destruction in France in the First World War as being outside the scope of the prohibition ... It appeared to be a widely shared assumption that battlefield damage incidental to conventional warfare would not normally be proscribed by this provision. What the article is primarily directed to is thus such damage as would be likely to prejudice, over a long-term, the continued survival of the civilian population or would risk causing it major health problems.[111]

---

[107] US COMMANDER'S HANDBOOK, para. 8.4; AMW MANUAL, commentary accompanying Rule 88. *See also* Rome Statute, Art. 8(2)(b)(iv).

[108] Hague Regulations, Art. 23(g); US COMMANDER'S HANDBOOK, para. 8.4; AMW MANUAL, Rule 88; ICRC CUSTOMARY IHL STUDY, commentary accompanying Rule 43. *See also* Rome Statute, Art. 8(2)(a)(iv).

[109] Geneva Convention IV, Art. 147; AMW MANUAL, commentary accompanying Rule 88. *See also* Rome Statute, Arts. 8(2)(a)(iv), 8(2)(e)(xii).

[110] Additional Protocol I, Arts. 35(3), 55. *See also* UK MANUAL, para. 5.29; CANADIAN MANUAL, para. 446; GERMAN MANUAL, para. 403.

[111] ICRC ADDITIONAL PROTOCOLS COMMENTARY, para. 1454.

7. The conjunctive nature of the phrase 'widespread, long-term, and severe' makes it clear that the Rule is only breached when the environmental damage is exceptionally serious.[112]

SECTION 10: DIPLOMATIC ARCHIVES AND COMMUNICATIONS

Rule 84 – Protection of diplomatic archives and communications

Diplomatic archives and communications are protected from cyber operations at all times.

1. This Rule is based on Articles 24 and 27 of the 1961 Vienna Convention on Diplomatic Relations and on the International Court of Justice's *Tehran Hostages* judgment.[113]

2. The International Group of Experts agreed that this Rule is applicable in both international and non-international armed conflicts.[114] With regard to diplomatic archives, the protection in Article 24 of the Vienna Convention on Diplomatic Relations expressly applies 'at any time and wherever they may be'. In particular, Article 45(a) provides that 'The receiving State must, even in case of armed conflict, respect and protect the premises of the mission, together with its property and archives.' As to official diplomatic communications, Article 27 is implicitly applicable at all times based on the Article's object and purpose, as well as its context. State practice supports the characterization of these rules as customary in character. For example, in 1990 the United Nations Security Council condemned violations of diplomatic premises during Iraq's invasion of Kuwait.[115] The Security Council demanded compliance with the Vienna Convention, notwithstanding the existence of an international armed conflict.[116]

---

[112] Under the Environmental Modification Convention, the corresponding criteria are disjunctive. Environmental Modification Convention, Art. II.

[113] *Tehran Hostages* case, paras. 61–2, 77, 86. *See also* Vienna Convention on Consular Relations Arts. 33, 35, 24 April 1963, 596 U.N.T.S. 261.

[114] At the time of drafting, the Netherlands voiced a dissenting viewpoint, arguing that only the law of armed conflict covered wartime relationships between States. *See Documents of the Tenth Session including the Report of the Commission to the General Assembly*, [1958], 2 YEARBOOK OF THE INTERNATIONAL LAW COMMISSION 126, UN Doc. A/CN.4/SER.A/1958/Add. No record of concurrence by other States exists.

[115] S.C. Res. 667, para. 1 (16 September 1990); S.C. Res. 674, para. 1 (29 October 1990).

[116] S.C. Res. 667, para. 3 (16 September 1990).

3.   The International Court of Justice has emphasized the receiving State's obligations *vis-à-vis* diplomatic documents and archives. During the 1980 seizure of the US embassy in Iran, diplomatic documents and archives were ransacked and disseminated.[117] The International Court of Justice held that

> By a number of provisions of the Vienna Conventions of 1961 and 1963, Iran was placed under the most categorical obligations, as a receiving State, to take appropriate steps to ensure the protection of the United States Embassy and Consulates, their staffs, their archives, their means of communication and the freedom of movement of the members of their staffs.[118]

4.   The protection accorded to diplomatic archives and communications includes respect for their confidentiality, integrity, and availability. This requires a party to a conflict to refrain from any action that would interfere with their transmission or reception or impugn their maintenance. This point is particularly relevant in the cyber context.

5.   The protection of enemy diplomatic cyber equipment and communications does not cease merely because an armed conflict (irrespective of location) has come into existence. Even the suspension of diplomatic relations does not deprive them of their protection.[119]

6.   If diplomatic cyber equipment and communications are misused during an armed conflict, they may, depending on the nature of the misuse, become military objectives since the law of diplomatic relations is not a self-contained normative regime. In such a case, they accordingly lose protection from cyber operations, including cyber attacks (Rule 30).

SECTION 11:   COLLECTIVE PUNISHMENT

Rule 85 – Collective punishment

Collective punishment by cyber means is prohibited.

1.   This Rule is based on Article 50 of the Hague Regulations, Article 87 of Geneva Convention III, Article 33 of Geneva Convention IV, Article 75(2)(d) of Additional Protocol I, and Article 4(2)(b) of Additional

---

[117] *Tehran Hostages* case, para. 24.   [118] *Tehran Hostages* case, para. 61.
[119] Vienna Convention on Diplomatic Relations, Art. 45.

Protocol II. It is recognized as customary international law applicable in international and non-international armed conflict.[120]

2.   The Rule prohibits the use of cyber means to impose retaliatory sanctions on persons or groups for acts in which they were not involved. The majority of the International Group of Experts agreed that, as noted in the ICRC commentary to Geneva Convention IV, the notion of prohibited collective punishment should be understood liberally. It 'does not refer to punishments inflicted under penal law ... [but rather to] penalties of any kind inflicted on persons or entire groups of persons ... for acts those persons have not committed'.[121] The ICRC Additional Protocols Commentary similarly notes that 'the concept of collective punishment must be understood in the broadest sense; it covers not only legal sentences but sanctions and harassment of any sort, administrative, by police action or otherwise'.[122] As an example, the majority of the Experts agreed that shutting off all Internet access in an area with the primary purpose of punishing its inhabitants for acts committed by some individuals is collective punishment. A minority of the Experts disagreed, taking the position that the term 'punishment' does not encompass the imposition of mere inconvenience or annoyance. However, all of the Experts concurred that, for instance, confiscation of all the personal computers in a village in retaliation for cyber attacks conducted by a small cell of insurgents would violate the prohibition on collective punishment.

3.   Collective punishment is to be contrasted with measures taken by the Occupying Power in accordance with Rules 87 to 90 to ensure its own security or to promote public order and the security of the population. It is also to be distinguished from actions justifiable under those Rules that are directed at individuals, but may have unintended or undesired effects on others.

4.   Although Article 50 of the Hague Regulations applies only in occupied territory, Article 33 of Geneva Convention IV applies to persons protected by that instrument in both occupied territory and a party's own territory.[123] Additionally, Article 75(2)(d) of Additional Protocol I and

---

[120] US COMMANDER'S HANDBOOK, paras. 11.3.1.1, 11.5; UK MANUAL, paras. 8.121.a, 9.4.d, 9.24.d, 15.38.b; CANADIAN MANUAL, paras. 1039, 1135, 1713; GERMAN MANUAL, paras. 507, 536; NIAC MANUAL, para. 1.2.4; ICRC CUSTOMARY IHL STUDY, Rule 103. See also ICTR Statute, Art. 4(b); Statute of the Special Court for Sierra Leone, Art. 3(b).
[121] ICRC GENEVA CONVENTION IV COMMENTARY at 225.
[122] ICRC ADDITIONAL PROTOCOLS COMMENTARY, para. 3055.
[123] For the definition of 'protected persons', see Geneva Convention IV, Art. 4.

Article 4(2)(b) of Additional Protocol II apply 'at any time and in any place whatsoever'. The International Group of Experts therefore agreed that this Rule is not limited in application to occupied territories.

SECTION 12: HUMANITARIAN ASSISTANCE

Rule 86 – Humanitarian assistance

Cyber operations shall not be designed or conducted to interfere unduly with impartial efforts to provide humanitarian assistance.

1. This Rule is based on Articles 23 and 59 of Geneva Convention IV and Articles 69 and 70 of Additional Protocol I. The Rule applies in international armed conflict and is customary in nature.[124]

2. The International Group of Experts did not achieve consensus on this Rule's application in non-international armed conflict. Some Experts argued it is inapplicable to such conflicts, except as treaty law for States Party to Additional Protocol II. Others took the position that the Rule is not only encompassed in Article 18(2) of Additional Protocol II, but also reflects customary international law for States not Party to that instrument.[125] A number of the Experts adopting the latter view emphasized, however, that delivery of humanitarian assistance requires the receiving State's consent.[126] With regard to consent, these Experts were split. Some took the position that such consent may not be withheld unreasonably,[127] while others argued that that the provision of humanitarian assistance is entirely at the discretion of the receiving State.[128]

---

[124] AMW Manual, Rules 102(a), (b) and accompanying commentary. *See also* Rome Statute, Art. 8(2)(b)(iii).

[125] Rome Statute, Art. 8.2(e)(iii); AMW Manual, commentary accompanying Rule 102(a)–(b); ICRC Customary IHL Study, Rules 31, 32. The present rule should be distinguished as oriented toward State action with respect to, tolerance of, and support for humanitarian assistance efforts, rather than the protection of humanitarian assistance objects. The International Group of Experts considered the present rule better adapted to the cyber context. *See also* UK Manual, para. 15.54; NIAC Manual, para. 5.1.

[126] Additional Protocol II, Art. 18(2). See also UK Manual, para. 15.54.

[127] UK Manual at 409, n. 129; AMW Manual, commentary accompanying Rule 100(a).

[128] This position can only be taken by States that are not Party to Additional Protocol II or by Parties thereto during a non-international armed conflict to which the treaty does not apply. ICRC Additional Protocols Commentary, para. 4885, explains that Art. 18(2) is not subject to unbridled discretion.

3. Although the ICRC Customary IHL Study provides that 'Objects used for humanitarian relief operations must be respected and protected',[129] this Rule is oriented toward State action regarding the tolerance of, and support for, humanitarian assistance efforts. The International Group of Experts considered the present formulation better adapted to the cyber context.

4. The prohibition set forth in this Rule applies to all territory. Article 23 of Geneva Convention IV guarantees 'free passage' to a broad range of relief consignments 'intended only for civilians of another High Contracting Party, even if the latter is its adversary'.[130] Combined with the provisions on ensuring that the population of occupied territory or territory otherwise under a party's control is properly provided with humanitarian assistance, the obligation to refrain from interference with humanitarian assistance knows no geographical limit.

5. The term 'humanitarian assistance' is employed here as a term of art. Not all efforts to provide materiel or support to a civilian population constitute humanitarian assistance for the purposes of the Rule. Rather, humanitarian assistance is to be understood as analogous to the term 'relief actions' found in Article 70 of Additional Protocol I. Efforts to deliver essential supplies and support that relieves suffering qualify. Examples of items that have a humanitarian character include 'food and medical supplies ... clothing, bedding, means of shelter or other supplies essential to ... survival'.[131]

6. The provision of humanitarian assistance is subject to the agreement of the parties to the conflict and therefore reasonable conditions may be imposed.[132] However, the conditions may not 'interfere unduly' with relief efforts. For the purposes of this Manual, the term means to conduct cyber operations arbitrarily to frustrate or prevent legitimate and impartial relief efforts or in a manner unsupported by valid military considerations.[133]

7. Consider an example in which State A is engaged in an international armed conflict with State B on the territory of State B. Several

---

[129] ICRC CUSTOMARY IHL STUDY, Rule 32.
[130] Art. 13 of Geneva Convention IV extends the Part (which contains Art. 23) to 'the whole of the populations of the countries in conflict'.
[131] Additional Protocol I, Art. 69(1).
[132] Additional Protocol I, Art. 70(1)–(3); UK MANUAL, para. 9.12.2; CANADIAN MANUAL, para. 1113; GERMAN MANUAL, para. 503.
[133] See also AMW MANUAL, commentary accompanying Rule 101.

non-governmental organizations have established an infrastructure for
humanitarian relief operations to assist State B's internally displaced
population. In its cyber operations against State B, State A is obligated
to avoid undue interference with the communications and other cyber
activities of the non-governmental organizations offering humanitarian
assistance.

6

Occupation

1. The concept of occupation does not extend to non-international armed conflicts.[1]

2. All members of the International Group of Experts agreed that territory is 'occupied' once it is actually placed under the authority of the hostile army. This occurs when the Occupying Power substitutes its own authority for that of the occupied territory's government, which must have been rendered incapable of performing public functions.[2] The occupation extends to the territory where such authority has been established and can be exercised. While some of the Experts were of the view that occupation includes situations in which a party to the conflict is in a position to substitute its authority,[3] others took the position that actual exercise of authority is a condition precedent to occupation.[4] Occupation ends as soon as the exercise of military authority over foreign territory ends or has otherwise become ineffective.[5]

3. There is no legal notion of occupation of cyberspace. Furthermore, cyber operations cannot alone suffice to establish or maintain the degree of authority over territory necessary to constitute an occupation. However, cyber operations can be employed to help establish or maintain the requisite authority, for example, by enabling the issuance of certain notices required by the law of occupation to the population. Conversely,

---

[1] Geneva Conventions I–IV, Art. 2. In that occupation is the exercise of authority of a State over another State's territory, it logically does not apply to non-international armed conflicts. *See also* AMW Manual, commentary accompanying Rule 100(a).

[2] Hague Regulations, Art. 43.

[3] International Committee of the Red Cross, Occupation and Other Forms of Administration of Foreign Territory 19 (Tristan Ferraro ed., 2012).

[4] These Experts relied on *Armed Activities in Congo* judgment, para. 173.

[5] Hague Regulations, Art. 42; *Armed Activities in Congo* judgment, para. 172; *Wall* Advisory Opinion, paras. 78, 89. For those who are of the view that occupation begins when a State is in position to exercise its authority, occupation would end when it is no longer in such a position.

cyber operations are capable of employment to disrupt or degrade computer systems used by an Occupying Power to maintain authority.

4. For the purposes of this chapter, the term 'protected persons' refers to the civilians who 'find themselves ... in the hands' of an Occupying Power of which they are not nationals.[6] This includes civilians in occupied territory.[7]

5. None of the Rules below relieve the Occupying Power of any obligations it would otherwise bear pursuant to the law of belligerent occupation. For example, the seizure of a government computer by occupation forces would be governed by the general rule regarding seizure of any government property set forth in Article 53 of the Hague Regulations. Similarly, the rules regarding compelled labour set forth in Article 51 of Geneva Convention IV and Article 23 of the Hague Regulations apply equally in relation to cyber activities.

6. Protected persons may under no circumstances renounce any of their rights under the law of occupation.[8]

7. The Rules set forth in this chapter are based solely on the extant law of occupation, principally that set forth in the Hague Regulations and Geneva Convention IV, both of which reflect customary international law. It must be understood that United Nations Security Council resolutions may sometimes modify the application of these traditional rules.

Rule 87 – Respect for protected persons in occupied territory

Protected persons in occupied territory must be respected and protected from the harmful effects of cyber operations.

1. This Rule is based on Article 27 of Geneva Convention IV.[9] The International Group of Experts agreed that it reflects customary international law.

2. Subject to special provisions related to health, age, and gender,[10] the Occupying Power must treat all protected persons with the same consideration, without any adverse distinction based, in particular, on

---

[6] Geneva Convention IV, Art. 4. Note, however, that, according to Art. 4, protection is not accorded if they are nationals of a neutral or co-belligerent State that has normal diplomatic representation in the State.

[7] Hague Regulations, Art. 42. The end of occupation must not be confused with the end of an armed conflict. Additional Protocol I, Art. 3(b).

[8] Geneva Convention IV, Art. 8.

[9] See also Hague Regulations, Art. 46 (concerning respect for family honour and rights of persons in occupied territory).

[10] Geneva Convention IV, Arts. 16, 24, 27.

race, religion, or political opinion.[11] Accordingly, blocking Internet access of an element of the civilian population defined by reference to race, religion, or political affiliation would be prohibited by this Rule. However, the Occupying Power may take such measures of control and security with respect to protected persons as may be necessitated by the conflict (Rules 88 and 90).

3. Protected persons in occupied territory must be allowed to transmit news of a strictly personal nature to members of their families, wherever they may be, and to receive news from them without undue delay.[12] Although the Occupying Power may permit such correspondence to consist of email correspondence or social media entries, it may impose restrictions on their transmission.[13] Similarly, they may limit Internet access to certain times of the day, prevent attachments from being forwarded, reduce the connection speed, or restrict the use of webcams. A means must remain, however, to enable family news to be transmitted on a periodic basis. For example, the occupation authorities may curb Internet traffic for security reasons, but allow family correspondence through the postal system.

4. The reference to 'respect' in this Rule denotes the obligation of the Occupying Power to avoid harming the civilian population as a result of any cyber operations it may conduct, subject to Rules 88, 89, and 90. By contrast, 'protected' refers to the obligation of the Occupying Power to take feasible measures to ensure the security and well-being of the civilian population with regard to cyber operations conducted by others, such as insurgents or criminals. The obligation to respect and protect necessarily involves compliance with the other Rules in this chapter.

5. Pursuant to Article 51 of Geneva Convention IV, only protected persons over eighteen years of age may be compelled to work under certain conditions.[14] It is forbidden to require children to undertake any cyber work, regardless of its purpose (Rule 78).

---

[11] Geneva Convention IV, Arts. 13, 27; UK MANUAL, para. 9.21.

[12] Geneva Convention IV, Art. 25; UK MANUAL, paras. 9.10, 9.10.1; GERMAN MANUAL, para. 538. Arts. 25 and 140 of Geneva Convention IV discuss the roles of neutral intermediaries and the Central Information Agency if it becomes difficult to exchange family correspondence through the ordinary post. In such circumstances, the use of email and texting is likely to provide a satisfactory solution, if available, and, in the case of occupation, if permitted by the Occupying Power.

[13] Geneva Convention IV, Art. 25.

[14] According to Art. 51 of Geneva Convention IV, the Occupying Power may compel protected persons over eighteen years of age to do 'work which is necessary either for the needs of the army of occupation, or for the public utility services, or for the feeding,

6. Article 23(h) of the Hague Regulations prohibits a party to the conflict from compelling enemy nationals to take part in military operations. Thus, although protected persons may have language skills, cultural understanding, knowledge as to computer systems operated by their own country, or other information that would enable the Occupying Power to undertake effective cyber military operations, such compulsory involvement is prohibited. The Group agreed that this prohibition extended to cyber activities that are preparatory to military operations, precautionary cyber measures to protect the Occupying Power's own computer networks, or general maintenance of the Occupying Power's computer networks that are used for military operations. Additionally, pursuant to Article 51 of Geneva Convention IV, the Occupying Power may not compel protected persons to serve in its armed or auxiliary forces.[15]

7. The Occupying Power shall, to the extent feasible in the circumstances and without any adverse distinction, ensure the continuance of computer operations that are essential to the survival of the civilian population of the occupied territory.[16] Examples may include, depending on the circumstances, the operation of SCADA systems necessary for the functioning of utilities such as power grids, water purification plants, and sewage processing facilities.

Rule 88 – Public order and safety in occupied territory

The Occupying Power shall take all the measures in its power to restore and ensure, as far as possible, public order and safety, while respecting, unless absolutely prevented, the laws in force in the country, including the laws applicable to cyber activities.

1. This Rule is based on Article 43 of the Hague Regulations and Articles 27 and 64 of Geneva Convention IV. It reflects customary international law.

2. The Occupying Power has an obligation to restore and ensure public order and safety, including administration of the territory for the population's benefit and maintenance of its critical infrastructure. This entails an obligation to restore and maintain cyber infrastructure essential

---

sheltering, clothing, transportation or health of the population of the occupied country'. *See also* UK Manual, para. 11.52; German Manual, para. 564.

[15] Geneva Convention IV, Art. 147; UK Manual, para. 11.53.a.

[16] *See* Additional Protocol I, Art. 69(1), which the International Group of Experts agreed reflects customary international law. *See also* Commentary accompanying Rule 81.

for the functioning of the occupied territory. Examples might include the transport and electricity systems and water supply network. Similarly, if the Occupying Power learns, for example, of websites or social media that are inciting sectarian violence or engaging in cyber crime, it has the obligation to do what it can to block or otherwise prevent such activities.

3. According to Article 43 of the Hague Regulations, the Occupying Power must, unless absolutely prevented, maintain the laws applicable in the occupied territory. The reference in Article 64 of Geneva Convention IV to 'penal laws' is widely accepted as extending to all the laws in force;[17] hence, domestic laws that regulate cyber activities retain their validity. Examples are penal laws on cyber crime or the interception of telecommunications, statutes that deal with Internet service providers, and laws that govern freedom of speech or intrusions into privacy.

4. This Rule encompasses laws that do not directly address cyber activities, but are relevant thereto. An example of such a law is one providing for freedom of religious expression. Absent a valid justification under the law of occupation, this Rule would preclude the Occupying Power from banning by cyber means the exercise of religious freedom.

5. The Occupying Power is entitled to curb the freedoms of expression and of the press in cyberspace, despite laws to the contrary, as necessary for its security.[18] This might be done, for example, by imposing censorship to counter resistance attempts to organize or regroup using social networking media. The Occupying Power may also take measures inconsistent with existing law if its computer networks outside occupied territory fall victim to cyber attacks launched from occupied territory.

6. The Occupying Power is entitled to repeal or suspend laws in force that prejudice its cyber operations or military communications in cases where they constitute a threat to its security. It may also repeal legislation that is inconsistent with its Geneva Convention IV obligations, or with other rules of international law.[19] For instance, the Occupying Power may enact legislation that replaces discriminatory domestic legislation that, if retained, would exclude certain groups of people, based on their

---

[17] ICRC GENEVA CONVENTION IV COMMENTARY at 335; GERMAN MANUAL, para. 547.

[18] See, e.g., UK MANUAL, para. 11.34. The UK Manual states: 'For legitimate reasons of security only, censorship may be imposed on the press, films, radio, television, theatres, and public entertainment, or to limit or prohibit telegram, postal, or telecommunications. To the same extent, existing press laws need not be respected, the publication of newspapers may be prohibited or subjected to restrictions, and the distribution of newspapers to unoccupied parts of the country or neutral countries may be stopped.'

[19] UK MANUAL, para. 11.25.

race, religion, or political affiliation, from expressing their opinions and beliefs. The Occupying Power may use cyber means to disseminate such new laws, and, consistent with international legal norms, to ensure compliance with them.

7. An Occupying Power may enact new laws if such action is required to enable it to ensure public order and safety, to fulfil its obligations under the law of occupation, or to maintain the orderly administration of the territory.[20] For example, the Occupying Power may adopt regulations aimed at countering cyber crime that is significantly harming the financial stability of the occupied territory.

Rule 89 – Security of the Occupying Power

The Occupying Power may take measures necessary to ensure its general security, including the integrity and reliability of its own cyber systems.

1. This Rule is based on Articles 27 and 64 of Geneva Convention IV. It reflects customary international law.[21]

2. This Rule envisages taking cyber measures with regard to the security of the Occupying Power in general. The concluding clause of the Rule emphasizes that its scope extends to the protection of the Occupying Power's cyber systems.

3. Examples of measures that might be taken in accordance with this Rule include steps to: shut down communications systems used to transmit information about the Occupying Power to insurgent forces; prohibit email references to military movements, posture, weapons, capabilities, or activities; implement militarily necessary restrictions on the use of certain servers; impose time restrictions on use of the Internet when military authorities need bandwidth; or place restrictions on use of the Internet by individuals that pose a security threat. Consider the example of an Occupying Power with reason to believe steganography is being used to pass bomb-making instructions to members of a resistance movement. If there is no effective way to determine which files contain the coded messages, the Occupying Power may prevent or restrict cyber communications by those it has reason to believe are involved in such activities. In limited circumstances, it may, to the extent

---

[20] Geneva Convention IV, Art. 64; Hague Regulations, Art. 43.
[21] UK MANUAL, paras. 11.15, 11.34–11.38; CANADIAN MANUAL, para. 1207.

necessary, restrict communications generally until the situation is resolved satisfactorily.

4.   The restrictions imposed on protected persons shall be no more than are necessary to address the legitimate security concerns of the Occupying Power.[22] The determination of necessity must be based on all attendant circumstances, such as the availability of other forms of communication.

Rule 90 – Confiscation and requisition of property

To the extent the law of occupation permits the confiscation or requisition of property, taking control of cyber infrastructure or systems is likewise permitted.

1.   This Rule is based on Articles 46, 52, 53, 55, and 56 of the Hague Regulations and Article 55 of Geneva Convention IV.[23] It reflects customary international law.[24]

2.   A distinction must be made between use of the terms 'confiscation' and 'requisition' in this Rule. The Occupying Power may confiscate State movable property, including cyber property such as computers, computer systems, and other computing and memory devices, for use in military operations. Private property may not be confiscated. Requisition by the Occupying Power is the taking of goods with compensation, or the taking of services.[25] Such taking is only permissible for the administration of occupied territory or for the needs of the occupying forces, and then only if the requirements of the civilian population have been taken into account.

3.   For the purposes of this Rule, the majority of the International Group of Experts agreed that, *sensu stricto*, data does not qualify as property. However, this fact does not preclude the Occupying Power from making use of State data for its military operations. A minority of the Experts was of the view that data can qualify as property.

4.   The Occupying Power is obliged to safeguard the capital value of immovable State property (as distinct from movable property) and

---

[22] 'What is essential is that the measures of constraint they adopt should not affect the fundamental rights of the persons concerned.' ICRC GENEVA CONVENTION IV COMMENTARY at 207.
[23] On the temporary requisition of hospitals, see Geneva Convention IV, Art. 57.
[24] See also Additional Protocol I, Art. 14; Geneva Convention IV, Art. 57; GERMAN MANUAL, paras. 552–61; ICRC CUSTOMARY IHL STUDY, Rule 51.
[25] On the requisition of labour, see Geneva Convention IV, Art. 51.

administer it with appropriate respect.[26] Such property includes the buildings in which cyber infrastructure is located. Whether that cyber infrastructure qualifies as immovable State property depends on whether it can be removed without substantially damaging the building. If it cannot be so removed, it is immovable property entitled to the protection of immovable State property. Accordingly, the Occupying Power would be prohibited from taking any actions that would reduce its capital value. Cyber infrastructure that can be removed without occasioning significant damage to the structure of the building is movable property subject to the rules set forth in the preceding paragraphs.

5. Based on Articles 46 and 52 of the Hague Regulations, private cyber property (or cyber services) must in principle be respected and may not be confiscated. It may only be requisitioned for the needs of the army of occupation and the administration of occupied territory. The property must be restored, and compensation fixed, when peace is made. For example, it would be appropriate to requisition a privately owned server in order to facilitate administration of the territory or to demand access to the Internet from a private Internet service provider when needed by the occupation force. Requisitions of goods and services must be in proportion to the occupied State's resources and may not oblige inhabitants to take part in military operations against their own country.[27]

6. It may be difficult to distinguish cyber property belonging to the State from private cyber property. Cyber infrastructure can be owned jointly in public–private partnerships or government cyber infrastructure can be established and maintained by private companies based on public concessions. When doubts arise about the private or public character of cyber assets, some States maintain a general presumption that it is public unless and until its private nature becomes evident.[28] Where both State and private interests in computers, computer networks, or other cyber property coexist, the property may be seized, but private interests therein must be compensated.[29]

7. Cyber property (including State cyber property) of municipalities and of institutions dedicated to religion, charity, education, and the arts

---

[26] Hague Regulations, Art. 55; UK Manual, para. 11.86.

[27] If they involve the requisition of foodstuffs or medicine, the requisitions are only permissible 'if the requirements of the civilian population have been taken into account'. Geneva Convention IV, Art. 55. See also UK Manual, para. 11.76.

[28] UK Manual, para. 11.90.

[29] UK Manual, para. 11.90; Canadian Manual, para. 1235.

and sciences shall be treated as private property.[30] As such, it may be requisitioned (and not confiscated) provided the preconditions mentioned above are fulfilled.

8. Based on Article 53 of the Hague Regulations, equipment adapted for the transmission of news may be seized even if it is private property. It must be returned to the owner and compensation paid when it is no longer needed. Today, every cell phone or computer connected to the Internet is capable of transmitting news. The Experts agreed that extending the application of this Rule to all such items would be contrary to the object and purpose of the underlying treaty provision from which the Rule derives. Therefore, 'equipment adapted for the transmission of news' should be understood as equipment that 'journalists' (Rule 79) use and that is operated by the organizations to which they belong.

9. The term 'taking control' refers to physical confiscation or requisition of property. The question in the cyber context is whether it extends to 'virtual' confiscation or requisition. The majority of the International Group of Experts agreed that it does to the extent that (1) the Occupying Power can employ the property for its own purposes, and (2) the owner is denied its use. The minority considered that physical possession of the property is an essential ingredient of this Rule.

10. Submarine cables (including those components on land) connecting occupied with neutral territory are subject to a special regime set forth in Article 54 of the Hague Regulations. They may not be seized or destroyed except in the case of absolute necessity and compensation must subsequently be paid. Since submarine cables are used for cyber communications, this point has particular relevance in the cyber context. The International Group of Experts came to no conclusion as to whether this customary norm applies more broadly to other objects necessary for cyber communications (e.g., satellite uplink and downlink stations) between occupied territories and neutral States.

---

[30] Hague Regulations, Art. 56; UK MANUAL, para. 11.76.1; GERMAN MANUAL, para. 559.

7

Neutrality

1. The law of neutrality applies only during international armed conflict. It is based on Hague Conventions V and XIII and customary international law.[1] The International Group of Experts unanimously agreed that the law of neutrality applied to cyber operations.

2. 'Neutral State' denotes a State that is not a party to the international armed conflict in question.[2] For the purposes of this Manual, 'neutral cyber infrastructure' means public or private cyber infrastructure that is located within neutral territory (including civilian cyber infrastructure owned by a party to the conflict or nationals of that party) or that has the nationality of a neutral State (and is located outside belligerent territory). 'Neutral territory' comprises the land territory of neutral States, as well as waters subject to their territorial sovereignty (internal waters, territorial sea and, where applicable, archipelagic waters) and the airspace above those areas.[3]

3. The law of neutrality regulates the relationship between the parties to an international armed conflict on the one hand and States that are not party to the conflict on the other. Its key purposes are to (i) protect neutral States and their citizens against the conflict's harmful effects; (ii) safeguard neutral rights, such as engaging in commerce on the high seas; and (iii) protect parties to the conflict against action or inaction on

---

[1] US COMMANDER'S HANDBOOK, Chapter 7; GERMAN MANUAL, paras. 1101–55; AMW MANUAL, sec. X. The UK Manual and the San Remo Manual recognize the continuing relevance of the law of neutrality throughout the documents, while the Canadian Manual devotes Chapter 13 to the topic. Note that neutrals are obligated to comply with the law of armed conflict in certain cases despite their non-belligerent status. Additional Protocol I, Art. 19; Geneva Convention I, Art. 4; Geneva Convention II, Art. 5.

[2] US COMMANDER'S HANDBOOK, para. 7.2; UK MANUAL, para. 12.11; CANADIAN MANUAL, para. 1302; GERMAN MANUAL, para. 1101; AMW MANUAL, Rule 1(aa); SAN REMO MANUAL, para. 13(d).

[3] See US COMMANDER'S HANDBOOK, para. 7.3; GERMAN MANUAL, paras. 1108, 1118; AMW MANUAL, commentary accompanying Rule 166; SAN REMO MANUAL, para. 14.

the part of neutral States that benefits their enemy. The global distribution of cyber assets and activities, as well as global dependency on cyber infrastructure, means that cyber operations of the parties to a conflict can easily affect private or public neutral cyber infrastructure. Accordingly, neutrality is particularly relevant in modern armed conflict.

4. The International Group of Experts was mindful of the fact that the law of neutrality developed based on situations in which entrance into or exit from a neutral State's territory is a physical act. The fact that cyberspace involves worldwide connectivity irrespective of geo-political borders challenges certain assumptions upon which the law of neutrality is based. For instance, a single email message sent from belligerent territory may automatically be routed through neutral cyber infrastructure before reaching its intended destination; the sender or the owner of the neutral cyber infrastructure cannot necessarily control the route it takes. The Rules set forth in this chapter have considered this reality. Given the difficulty of controlling cyber infrastructure and routes, any conclusions about violations of a State's neutrality or whether a neutral State has violated its obligations under the law of neutrality should only be arrived at after careful consideration.

5. Cyber infrastructure located within the territory of a neutral State is not only subject to that State's jurisdiction, but also protected by that State's territorial sovereignty. It is considered neutral in character irrespective of public or private ownership or of the nationality of the owners (provided that it is not used for the exercise of belligerent rights, Rule 94).

6. The term 'exercise of belligerent rights' is synonymous with the terms 'hostile act' in Hague Convention V and 'act of hostility' under Hague Convention XIII.[4] The International Group of Experts decided to use 'belligerent rights' in this chapter to avoid confusion with the term 'hostile act', which is an operational term of art. Exercise of belligerent rights is accordingly to be understood in the broadest sense as actions that a party to the conflict is entitled to take in connection with the conflict, including cyber operations. Belligerent rights are not limited to 'attacks' as defined in Rule 30, but it should be noted that the term does not extend to espionage conducted against the neutral State.

---

[4] Hague V, Art. 10; Hague Convention XIII, Art. 2. *See also* SAN REMO MANUAL, paras. 15, 16.

Rule 91 – Protection of neutral cyber infrastructure

The exercise of belligerent rights by cyber means directed against neutral cyber infrastructure is prohibited.

1.   It is a well-established principle of the law of neutrality that parties to the conflict are prohibited from conducting hostilities within neutral territory. The inviolability of neutral territory is laid down in Article 1 of Hague Convention V and Article 1 of Hague Convention XIII. The norm is customary in character.[5]

2.   Neutral cyber infrastructure physically located in international airspace, outer space, or high seas areas is protected by virtue of the State of nationality's sovereignty.

3.   The term 'directed against' refers to an operation intended to detrimentally affect neutral cyber infrastructure. As to operations passing through such infrastructure or employing it for operations against the enemy, see Rule 92.

4.   The International Group of Experts struggled with the situation in which a cyber attack against a military objective in belligerent territory has spill-over effects in neutral territory. For example, a cyber attack on a server in belligerent territory could significantly affect services in neutral territory. The Experts agreed that if such effects are not foreseeable, the attack does not violate the law of neutrality. As to effects that are foreseeable, the Group of Experts noted that the law of neutrality seeks to balance the right of belligerents to effectively conduct military operations with the right of neutral States to remain generally unaffected by the conflict. Each case must be assessed on its own merits by balancing these competing rights. The Experts agreed that the effects on the neutral State to be considered in making this assessment are not limited to physical effects. They also agreed that in practice, States would be unlikely to regard *de minimis* effects as precluding the prosecution of an otherwise legitimate attack.

5.   It is important to note that neutral cyber infrastructure located in neutral territory may lose its protection under Rule 94. Moreover, neutral cyber infrastructure located outside neutral territory, such as undersea cables, may be attacked if it constitutes a lawful military objective. It may also be subject to capture.

---

[5]   US COMMANDER'S HANDBOOK, para. 7.3; UK MANUAL, para. 1.43; GERMAN MANUAL, paras. 1108, 1118, 1149; SAN REMO MANUAL, para. 15; Hague Air Warfare Rules, Arts. 39, 40.

Rule 92 – Cyber operations in neutral territory

The exercise of belligerent rights by cyber means in neutral territory is prohibited.

1. This Rule is based on Articles 2 and 3 of Hague Convention V and Articles 2 and 5 of Hague Convention XIII. It reflects customary international law.[6] Whereas Rule 91 addresses operations against neutral cyber infrastructure, this Rule deals with the use of such infrastructure on neutral territory by a belligerent.

2. Rule 92 prohibits the armed forces of a party to the conflict from conducting cyber operations from neutral territory. In addition to conducting cyber operations from within neutral territory, it encompasses remotely taking control of neutral cyber infrastructure and using it for such purposes.

3. Although the Rule only addresses the exercise of belligerent rights in neutral territory, it would also constitute a breach of neutrality to use neutral non-commercial government cyber infrastructure that is located outside neutral territory (but not within belligerent territory) for belligerent purposes. For instance, it is prohibited to route military communications through cyber systems aboard a neutral State's government ships or State aircraft because those platforms enjoy sovereign immunity (Rule 4).

4. Using a public, internationally and openly accessible network such as the Internet for military purposes does not violate the law of neutrality. This is so even if it, or components thereof, is located in neutral territory. Although there is no express treaty law directly on point, the majority of the International Group of Experts agreed that Article 8 of Hague Convention V, which provides that a neutral Power need not 'forbid or restrict the use on behalf of the belligerents of telegraph or telephone cables or of wireless telegraphy apparatus belonging to it or to companies or private individuals', can be applied to cyber communications systems. They further agreed that the Article reflects customary international law.[7] A minority of the Experts would limit the application of Article 8 to the items referred to therein.

---

[6] US COMMANDER'S HANDBOOK, para. 7.3; UK MANUAL, para. 1.43.b; CANADIAN MANUAL, para. 1304; GERMAN MANUAL, paras. 1108, 1120, 1150; AMW MANUAL, Rule 167(a) and accompanying commentary; SAN REMO MANUAL, para. 15.

[7] *See* AMW MANUAL, Rule 167(b).

5.   The International Group of Experts considered the issue of transmission of cyber weapons (Rule 41) across neutral territory. Most Experts
took the position that such transmission by cyber means is prohibited
based on Article 2 of Hague Convention V, which prohibits movement of
munitions of war or supplies across the territory of a neutral Power.
A minority of Experts pointed to Article 8 of Hague Convention V as
providing an express exception to the general rule.[8]

Rule 93 – Neutral obligations

**A neutral State may not knowingly allow the exercise of belligerent
rights by the parties to the conflict from cyber infrastructure located
in its territory or under its exclusive control.**

1.   This Rule, which reflects customary international law,[9] is derived
from Article 5 of Hague Convention V, according to which '[a] neutral
Power must not allow any of the acts referred to in Articles 2 to 4 to
occur on its territory'. In the context of cyber operations, it is of importance to note that according to Article 3 of Hague Convention V,

> belligerents are … forbidden to:
>
> (a) Erect on the territory of a neutral Power a wireless telegraphy station
>   or other apparatus for the purpose of communicating with belligerent
>   forces on land or sea;
> (b) Use any installation of this kind established by them before the war
>   on the territory of a neutral Power for purely military purposes, and
>   which has not been opened for the service of public messages.

2.   Adapting the object and purpose of Hague Convention V to cyber
operations, a neutral State may not allow a party to the conflict to use its
pre-existing cyber infrastructure on neutral territory for military purposes or to establish any new cyber infrastructure for said purposes.
3.   The obligation set forth in this Rule extends not only to a party's
cyber infrastructure on neutral territory, but also to the exercise of
belligerent rights employing other cyber infrastructure located there.
An exception applies to public, internationally and openly accessible
networks, such as the Internet, which may be used for military

---

[8] This was the position adopted in the AMW Manual. AMW MANUAL, commentary
accompanying Rule 167(b).
[9] US COMMANDER'S HANDBOOK, para. 7.3; UK MANUAL, para. 1.43.a; GERMAN MANUAL,
para. 1111; AMW MANUAL, Rule 168(a); SAN REMO MANUAL, para. 22. *See also* this Rule's
peacetime counterpart, Rule 5 of this Manual.

communications (Rule 92). To the extent that a neutral State does place restrictions on the use of such networks, these restrictions must be impartially applied to all parties to the conflict.[10] As noted with regard to Rule 92, the International Group of Experts was divided as to whether the transmission of cyber weapons across neutral territory using such a network is prohibited. It was similarly divided as to whether a neutral State is obligated to prevent such transmission.

4. The phrase 'under its exclusive control' is employed here to refer to non-commercial government cyber infrastructure (Rule 4). With regard to such infrastructure, this Rule applies regardless of its location because the obligation derives from the infrastructure's government character.

5. Rule 93 presupposes knowledge, whether actual or constructive, by the organs of the neutral State. A neutral State has actual knowledge if its organs have detected a cyber operation conducted by a party to the conflict originating from its territory or if the aggrieved party to the conflict has credibly informed the neutral State that a cyber operation has originated from its territory. Constructive knowledge exists in situations in which a State should reasonably have known of the activity. The International Group of Experts was split as to whether the extension to constructive knowledge implies a duty on behalf of the neutral State actively to monitor, to the extent feasible, the use of cyber infrastructure on its territory. Whereas some members took the position that it does, and that therefore a neutral State must exercise due diligence in monitoring for belligerent activity,[11] others suggested that no such duty exists.

6. The phrase 'may not knowingly allow' implies a duty on the part of neutral States to take all feasible measures to terminate any exercise of belligerent rights employing cyber infrastructure falling within the scope of this Rule.[12] However, the International Group of Experts could achieve no consensus as to the existence of a duty to take measures to prevent the exercise of belligerent rights before it occurs, in particular by monitoring cyber activities. Some Experts took the position that this obligation is implied in the duty to 'not knowingly allow'.[13] These Experts suggested that to the extent preventive measures such as monitoring are feasible they are required. Feasibility is, of course, dependent on the attendant

---

[10] Hague Convention V, Art. 9.   [11] AMW MANUAL, Rule 170(b).

[12] US COMMANDER'S HANDBOOK, para. 7.3; GERMAN MANUAL, paras. 1109, 1125, 1151; AMW MANUAL, commentary accompanying Rule 168(a); SAN REMO MANUAL, paras. 15, 18, 22. *See also* Hague Air Warfare Rules, Arts. 42, 47.

[13] Hague XIII, Art. 8; AMW MANUAL, Rule 170(b).

circumstances, such as the technological capacity of the State concerned. Other Experts rejected this position, arguing that the sole duty of the neutral State is to terminate use, as distinct from preventing it. These Experts pointed, in particular, to the practical difficulties inherent in complying with any duty to determine the belligerent character of a packet traversing its networks.

7.   Measures taken by a neutral that are in compliance with this Rule do not constitute a hostile act and, a fortiori, do not constitute an armed attack (Rule 13) against the party to the conflict violating its neutrality.[14] As to activities on neutral territory that do not have belligerent nexus, see Rule 5.

Rule 94 – Response by parties to the conflict to violations

If a neutral State fails to terminate the exercise of belligerent rights on its territory, the aggrieved party to the conflict may take such steps, including by cyber operations, as are necessary to counter that conduct.

1.   This Rule is generally accepted as customary international law. It provides an aggrieved party to the conflict with a remedy for the enemy's unlawful activities on neutral territory or belligerent use of neutral cyber infrastructure that remains unaddressed by the neutral State.[15] It is a form of 'self-help'.

2.   The object and purpose of this Rule is to redress the disadvantage suffered by a party through its enemy's violation of the law of neutrality. It does not apply to every violation of neutrality, but rather only to those that negatively affect the opposing party. Any other violations are exclusively the concern of the neutral State. For instance, a denial of service operation by one party against neutral cyber infrastructure does not necessarily result in a military advantage *vis-à-vis* its enemy. In such cases, the enemy is not entitled to terminate the denial of service operation under this Rule. Any response would be reserved exclusively to the neutral State.

3.   The operation of this Rule depends upon two criteria. First, the violation of the neutral State's territory must be 'serious'. Minor violations do not trigger the application of this Rule.[16] In other words, the

---

[14] Hague Convention V, Art. 10; SAN REMO MANUAL Rule 22 and accompanying commentary.

[15] US COMMANDER'S HANDBOOK, para. 7.3; UK MANUAL, para. 1.43(a); CANADIAN MANUAL, para. 1304(3); AMW MANUAL, Rule 168(b); SAN REMO MANUAL, Rule 22.

[16] SAN REMO MANUAL, Rule 22.

party violating the neutral status must, by that violation, gain a meaning-ful military advantage over the adversary. Seriousness cannot be deter-mined *in abstracto*; it depends upon the circumstances ruling at the time. It may be based on either the pervasiveness of the violation or on the advantage that accrues to the violator because of that violation. For example, establishing the capability to hack into personal email accounts of low-level members of the enemy armed forces does not trigger this Rule. By contrast, assume that one of the parties to the conflict has diminished cyber capability because of the hostilities. Use by that party of neutral cyber infrastructure in order to undertake cyber operations against the enemy would trigger it.

4.   Second, the exercise of belligerent rights on neutral territory by a party to the conflict must represent an immediate threat to the security of the aggrieved party and there must be no feasible and timely alternative to taking action on neutral territory.[17] Therefore, the Rule only applies if the neutral State is either unwilling or unable to comply with its obliga-tions under Rule 93. When this is the case, the aggrieved party is entitled to terminate a violation of neutrality by its adversary once the neutral State has exhausted all measures at its disposal to do so, but has been unsuccessful. Obviously, the aggrieved party may also act when the neutral State does nothing to terminate the violation.

5.   Measures of self-help are subject to a requirement of prior notification that allows a reasonable time for the neutral State to address the violation. Only if the violation immediately threatens the security of the aggrieved party may that party, in the absence of any feasible and timely alternative, use such immediate force as is necessary to terminate the violation.

6.   Consider the example of a belligerent that is routing cyber oper-ations against its enemy through a server in a neutral State. The enemy State complains to the neutral State and demands that it prevent this use of its cyber infrastructure. If the neutral State fails to terminate the operations in a timely manner, the aggrieved belligerent may lawfully launch a cyber operation to destroy the server's functionality.

Rule 95 – Neutrality and Security Council actions

A State may not rely upon the law of neutrality to justify conduct, including cyber operations, that would be incompatible with

---

[17] SAN REMO MANUAL, Rule 22.

preventive or enforcement measures decided upon by the Security Council under Chapter VII of the Charter of the United Nations.

1.   This Rule is based on Article 25 of the United Nations Charter, which requires Member States to comply with Security Council decisions set forth in its resolutions. It also derives from Article 103 of the Charter, which makes treaty obligations such as those arising from Hague Conventions V and XIII inapplicable in the face of Security Council action under Chapter VII.[18] Subject to *jus cogens*, the same holds true for obligations under customary international law incompatible with Security Council decisions.

2.   Rule 95 applies both when the Security Council responds to a breach of the peace or an act of aggression (by deciding upon an enforcement measure) and when the Council takes measures in the face of a threat to the peace.[19] It operates in three situations. First, if a Security Council resolution requires States to take a particular action, they may not rely on the law of neutrality to avoid doing so. Second, a Security Council resolution may prohibit the taking of a certain action by States. The law of neutrality offers no justification for engaging in such conduct. Third, States are prohibited by this Rule from engaging in any activities that might interfere with actions taken by other States pursuant to a Security Council resolution.

3.   Consider a situation in which the Security Council has determined that a particular State involved in an armed conflict has engaged in an act of aggression. Among other acts, the State is conducting highly destructive cyber attacks against its opponent's military cyber infrastructure. In response, the Security Council passes a resolution authorizing all Member States to employ their cyber assets and capabilities to terminate the attacks. States acting in compliance with this resolution would not be in breach of their obligations under the law of neutrality.

---

[18] *See also* GERMAN MANUAL, para. 1103; AMW MANUAL, Rule 165; SAN REMO MANUAL, paras. 7–9.

[19] UN Charter Art. 39 (setting forth these situations).

GLOSSARY

Active Cyber Defence: A proactive measure for detecting or obtaining information as to a cyber intrusion, cyber attack, or impending cyber operation, or for determining the origin of an operation that involves launching a pre-emptive, preventive, or cyber counter-operation against the source.

Automatic Identification System (AIS): A tracking system used for identifying and geo-locating ships. Ships equipped with AIS equipment electronically exchange data about their identity and location with other ships and AIS base stations. The system is also used in vessel traffic management and other applications.

Bandwidth: The capacity of a communication channel to pass data through the channel in a given amount of time, usually expressed in bits per second.

Botnet: A network of compromised computers, 'the bots', remotely controlled by an intruder, 'the botherder', used to conduct coordinated cyber operations or cyber crimes. There is no practical limit on the number of bots that can be 'recruited' into a botnet.

Close Access Operation: A cyber operation requiring physical proximity to the targeted system.

Cloud Computing: A model for enabling ubiquitous, convenient, on-demand network access to a shared pool of configurable computing resources (such as networks, servers, storage, applications, and services) that can be rapidly provisioned and released with minimal management effort or service provider interaction. Cloud computing allows for efficient pooling of computer resources and the ability to scale resource to demand.[1]

Common Criteria: Governing document that provides a comprehensive, rigorous method for specifying security function and assurance requirements for products and systems.[2]

---

[1] Drawn from The National Institute of Standards in Technology, US Department of Commerce, definition of Cloud Computing, Special Publication 800-145, September 2011.
[2] NIA GLOSSARY.

Computer: A device that processes data. The device may be stand-alone (e.g., a tablet computer, smartphone, network server) or embedded in another device (e.g., a microcontroller in a missile, radar system, or aircraft).

Computer Emergency Response Team (CERT): A team that provides initial emergency response aid and triage services to the victims or potential victims of cyber operations or cyber crimes, usually in a manner that involves coordination between private sector and government entities. These teams also maintain situational awareness about hacker activities and new developments in the design and use of malware, providing defenders of computer networks with advice on how to address security threats and vulnerabilities associated with those activities and malware.

Computer Network: An information infrastructure used to permit computers to exchange data. The infrastructure may be wired (e.g., Ethernet, fibre-optic), wireless (e.g., Wi-Fi), or a combination of the two.

Computer Resources: The storage, processing, and communications capacity of a computer.

Computer System: One or more interconnected computers with associated software and peripheral devices. It can include sensors and/or (programmable logic) controllers, connected over a computer network. Computer systems can be general purpose (for example, a laptop) or specialized (for example, the 'blue force tracking system').

Critical Infrastructure: Physical or virtual systems and assets under the jurisdiction of a State that are so vital that their incapacitation or destruction may debilitate a State's security, economy, public health or safety, or the environment.

Cyber: Connotes a relationship with information technology.

Cyber Attack: See Rule 30.

Cyber Espionage: See Rule 66.

Cyber Infrastructure: The communications, storage, and computing resources upon which information systems operate. The Internet is an example of a global information infrastructure.

Cyber Operations: The employment of cyber capabilities with the primary purpose of achieving objectives in or by the use of cyberspace.

Cyber Reconnaissance: The use of cyber capabilities to obtain information about activities, information resources, or system capabilities.

Cyber System: See 'computer system'.

Cyberspace: The environment formed by physical and non-physical components, characterized by the use of computers and the electro-magnetic spectrum, to store, modify, and exchange data using computer networks.

Data: The basic elements that can be processed or produced by a computer.

Data Centre: A physical facility used for the storage and processing of large volumes of data. A data centre can be used solely by users belonging to a single enterprise or shared among multiple enterprises as in cloud computing data centres. A data centre can be stationary or mobile (e.g., housed in a cargo container transported via ship, truck, or aircraft).

Database: A collection of interrelated data stored together in one or more computerized files.[3]

Denial of Service (DoS): The non-availability of computer resources to the intended or usual customers of a computer service, normally as a result of a cyber operation.

Distributed Denial of Service (DDoS): A technique that employs two or more computers, such as the bots of a botnet, to achieve a denial of service from a single or multiple targets.

Domain: An environment or context that includes a set of system resources and a set of system entities that have the right to access the resources as defined by a common security policy, security model, or security architecture.[4]

Domain Name: A unique, alphabetic human-readable name for a computer. All computers that are addressable via the Internet have both a domain name and a corresponding numeric Internet protocol (IP) address. A Domain Name Server (DNS) uses a lookup table to translate the domain name into an IP address and vice versa. The Internet Assigned Numbers Authority (IANA) is the central authority for assigning domain names and IP addresses. The term 'top-level domain name' refers to the highest level in the hierarchy of the Internet domain name system. Examples include: '.org', '.int', and '.mil'.

Domain Name Extensions: Extensions at the end of a domain name. Examples of top-level domain extensions include '.com' (generic extension), '.mil' (sponsored extension), and '.uk' (country code extension for the United Kingdom).

Electronic Warfare: The use of electromagnetic (EM) or directed energy to exploit the electromagnetic spectrum. It may include interception or identification of EM emissions, employment of EM energy, prevention of hostile use of the EM spectrum by an adversary, and actions to ensure efficient employment of that spectrum by the user-State.

Hacker: A person who gains or attempts to gain unauthorized access to hardware and/or software.

Hacktivist: A private citizen who on his or her own initiative engages in hacking for, inter alia, ideological, political, religious, or patriotic reasons.

Hardware: The physical components that comprise a computer system and cyber infrastructure.

---

[3] Glossary of Software Engineering Technology, Institute of Electrical and Electronics Engineers (IEEE) Std 610.12 (28 September 1990).

[4] NIA GLOSSARY.

High-Performance Computing: High-speed computing that utilizes supercomputers or clusters of networked computers. High-performance computing may be enabled by grid-computing, that is, the use of distributed, loosely coupled, heterogeneous networked computers to perform very large computing tasks.

Honeynet: A virtual environment consisting of multiple honeypots, designed to deceive an intruder into thinking that he or she has located a network of computing devices of targeting value.

Honeypot: A deception technique in which a person seeking to defend computing devices and cyber infrastructure against cyber operations uses a virtual environment designed to lure the attention of intruders with the aim of: deceiving the intruders about the nature of the environment; having the intruders waste resources on the decoy environment; and gathering counter-intelligence about the intruder's intent, identity, and means and methods of cyber operation. The honeypot can be co-resident with the real targets the intruder would like to attack, but the honeypot itself is isolated from the rest of the systems being defended via software wrappers, separate hardware, and other isolation techniques such that the intruder's operations are contained.

Internet: A global system of interconnected computer networks that use the standard Internet protocol suite.

Internet Protocol (IP): A protocol for addressing hosts and routing datagrams (i.e., packets) from a source host to the destination host across one or more IP networks.

Internet Protocol (IP) Address: A unique identifier for a device on the Internet.[5]

Internet Service Provider (ISP): An organization that provides the network connectivity that enables computer users to access the Internet.

Jamming: An activity the purpose of which is interference with the reception of broadcast communications.

Logic Bomb: Malware that is designed to initiate a malicious sequence of actions if specified conditions are met.

Malicious Logic: Instructions and data that may be stored in software, firmware, or hardware that is designed or intended adversely to affect the performance of a computer system. The term 'logic' refers to any set of instructions, be they in hardware, firmware, or software, executed by a computing device. Examples of malicious logic include Trojan horses, rootkits, computer viruses, and computer worms. Firmware comprises a layer between software (i.e., applications and operating systems) and hardware and consists of low-level drivers that act as an interface between hardware and software.

Malware: See 'malicious logic'.

---

[5] *See* Internet Assigned Numbers Authority, Glossary of terms *available at*: www.iana.org/glossary.

Network Node: An individual computer within a network.

Network Throttling: Also known as 'bandwidth throttling' and 'network bandwidth throttling', a technique used to control the usage of bandwidth by users of communications networks.

Passive Cyber Defence: A measure for detecting and mitigating cyber intrusions and the effects of cyber attacks that does not involve launching a preventive, pre-emptive or countering operation against the source. Examples of passive cyber defence measures are firewalls, patches, anti-virus software, and digital forensics tools.[6]

Rootkit: Malware installed on a compromised computer that allows a cyber operator to maintain privileged access to that computer and to conceal the cyber operator's activities there from other users of that or another computer.

Server: A physical or virtual computer dedicated to running one or more computing services. Examples include network and database servers.

Server Farm: A form of cluster computing in which a large number of servers are collocated in a data centre.

Smartphone: A mobile phone that, unlike a traditional feature mobile phone, is built on top of a mobile computing platform that enables the phone to run third-party applications. For example, smartphones have one or more web browsers and can download or run applications via the Internet.

Sniffer: Software used to observe and record network traffic.

Social Networking Media: An online service that provides a medium for social interaction (e.g., Facebook and Twitter).

Software: The non-physical components of a computer system and of cyber infrastructure. These components include programs, applications, and related data.

Software Agent: A computer process, managed by a computer operating system, which performs one or more tasks on behalf of a human user. It is possible for software agents to operate autonomously or to communicate and coordinate their actions with other software agents in a distributed computing environment. For instance, software agents are used for executing queries across distributed repositories of information available via the World Wide Web (WWW).

Spoofing: Impersonating a legitimate resource or user to gain unauthorized entry into an information system or to make it appear that some other organization or individual has initiated or undertaken certain cyber activity.

Steganography: The use of encoding techniques for hiding content within other content. For example, there are computer-based steganographic techniques and tools for embedding the contents of a computer file containing

---

[6] This term should be distinguished from the legal term of art 'passive precautions' (Rule 59).

engineering diagrams and text into an image file (e.g., a JPG document) such
that the existence of the engineering data in the image file is difficult for the
observer to detect.

Stuxnet: A computer worm that was designed to target software and equipment
comprising Siemens Corporation developed Supervisory Control and Data
Acquisition (SCADA) systems. The payload of the Stuxnet malware included
a programmable logic controller rootkit. Stuxnet came to light after it was
discovered that it had been used to target Iranian facilities at which Siemens
SCADA systems are used to control centrifuges involved in the enrichment of
uranium.

Supervisory Control and Data Acquisition (SCADA):   Computer systems and
instrumentation that provide for monitoring and controlling industrial, infrastructure, and facility-based processes, such as the operation of power plants,
water treatment facilities, electrical distribution systems, oil and gas pipelines,
airports, and factories.

Virus: Self-replicating malicious code that attaches itself to an application program or other executable system component and leaves no obvious signs of its
presence.[7]

Website: A set of related web pages containing information. A website is hosted
on one or more web servers. A website is accessed via its Uniform Resource
Locator (URL). The World Wide Web (WWW) is comprised of all of the
publicly accessible websites.

Wi-Fi: A type of high-speed wireless networking based on the Institute of
Electrical and Electronics Engineers (IEEE) 802.11 standards.

Worm: Malware that is able to copy itself from one computer to another, unlike
a virus that relies on embedding in another application in order to propagate
itself from one computer to another.

XML Tag: A markup construct that is part of the open standard known as the
Extensible Markup Language (XML). The tag is both human- and machine-
readable and used to encode the syntactic parts of the content of a document.
For example, in the electronic version of this Manual, a string of text containing a legal term of art could be delimited by the opening and closing
tags <legal-term> and </legal term>, for example <legal-term> necessity
</legal term>.

---

[7] NIA GLOSSARY.

INDEX